"Wonderful material and a wonderful ministry! I'm a chaplain in a military unit and I've started e-mailing this web site to many individuals that can benefit from it both as participants in their own marriages and as ministers to others. The surveys are unsurpassed in their practical approach to the marriage relationship! I've never seen better!"

"I am twenty-six, contemplating marriage, and have found your site a great resource for resolving, or attempting to resolve, the issues we need to before we get married. Keep up the great work and the most informative site I have seen on the web."

"Being in a second marriage for both my husband and me, we are thankful for your wise words of advice in order not to end up in the same place as we did in our first marriages."

"Dr. Harley, you saved our marriage."

"Your words made me cry but also give me hope and encouragement to keep trying. Thank you."

"This is a phenomenal resource for people who want to improve their love relationship."

"I just want to let you know that your work is appreciated and to say thank you for the help it has brought to our marriage."

"This web site has probably saved a marriage. I needed some help quick and found some hope."

"I was feeling shaky about my marriage and so happy to find your information so I at least have a clue of where to begin. Your writings make so much sense—this is really what marriage is all about."

"Thanks for saving my marriage."

"Your web site is excellent. I just wanted to let you know that I appreciate your hard work and the valuable information that you have shared with me."

Your

Love

and Marriage

Your
Love
and Marriage

Dr. Harley Answers Your Most
Personal Questions

Willard F. Harley, Jr.

Fleming H. Revell
A Division of Baker Book House Co
Grand Rapids, Michigan 49516

Published by Fleming H. Revell
a division of Baker Book House Company
P.O. Box 6287, Grand Rapids, MI 49516-6287

Printed in the United States of America

Library of Congress Cataloging-in-Publication Data

Harley, Willard F.
    Your love and marriage: Dr. Harley answers your most personal questions / Willard F. Harley, Jr.
        p. cm.
    ISBN 0-8007-5642-8 (paper)
    1. Love—Computer network resources. 2. Intimacy (Psychology)—Computer network resources. 3. Marriage—Computer network resources. I. Title.
HQ801.H3274 1997
025.06′3067—dc21   97-21312

"Why Women Leave Men" in appendix F is edited and reprinted with the permission of *New Man*.

For current information about all releases from Baker Book House, visit our web site:
http://www.bakerbooks.com

Contents

Part 1
Introduction

How to Use This Book

*T*his book is a little unusual. It's laid out in the same way as my web site—Marriage Builders. As in the web site, I suggest that you become familiar with my basic concepts of marriage before reading my answers for solving marriage problems. I have summarized my basic concepts in the next chapter of this book.

After you have read my basic concepts, you are ready to create a strategy that will solve any marital conflict you may have. To assist you in creating that strategy, you should read the letters I've received from those having similar conflicts and my answers that suggest solutions to their problems.

The table of contents will help you find the topics that are related to your conflict. The book contains five sections that deal with a variety of topics: infidelity, sexual adjustment, marital negotiation, living together before marriage, and keeping love in your marriage. Each section is further divided into more specific areas of concern with several letters in each one.

When you find topics that are related to your particular conflict, go directly to them and read the questions and answers regarding strategy. On the Marriage Builders web site, if a person has trouble creating a plan after reading the basic concepts and the related Q&A columns, I encourage the reader to e-mail me, telling me about his or her particular problem and I try to offer an effective approach in my response.

You are welcome to do the same thing. After reading this book, if you are having difficulty creating a plan to resolve your conflict, e-mail your problem to me at bharley@marriagebuilders.com and I will try to offer you a plan. A more interactive alternative is to discuss your problem with one of the Marriage Builders counselors by telephone (1-888-639-1639).

The goal of this book is to help you discover a plan that will guide you and your spouse in resolving your marital conflict and will restore love to your marriage. As you read about the marital struggles of others and consider the plans I've suggested to help them overcome their conflicts, you will be in a good position to know how to resolve your own conflicts and restore love to your marriage.

My Basic Concepts of Marriage

My basic concepts of marriage have developed over the years as I have counseled hundreds of couples in an attempt to help them save their marriages. These concepts address important aspects of relationship and marriage building, such as why people fall in love, why they fall out of love, what they want most in marriage, what drives them out of marriage, and how a bad marriage can become a great marriage.

When I was nineteen, a married friend told me his marriage was in trouble and he asked for my advice. The advice didn't seem to help—his marriage ended in divorce. Why couldn't I help? What was it about my friend's marriage that made divorce seem so inevitable?

My failure to help my friend convinced me that I didn't have what it takes to be a marriage counselor. Over the next ten years I was curious to know what would have helped my friend and countless other couples having problems. I read as much as I could and was even supervised by a professor of marriage and family therapy. What I discovered was that my approach was not the only one that was ineffective. The approaches of the experts were ineffective too!

The more I looked into the methods of other marriage counselors, the more I came to realize that marital therapy in general wasn't working. In fact I learned that marriage counseling had the lowest success rate of any form of counseling: In one study only 25 percent of those seeking help from a variety of marriage counselors felt that it did them any good.

Now there was a challenge if I'd ever had one! By the time I was thirty-two, I had discovered why I and so many other marital therapists were having so much trouble. We had failed to understand what made marriages work. And I discovered it by simply listening to couples tell me what it would take to straighten out their marriages. Their answer: Teach my spouse to meet my emotional needs. Almost every couple reported that their emotional needs were no longer being met in their marriage. And the love that they had for each other was replaced by indifference and, in some cases, hatred.

When they first married, the couples found each other irresistible because they had been so effective in meeting each other's needs. But over time they stopped caring for each other and were making each other miserable. Divorce seemed to be their only escape from the unhappiness of marriage and their only hope of someday having their needs met by someone else.

It became clear to me that when the emotional needs of spouses are not met, the marriage is in danger of dissolution. If emotional needs are met again, however, the danger passes. It is that simple. I began to recognize the importance in marriage counseling of attacking the emotional issues of need fulfillment rather than rational issues, such as communication or commitment.

Couples came to me with a common complaint: "I'm no longer in love." It was hard for them to understand how their feelings toward each other could have changed so much after marriage. Before they were married, they could not live without each other; now they could not stand each other.

To help couples understand the rise and fall of their feelings of love, and how that rise and fall is related to the way they treat each other, I created the concept of the Love Bank, my first basic concept.

The Love Bank

We all have a Love Bank, and the people we know have accounts in it. When people do things that make us feel good, "love units" are deposited, and when they do things that make us feel bad, love units are withdrawn. We are emotionally attracted to, or love, people with large balances in our Love Bank and we are repulsed by, or hate, those with negative balances. This is the way our emotions encourage us to be with people who treat us well and avoid those who hurt us.

With a member of the opposite sex, when a certain threshold is reached—say 1,000 love units—the emotional reaction we call romantic love is triggered. It is a feeling of incredible attraction. As long as the love units balance stays above 1,000 (an arbitrary number), we're in love. If the feeling of romantic love is the objective in marriage, a couple need to raise their balances in each other's Love Bank to 1,000 and keep them there.

How can a couple keep their Love Bank balances high enough to experience romantic love? There are two important considerations—deposits and withdrawals. Couples need to learn how to deposit as many love units as possible but they also should learn to avoid withdrawing love units.

Couples deposit love units by meeting each other's emotional needs (I'll explain that in the next section) and they avoid withdrawing them by overcoming habits that hurt each other (I call them Love Busters and I'll explain them later).

The only way to deposit love units continually and efficiently is to learn to meet your spouse's *most important emotional needs*. That's the second concept I'll introduce to you.

The Most Important Emotional Needs

What is an emotional need? It is a craving that, when satisfied, leaves you with a feeling of happiness and contentment and, when unsatisfied, leaves you with a feeling of unhappiness and frustration. There are probably thousands of emotional needs—a need for birthday parties, peanut butter sandwiches, Monday Night Football, garage sales. I could go on and on. Each of us has some of them and not others. But there are only a very few emotional needs that, when met by someone of the opposite sex, make us so happy that we fall in love with the person who meets them. I call those our *most important* emotional needs. Those are the ones that deposit the most love units in our Love Banks.

Whenever a husband and wife come to me for help, I first identify their most important emotional needs, what each of them can do for the other that will make them the happiest and most contented. Then I help them learn to meet those emotional needs. If they learn to do it, they begin depositing love units and eventually they are in love with each other.

By privately discussing emotional needs with hundreds of men and women, I have discovered that there are ten emotional needs that most people have: the need of admiration, affection, conversation, domestic support, family commitment, financial support, honesty and openness, physical attractiveness, recreational companionship, and sexual fulfillment.

I have also made a revolutionary discovery that has helped me understand why it is so difficult for men and women to meet each other's needs. Whenever I ask couples to list their needs according to their priority, men list them one way and women the opposite way. The five *most important* emotional needs of men are usually the *least important* for women, and vice versa.

What an insight! No wonder men and women have so much difficulty meeting each other's needs: They are unable to empathize with each other. They do for each other what they would appreciate the most, but it turns out that their efforts are misdirected. What one spouse appreciates the most, the other appreciates the least!

Of course everyone's unique. While men on average pick a particular five emotional needs and women on average pick another five, any particular man or woman can and do pick all sorts of combinations. Therefore, each spouse's list of important emotional needs reflects what he or she appreciates the most. When those needs are met, he or she will be in love with the one who meets them.

These conclusions are given in my book *His Needs, Her Needs,* where I explain how couples build romantic love by learning how to meet each other's most important emotional needs.

If you would like to identify your own most important emotional needs, and those of your spouse, make two enlarged copies of the Emotional Needs Questionnaire that is provided in appendix B and then fill them out. To help you better understand these needs, I have written a short description of each of them in appendix A.

Love Busters

Meeting important emotional needs is only half of the story, however. While that's how couples deposit love units, they must be sure that they're not depositing them into a sieve: They must avoid withdrawing love units. Couples often get into the habit of doing things that hurt each other. I call these habits Love Busters because they drain love units out of the Love Bank.

Whenever you do something that makes your spouse unhappy, you withdraw some love units. A single careless act is bad enough, but if you repeatedly do something that makes your spouse unhappy, your Love Bank withdrawals can become serious enough to threaten your love for each other. I call behavior that causes repeated withdrawals Love Busters because they destroy romantic love.

In the simplest terms, Love Busters are those things you do on a regular basis that make your spouse unhappy. They will rob enough love units from your account in your spouse's Love Bank to destroy romantic love.

From my work with couples over the years, I have identified five categories of behavior that are Love Busters: angry outbursts, disrespectful judgments, annoying behavior, selfish demands, and dishonesty. Each category represents a type of thoughtless behavior that tends to ruin marriages.

If you would like to identify Love Busters that are withdrawing love units in your relationship, there is a copy of the Love Busters Questionnaire in appendix D. Make two enlarged copies of the questionnaire, one for you and one for your spouse.

Next let me introduce to you a rule that will help you overcome all of your Love Busters. I call it the Policy of Joint Agreement.

The Policy of Joint Agreement

I help couples avoid Love Busters with my Policy of Joint Agreement: *Never do anything without an enthusiastic agreement between you and your spouse.* This rule teaches couples to become thoughtful and sensitive to each other's feelings. If they follow the Policy, they avoid countless Love Busters because they won't ever mutually agree to behavior that hurts one of them. It helps plug up the holes in the sieve of the Love Bank that cause most couples to drift into incompatibility.

My Policy of Joint Agreement encourages couples to consider each other's happiness as equally important. They are a team and both should try to help each other and avoid hurting each other. It just makes good sense. When one spouse considers his or her own interests so important that he or she runs roughshod over the interests of the other, it's a formula for marital disaster, and yet some of the most well-intentioned couples do it from their honeymoon on.

When couples start to follow the Policy of Joint Agreement, however, they gradually throw out all their thoughtless habits and activities and replace them with habits and activities that take each other's feelings into account. That's what compatibility is all about—building a way of life that is comfortable for both spouses. When a couple create a lifestyle that they each enjoy and appreciate, they build compatibility into their marriage.

The most powerful incentive for following the Policy is that it helps create and sustain romantic love. Once the Policy of Joint Agreement is acted on, it helps insulate a couple from many of the destructive forces that are ruining marriages. It helps couples learn to meet each other's needs in ways that are mutually fulfilling and enjoyable.

Spouses that follow the Policy and meet each other's needs fall in love and stay in love with each other. It's so simple: Follow the Policy of Joint Agreement and watch your marriage flourish. As you may have already suspected, however, the Policy isn't very easy to follow. I have developed the concept of the Giver and the Taker to show couples what they're up against.

The Giver and the Taker

Have you ever suspected your spouse of having two personalities—one that is caring and considerate and one that seems impossible to get along with? I'm sure you've not only noticed, but you've probably been horrified by the impossible one. I call these two personalities the Giver and the Taker.

We all have them, a Giver and a Taker, and they make marital problem solving much more difficult than it should be. To help you understand why it's so difficult to communicate in marriage and why the

Policy of Joint Agreement is so hard to follow, I'll explain to you who these characters are and how they make marriage so difficult.

The Giver is the part of you that follows this rule: Do whatever you can to make the other person happy and avoid anything that makes the other person unhappy. It's the part of you that wants to make a difference in the lives of others. It grows out of a basic instinct that we all share, a deep reservoir of love and concern for those around us.

But giving is only half of the story. The other half is the Taker. It's the part of you that follows this rule: Do whatever you can to make you happy and avoid anything that makes you unhappy. It's the part of you that wants you to get as much from life as possible and it grows out of your basic instinct for self-preservation.

In everyday life our Giver and Taker usually solve problems together. They recognize our need to give and take simultaneously. For example, when we buy groceries, we give money and take groceries. We don't give more money than the grocer asks for and we don't take groceries without paying for them.

In marriage a strange thing happens to the way our Giver and Taker operate. They seem to work independently of each other. Either the Giver is in charge, and we give unconditionally to our spouse, or the Taker is in charge, and we take what we want from our spouse without giving anything in return.

When the Giver is in charge, we are loving and considerate. But we tend to make personal sacrifices to see to it that our spouse is happy and fulfilled. Our Taker is not there to defend our personal interests. We love unconditionally when guided by our Giver, because our Giver does not care how we feel.

But when the Taker is in charge, we are rude, demanding, and inconsiderate. All we seem to think about is ourselves and what our spouse can do to make us happy. We expect our spouse to make sacrifices for us because our Taker doesn't care how our spouse feels.

I want to emphasize to you that this is normal behavior in marriage. You might think you're married to a crazy person or you may think you're crazy, but let me assure you, marriage is one of the very few conditions that bring out the pure Giver and Taker in each of us. And that usually makes us seem much crazier than we really are.

It should come as no surprise to you that it isn't the Giver that ruins marriages—it's the Taker. But the Giver plays a very important role in creating the problem. It's the effort of the Giver to give our spouse anything he or she wants that sets up the Taker for its destructive acts. After you have been giving, giving, giving to your spouse, and receiving little in return (because you haven't bargained for much), your Taker rises up to straighten out the situation. It sees the unfairness of it all and steps in to balance the books. Instead of coming to a more equitable arrangement, where you get something for what you give, the Taker just moves the Giver out of the picture altogether. It says, "I've been giving enough; now it's time to take."

Sound familiar? We've all been through it, but it doesn't work. All our Taker does is arouse our spouse's Taker, and the first thing we know, we're having a fight.

But I'm getting a little ahead of myself. Before you can understand fully how our Taker makes us argue instead of negotiate, I need to explain to you the concept of the Three States of Marriage.

The Three States of Marriage

This concept is more complicated than those I've shared with you so far but it's absolutely crucial to your understanding of how you and your spouse can resolve your conflicts. So bear with me.

Some of the brightest people I know become idiots when faced with marital conflict. I've seen this happen in case after case. An intelligent man listens to his wife talking about her needs, her desires, her interests—and it's as if she's speaking a foreign language. A brilliant woman hears her husband describe his perspective and she doesn't get it.

What makes marital communication so tough? Is it that men and women just can't communicate? Or is there something about marriage that blurs their thinking? Having spent decades counseling couples who seem communicationally challenged, I am thoroughly convinced that it is marriage itself (or more specifically, romantic relationships) that makes communication difficult, and not differences between men and women. The men I counsel have very little trouble resolving conflicts with women, and the wives are usually just as good at negotiating with men. It's conflicts they have with each other that seem impossible to resolve.

My experience trying to help couples negotiate has led me to the conclusion that, left to their own devices, they negotiate from one of three states of mind, each having its own unique negotiating rules and its own unique emotional reactions. I call them States of Marriage: intimacy, conflict, and withdrawal. Negotiations are very different for each of these States of Marriage.

The First State of Marriage: Intimacy

The most essential prerequisite for the state of intimacy is the feeling of being in love. As I discussed earlier in the section on the Love Bank, you have that feeling when your spouse has deposited a certain number of love units into your Love Bank.

In this most enjoyable state of a relationship, spouses follow the rule of the Giver: Do whatever you can to make the *other person* happy, and avoid anything that makes the *other person* unhappy. When both partners follow this rule, both are getting their emotional needs met, and all is well with the world. Giving to each other seems almost instinctive. Spouses both have a great desire to make each other happy in any way they can and want to avoid hurting each other at all costs.

As they protect each other, trust builds. They can share their deepest feelings, becoming emotionally vulnerable, because they know that they both have each other's best interest at heart. They feel so close to each other that to hurt the other person would be the same as hurting themselves.

Conversation in the state of intimacy is respectful and nonjudgmental. The partners also express their deepest love for each other and gratitude for the care they are receiving. By lowering their defenses and forming a close emotional bond, they feel even greater pleasure when they meet each other's needs. This is the way marriage was meant to be.

Negotiation in this State of Marriage is controlled by the Giver and the Giver's rule. When one spouse expresses a desire, the other rushes to fulfill it. There is no thought of repayment, because the Giver's care is unconditional. As long as both spouses are in the same state, there's actually nothing to negotiate—they give each other anything that's possible and they do it unconditionally.

The Second State of Marriage: Conflict

Suppose, while a couple is in the state of intimacy, the husband is unintentionally inconsiderate. He promised to pick up orange juice on the way home from work and forgot. Or perhaps, through no fault of her own, the wife is ineffective in meeting one of her husband's most important emotional needs, causing him frustration. Because of their vulnerability and close emotional bonding, every negative experience feels like a stab in the back.

"Why are you treating me this way?" The slumbering Taker has been alerted to your pain. "I haven't done anything to hurt you."

If this was just a temporary lapse, if the errant partner is still in a giving mood, apologies abound and efforts are made to compensate for the pain. The husband promises that he will be more thoughtful in the future and the wife makes an effort to meet her husband's unmet need. The Takers are satisfied that all is well and go back to sleep, leaving the Givers in charge and keeping the couple in the state of intimacy.

But what happens if there are no apologies? What if the damage is not repaired quickly? What if one partner continues to be thoughtless?

As soon as you can say, "bull in a china closet," out comes the Taker, drawing you into the second State of Marriage, conflict. Now the Taker's rules and emotional reactions prevail.

Instinctively you adapt the Taker's rule: Do whatever you can to make *you* happy, and avoid anything that makes *you* unhappy. When one spouse follows this new rule, it isn't long before the other spouse's Taker pushes the Giver aside and is ready for battle. In this State of Marriage partners are no longer willing to meet each other's needs but demand that their own needs be met first. They no longer guarantee protection. Instead, they threaten each other with pain unless their demands are met.

In the state of conflict, conversation tends to be disrespectful, resentful, and even hateful. Mutual care and concern have been replaced by mutual self-centeredness. Your Taker no longer trusts your spouse to look after your interests but pulls out all the stops to see to it that you are treated fairly. The problem, of course, is that your Taker does not know how to treat your spouse with that same fairness. From your Taker's perspective, fairness is getting your way at all costs.

In the state of conflict, couples are still emotionally bonded and that makes the pain of thoughtlessness even worse. Love units are withdrawn at a very fast rate. The couple may still hope that the hurting will stop and there will be a return to the state of intimacy but they don't trust each other to stop the madness. Occasionally one spouse may revert to the state of intimacy, but if peace is to return, they must both do it simultaneously. The only way to calm down both spouses' Takers is for both of them to be protected at the same time.

Couples can return to the state of intimacy from conflict, if and only if they stop hurting each other and return to meeting each other's emotional needs again.

This is extremely difficult because in the state of conflict your Taker urges you to return pain whenever you receive it. So for most couples the state of conflict inspires them to be shortsighted. Instead of wanting to meet each other's needs, they want their own needs met before they'll do anything. That makes resolving the conflict seem almost impossible, because our Taker would rather fight than try to make the other spouse happy.

In the state of intimacy negotiations really don't work, because each spouse is trying to out-give the other. They are both happy with the arrangement, but it's not what I consider bargaining. It's like giving away the store!

However, negotiations in the state of conflict don't work either. Each spouse is trying to out-take the other. There is no effort to make the other spouse happy, only the self-centered effort of pleasing self at the other person's expense. It's like robbing the bank.

The Third State of Marriage: Withdrawal

If reason does not prevail, couples eventually enter the third State of Marriage, withdrawal. The Takers are still in charge, but they adopt a new strategy. In the state of conflict the strategy is *fight*. But in the state of withdrawal the strategy is *flight*.

When you're in the state of conflict, your Taker tries to force your spouse to meet your needs, making demands and threatening your spouse with pain to get its way. But if that doesn't work—if your spouse does not meet your needs—your Taker suggests a new approach to the problem: withdrawal. It tries to convince you that your spouse is not worth the effort.

In the state of withdrawal, spouses no longer feel emotionally bonded or in love, and emotional defenses are raised. Neither one wants to try to meet the other's needs, and both have given up on attempts to get their own needs met by the other. One becomes two. They are completely independent, united only in living arrangements, finances, and child rearing, although they often have to keep up appearances for neighbors and friends.

When one spouse enters the state of withdrawal, the other usually follows. After all, what is the point? If she is meeting none of his needs and rebuffing every effort he makes to meet hers, he might as well give up too. The thoughtless behavior by each spouse toward the other becomes too great to bear, so they stop caring. Trust is a faint memory.

Emotional needs can be met only when we are emotionally vulnerable to someone who meets those needs. When we are in the state of withdrawal, our emotional needs cannot be met. Couples in withdrawal are really in a state of emotional divorce. When they've been in withdrawal for any length of time, they will sleep in separate rooms, take separate vacations, and eat meals at different times. They will not communicate unless they must. If those conditions don't work, they either separate or obtain a legal divorce.

If negotiations aren't successful in the states of intimacy and conflict, they certainly don't work in the state of withdrawal. In intimacy couples must only ask and they receive. In conflict they fight to get what they want, and the bargain is usually unfair. But in withdrawal, there are no discussions, no bargaining, not even arguing. In that state, a spouse is unwilling to do anything for his or her spouse or let the spouse do anything in return.

Getting Back to Intimacy

Marriage partners do not necessarily experience the same State of Marriage at the same time. One spouse may mar the peace and tranquility of intimacy and cause the other spouse to enter into the state of conflict. That's when complaints, nagging, and arguments start. As these disagreements escalate, the other spouse is dragged into the conflict as well, and then both spouses behave selfishly.

Typically, if they fail in their efforts to resolve the conflict and if the unpleasant effects escalate, one spouse will go into withdrawal first and raise his or her emotional barriers. The spouse that remains in the state of conflict continues to argue, while the withdrawn spouse tries to escape. If the arguing spouse persists, the withdrawn spouse may be goaded to reenter the conflict state and fight back. Or the arguing spouse may give up and enter the withdrawal state too.

One spouse may also lead the other on the road back from withdrawal to conflict and eventually to intimacy. While in withdrawal, a husband may decide to make a new effort to restore intimacy and he tosses out an olive branch. That effort places him back into the conflict state, leaving his wife in withdrawal.

Suppose his effort is an encouragement to her and she joins him in the state of conflict. Now they are both willing to have their needs met by the other, but their Takers encourage them to fight about it, rather than negotiate fairly and peacefully.

This step from withdrawal to conflict is a positive one, a step in the right direction. Withdrawal may seem more peaceful, but it is actually a shutting down of the marriage. A return to the conflict state is a sign that the partners have restored hope—they think they can get what they want from each other. They are lowering their emotional defenses and taking the risk of getting close to each other again.

While fighting and arguing is instinctive in the conflict state, one spouse can lead the other back to intimacy by resisting the Taker's temptation to fight. It takes two to fight, and if one spouse makes an effort to avoid making hurtful and judgmental statements, and tries to meet the other's needs, the other usually calms down and does the same thing.

Once they see each other's caring efforts and rebuild their Love Bank accounts, they reenter the intimacy state. But there's an irony that trips up some couples. Which spouse do you think is the first to move back into the state of intimacy, the one who makes the first effort to meet the other's needs or the recipient of that effort? You may have guessed it. The recipient of care is usually the first to return to the state of intimacy, and not the one who makes the greatest effort to save the relationship.

If you set a good example by meeting your spouse's needs first, alas, that usually means that your own needs are met last. Your Taker is not pleased with this arrangement and may try to sabotage it. You will need to make a deliberate and patient effort to override the Taker's instinct to retreat back to fighting and name-calling. But if you resist that instinct to argue and instead focus attention on meeting your spouse's needs, your spouse will be encouraged to meet your needs. When both your needs and your spouse's needs are finally met, the struggle is over. You will have restored intimacy.

The passage from intimacy, through conflict, to withdrawal can be almost effortless, but it takes quite a bit of work to climb back up that hill. While one of you can pull you both back up the hill, it's a lot easier when you both work together.

Successful negotiation, as I see it, is a bargain that benefits both spouses and doesn't hurt either spouse. When you are in the state of intimacy, neither spouse wants to see *the other* hurt. In the state of conflict, neither wants to *be* hurt. Actually both objectives are important, and that's why I created the Policy of Joint Agreement— it takes the best from both our Giver and our Taker.

The Policy of Joint Agreement also avoids the worst in our Giver and Taker. In the state of intimacy, we are willing to be hurt ourselves to make the other person happy. In the state of conflict, we are willing to see our spouse suffer so we can be happy. Neither of these are worthy objectives because in both cases someone gets hurt.

In marriage your interests and your spouse's interests must be considered simultaneously. One of you cannot afford to suffer for the benefit of the other, even willingly, because when either of you suffers, your marriage suffers. You're a team, not two individuals, and your joint success will determine the success of your marriage. The Policy of Joint Agreement helps you maintain that perspective.

Remember to go by the Policy—never do anything without an enthusiastic agreement between you and your spouse—whenever you negotiate with your spouse. When you follow the Policy, your Giver will encourage you to make your spouse happy, but your Taker will protect you from agreeing to something that is not in your best interest.

The Policy of Joint Agreement keeps the excesses of our Giver and Taker in check. It prevents us from giving so much that we'll resent it later, or taking so much that we hurt our spouse. It forces us into the balance we need in marriage to create and sustain compatibility and the feeling of romantic love.

I have one more basic concept to introduce to you. It is the Rule of Honesty. Without it, the Policy of Joint Agreement will not work. When you follow this rule and the Policy of Joint Agreement, your marriage will be utterly sensational!

The Rule of Honesty

Most couples do the best they can to make each other happy. But their efforts, however sincere, are often misdirected. They aim at the wrong target. Ignorance, not lack of effort, causes their ultimate downfall.

Couples are ignorant not only of ways to improve their marriage, they are often ignorant of the problems themselves. To avoid conflict, they sometimes deliberately misinform each other as to their feelings, activities, and plans. This not only leads to a withdrawal of love units, when the deception is discovered, but it also makes marital conflicts impossible to resolve. As conflicts build, romantic love slips away.

To help couples understand its importance, I've created the Rule of Honesty for successful marriages: *Reveal to your spouse as much information about yourself as you know: your thoughts, feelings, habits, likes, dislikes, personal history, daily activities, and plans for the future.*

To help explain this rule, I have broken it down into five parts:

Emotional Honesty: Reveal your emotional reactions—both positive and negative—to the events of your life, particularly to your spouse's behavior.

Historical Honesty: Reveal information about your personal history, particularly events that demonstrate personal weakness or failure.

Current Honesty: Reveal information about the events of your day. Provide your spouse with a calendar of your activities, with special emphasis on those that may affect your spouse.

Future Honesty: Reveal your thoughts and plans regarding future activities and objectives.

Complete Honesty: Do not leave your spouse with a false impression about your thoughts, feelings, habits, likes, dislikes, personal history, daily activities, or plans for the future. Do not deliberately keep personal information from your spouse.

To some extent this rule seems like motherhood and apple pie. Who would argue that it's not a good idea to be honest? But in my years of experience as a marriage counselor, I have found that many clients consider dishonesty a good idea under certain conditions. Moreover, pastors and counselors often advise dishonesty.

Granted, dishonesty may seem like a good short-term solution to marital conflict. It will probably get you off the hook for a few days or months. But it's a terrible long-term solution. If you expect to live with each other for the next few years, dishonesty can get you into a great deal of trouble.

Because there are so many who advocate dishonesty in marriage, I have written a defense and explanation of the five parts of my Rule of Honesty. You will find this in appendix E.

Throughout my years of counseling, these basic concepts have helped me guide couples from the edge of marital disaster to the security of marital happiness. Not only do these concepts explain how couples create their marital problems, but they also point the way to solutions.

The letters that follow represent the most common marital conflicts. My answer to each letter explains how my basic concepts are to be used to resolve the conflict and restore love to the marriage. Somewhere in this book, the conflicts you have in marriage are probably addressed and solutions to your problems are suggested. Even if you cannot find an example of your particular conflict, you should be able to use the same basic concepts to solve your problem and restore love to your marriage.

Part 2

How to Survive Infidelity

What to Do with an Unfaithful Husband

The following four letters are from women whose husbands are having an affair. These letters will not only help you see how cruel infidelity is, but they will show you that reconciliation is neither hopeless nor masochistic.

Dear Dr. Harley,

This past summer my husband of fourteen years confessed he had been having an affair with a woman from work for the past two years. He has contemplated leaving me and our two children many times but could not bring himself to do it. He claims he loves us and cares about us but he is not in love with me.

Our love relationship started going downhill after we had our children, with all the pressures of family life. But it didn't really get bad until after he started the affair. Our power struggle has always been between his not having enough sex and my not having enough affection. We recently read your book "His Needs, Her Needs" and agree that we were both at fault.

I find this all easy to see from a logical point of view, but my husband is seeing everything from an emotional point of view. He feels love for the other woman and he doesn't feel love for me. He says he has not been seeing her, even though they work at the same place. I believe he is sincere about it. We have been just riding it out until our emotions start to level out but we are both growing impatient.

I have suggested counseling, but my husband is reluctant because he says he knows what his feelings are. I asked him, "If we could restore the intimacy we once had, would you want to stay with me?" He said, "Yes." My husband is a truly wonderful person with qualities that are hard to find. I love him more than anything and the last thing I want is for him to move out, but the tension is so high. Sometimes we do relax and have a great time but that seems to scare him and he gets depressed and withdraws again.

Right now I feel like the only way to win his heart back is to separate for a while. It would mean that the kids and I would have to move back to my family, out of state. He feels that would be unfair. He doesn't want his life disrupted like that. He wants to have access to his children. The move would be really hard on all of us but I cannot stand thinking of staying here with all our memories while he is so distant. I need the love and support of my family. My real question is would counseling help at this point considering his emotional state, or am I better off letting him find out what his real feelings are for me by separating?

I don't want another marriage to end up in divorce because of a communication problem. But my husband feels the love is too long gone to get it back.

W. M.

Dear W. M.,

As you know from having read my book, I advise your husband to never see his lover again. He must move to another job and possibly to another state before he can reconcile with you. Otherwise, he will continue to love her and be unable to resist seeing her from time to time. Even if your marriage improves, he may never be able to overcome his feeling of love for this other woman unless he stops seeing her.

From your description, it seems that he is unlikely to accept my advice—at least at this time. All of his talk about the way he feels proves that he is addicted to his lover. So I recommend to you a three-step plan.

The *first step* is to be the very best wife you can possibly be. Do everything you can to meet his needs and don't do anything to upset him. Set a period of time that you think you can do this without getting too upset, say, six months. Once in a while tell him that you think both of you need a fresh start somewhere else.

If he does not respond to your kindness and respectful suggestions within the period of time you set for yourself, you're ready for the *second step:* Pack up yourself and your children and move near your family and friends for their support. It should be far away from his lover—another city or even another state. Have absolutely nothing to do with your husband. Don't talk to him; don't see him.

If you are forced to say something to him, tell him that you love him and hope he can free himself from the addiction of his affair. Let him know that the only way you will consider restoring your relationship with him is for him to quit his job and move to where you are. There you will start life over again. Be certain that your words and tone of voice communicate your care for him, not your anger.

Your husband is not likely to agree to your ultimatum right away. He will try to develop a relationship with his lover first. The relationship probably won't work because he needs both you and her. She meets some of his needs and you meet others. This is true in the vast majority of cases. Eventually he will discover how much he misses you.

In the event that he stays with his lover and he does not come back to you, you avoid untold sorrow trying to reach a man who is in love with another woman. As you wait for his decision and go through this crisis, it is very important to surround yourself with your family and friends. Then, if he chooses his lover, the experience will be much harder on him than on you.

If he eventually agrees to your terms, you begin the *third step,* which is to start again with a new commitment to meet each other's needs and avoid Love Busters—in a new location.

At first, he will be depressed because he misses his lover. He will go through a grieving process that usually lasts a few weeks. For some, it takes as long as a year to overcome, but this is quite rare. His affair is an addiction, and the withdrawal from his lover puts him into a very painful emotional state. If he calls his lover on the telephone, or inadvertently sees her, the clock is set back to zero, and the period of withdrawal begins again. That's why he must avoid all contact with her for the rest of his life.

After the period of withdrawal has ended, he will open his heart to you and give you a chance to meet his need for sex and the other needs his lover met. He will also learn to meet your needs, particularly your need for affection. You will have an opportunity to build a new lifestyle together, one that fits your needs so well that it will affair-proof your marriage.

Dear Dr. Harley,

My husband and I have had a difficult marriage of seven years as well as three years of living together before marriage. About six months ago he informed me that he was very close to a woman in a nearby office. He said he was unsure of how he felt about her. After a week or so of "discussing" this situation, we agreed to work on our marriage if for no other reason than for our four-year-old son.

My husband promised not to talk with the other woman other than in passing but he did nothing to improve our relationship at home. He essentially moped around the house and pouted as if he had lost his best friend. I tried showering him with affection and attention and later found out he considered it "too much."

During this time we saw a counselor. My husband did not consider himself to be at fault for his relationship with the other woman. He thought the kiss they shared was nothing. But last week he informed me that he is in love with her and "loves" me only because I am our son's mother. I threw him out of the house.

He discussed the situation with the other woman, and they decided that too many lives would be negatively affected by a relationship between them. She has asked for a transfer to a different location to eliminate their daily contact. My husband wants to come home. He doesn't know if he will ever love me as a wife again but he wants to keep his family together. He is unsure how he will deal with his feelings for this woman.

I have not a clue as to what to do. Is it possible for him to love me again? Any insight or revelation will be appreciated! I look forward to your response.

M. S.

Dear M. S.,

Your approach to the problem has been quite reasonable. First, in an effort to win him back to you, you tried to meet needs that your husband's lover was meeting. But he was in a state of withdrawal and wouldn't let you meet his needs. Then you asked him to leave when you found his relationship with the woman increasing in intensity. It's what I recommend in chapter 13 (How to Survive an Affair) of *His Needs, Her Needs.*

He reacted to your rejection in a reasonable way too. He discussed it with his lover, they decided to try to end the relationship, she moved to another location, and he is wanting to return to you.

So far, so good. Now, what's the next step?

First, let me give you an overview of what it is you are up against. An affair is often more than a choice; it's an addiction. Even though your husband knows what he should do, he will have great difficulty doing it, because he's addicted.

Your husband probably does love you (even though he didn't sound too convincing) and cannot imagine leaving you. Furthermore, he does not want his family broken up and he has decided to make his marriage with you work. But in spite of his resolve, he is suffering from the effects of his addiction. He is powerless to resist his lover.

Not everyone involved in an affair is addicted, of course, just like not all people who get drunk every weekend are alcoholics. I have treated many "alcoholics" who simply made a decision in my office to stop drinking. Even though they were suffering the physical effects of years of drunkenness, from that day forward they never had another drink. They told me they had almost no craving for liquor after they stopped drinking. I don't consider these people addicts. I believe their drinking was something they could have always stopped at any time because they were never addicted. The proof was in the fact that they actually stopped cold turkey and suffered no withdrawal symptoms. Another proof was that they were able to avoid alcohol for the rest of their lives. I have known some of them to remain sober for more than twenty years.

It can be the same with cigarette smokers. Rush Limbaugh claims that after years of smoking he simply gave it up one day and has never smoked since. I know of many people like Rush who, in my judgment, were never addicted to nicotine. That's why they were able to give up smoking with relative ease.

Affairs can be the same, particularly when a spouse is not in love with his lover. Many affairs are one-night stands, and a spouse has sex only once with someone who happens to be available. Even when it is repeated, a relationship of sexual convenience, without the feeling of love, is often easy to stop when it is exposed. That sort of relationship is not an addiction, although it is still devastating to the other spouse.

It's difficult to know whether or not a relationship *is* an addiction until a husband has left his lover for good. An addicted husband will claim that he does not love the other woman as a way to deflect attention from the relationship. Then when everything is back to normal at home, he gets back together with her. Addicts are notorious liars, and the appearance of sincerity is their specialty.

An alcoholic that I once counseled told his wife that he had simply made the decision to give up drinking. He was convincing for two years. But one day he was rushed to the hospital for drinking window washer fluid. Unknown to him, his brother had filled the container with the real thing, and he just about killed himself drinking it. From that day on, his wife knew he was an addict, and he voluntarily admitted himself into treatment.

In your case, your husband is most certainly addicted because he loves the other woman and he had so many withdrawal symptoms when he tried to leave her. So let's look at ways that addicts must be treated to help them overcome their addiction. Having owned and operated chemical dependency treatment programs, I am well aware of the most successful methods.

To be on the safe side, I usually assume that an affair is an addiction. If I'm right, we get to the root of the problem without wasting valuable time. If I'm wrong, going through the steps necessary to avoid seeing the former lover, which should be done whether or not it's an addiction, is simply easier for the straying spouse to do. Also, if it's not an addiction, the wayward spouse simply doesn't experience any of the symptoms of withdrawal when separated from his lover.

Treatment for addiction to drugs or alcohol begins by simply separating a person from the addicting substance. There is a period of withdrawal, but after that, the person is no longer physically addicted. From there, treatment usually focuses on helping addicts resist the temptation to go back to the addicting substance. Support groups usually try to help build values and moral character that prevent a relapse. The goal of most successful programs is to help an addict completely avoid the addicting substance for the rest of his or her life.

The first step, separating a person from the addicting substance, is essential to treatment. In many cases, a person must be hospitalized to ensure compliance with this step. Once physiological addiction has ended, addicts are in a better position to control their impulse to use the addicting substance again. They must understand that any use of it will ultimately lead to physical addiction again, so therapy usually focuses on abstinence.

One sure cure for addicts is to have them live in a place where the addicting substance is simply unavailable to them. This is enforced prohibition. In the case of infidelity, it is relatively easy to find a place that is free of the addicting agent. In fact, any place will do, as long as it's not where the lover resides. Unlike drugs and alcohol that are readily available almost everywhere, the object of the addiction in an affair, the lover, is in only one place. It's easy to remove the temptation because you know where the lover is, and where he or she isn't.

Since an affair is usually an addiction, it is unlikely that your husband will be able to establish a meaningful relationship with you until his friend is no longer available to him. She is in a new location at work, but I doubt that they will be able to avoid making contact with each other. So the first thing you and he need to discuss is moving to a place where he cannot easily make contact with her.

I recommend moving to another state. While that may sound drastic, moves are not all that unusual in America today. In fact a move may revitalize your marriage. It may help you form a lifestyle that you both enjoy much more than the one you have now.

At first your husband will go through a period of depression and won't be much fun to be around. You've already experienced some of his moping when he was going through withdrawal a few weeks ago. Well, he will go through it again when he first comes home to you. Those who let themselves be trapped in an affair pay a terrific price. Many of those I've counseled wished they were dead. But when the period of withdrawal is over, they have a chance to make their marriage better than it's ever been.

Then what's the next step? How can you restore the love you had for each other?

You should be complimented on your willingness to work things out with him. You have had to put up with frustration, humiliation, and very hurt feelings to try to prevent your family from breaking up. But you should acknowledge an important reason that he had the affair: You have not been meeting at least one of his most important emotional needs. His feelings for you are not what they should be because of it.

The purpose of my Emotional Needs Questionnaire (appendix B) is to help spouses identify their most important emotional needs so that the other spouse can learn to meet those needs. While your husband is still separated from you, ask him to fill out a questionnaire. His lover apparently met some needs that you didn't meet. You must learn to meet each other's most important emotional needs and then you will have the marriage you have always wanted.

It's entirely possible that your four-year-old child has something to do with your failure to meet your husband's emotional needs. What changed between you and your husband when your child arrived that could account for his missing out on something? Certainly the availability of privacy changed. Maybe you didn't have much time with each other to talk, to connect emotionally.

You say that your seven years of marriage were difficult as were the three years you were living together. Have you both been the victims of Love Busters? Have you been destroying your relationship with angry outbursts, disrespectful judgments, or selfish demands?

Make two copies of my Love Busters Questionnaire (appendix D) so that both of you can identify Love Busters that may be wrecking everything you are trying to create. Even if you know how to meet each other's emotional needs, Love Busters can make all your efforts worthless. On the other hand, if you know how to throw the rascals out, what you build will stay put. The love units you deposit by meeting each other's emotional needs will accumulate in the Love Bank, and you will both be in love with each other once more.

Dear Dr. Harley,

My husband had an affair with a coworker about ten months ago. The affair is over but they both still work in the same office building. After reading your book "His Needs, Her Needs," I feel that my needs were never really met in our relationship. Now my biggest need is for him to prove he really loves me and cares about me and will put my needs above anything else.

My greatest need is for him to confront this woman and tell her what a mistake their relationship was and how much he really loves me and his family. Am I wrong or out of line?

He is scared to death she will file a sexual harassment charge against him. He says that is why he can't do it. I feel that his account in my Love Bank is in the negative and this is the only way he can begin making new deposits after what he has done. Am I totally wrong? Am I looking at this from the wrong perspective?

I guess you could say I ended the affair because I discovered it. My husband has always been a very weak, needy person. He thought he loved this woman. He would have left me the night I found out except she didn't want him to come to her. My husband is so needy he couldn't stand the idea of being alone so he stayed with me.

We are still together but there is so much pain and anger on my side it gets in the way. He feels he can't quit his job because he wouldn't find another one. I don't really want him to quit either, because the only need of mine he meets is financial security. If he couldn't find another job, I'd have no reason at all to be with him.

If anyone should have had an affair, it's me. I am in desperate need of help. Counselors in the past seemed to only make things worse. Can you help me?

B. T.

Dear B. T.,

When one spouse has an affair, it is common that the other spouse is just as likely to have one. Often only a lack of opportunity prevents it. Regretfully ethical standards seem to have little to do with it. You are both vulnerable to an affair because you are both failing to meet each other's emotional needs.

In spite of your anger, you and your husband should come to grips with what's missing in your marriage and work together to make the necessary changes. You might find *Give and Take: The Secret to Marital Compatibility* helpful because it deals with how to learn to meet each other's needs when you don't feel like it.

You describe a need that all of us have: the need to be loved. What you want is assurance that your husband cares more about you than anyone else, particularly his coworker. So you want him to tell her that he really loves you, not her. He has reason to fear a sexual harassment charge from what he's done in the past, but there's little risk that the conversation you have in mind would inspire one. His biggest problem is that he probably loves her more than he loves you, and he cannot in all honesty tell her otherwise.

My advice is that he should never have another conversation with her again, certainly not one about his feelings toward her. Fortunately the woman at work seems to have rejected him. Thankfully most affairs end that way. You have both missed a bullet. But if you don't straighten things out with him, he'll keep looking, and it will only be a matter of time before he finds someone who won't let him go so easily.

Don't ask your husband to make all the changes; you have to make some too. From the way you describe your husband, I would assume that you are tempted to smother him in Love Busters: angry outbursts, disrespectful judgments, and selfish demands. You have been deeply hurt and you want to retaliate but you'll only be doing your-self harm if you make him suffer for what you've been through. Resist the temptation because it's in your best interest for him to love you and care for you. He won't do either unless you deposit love units in his Love Bank (by meeting his emotional needs) and avoid with-drawing love units from his Love Bank (by not indulging in Love Busters).

Your husband's affair can be the catalyst that either improves or ends your bad marriage. If you both decide to make permanent changes in the way you treat each other, your love for your husband will return, and your anger toward him will end. Believe it or not, after you and your husband learn to take good care of each other, you will look back at this experience and view it as a positive turn-ing point in your relationship.

Dear Dr. Harley,

My husband has been having an affair since January. We have been married for almost nine years and we have two children. He has been living with his brother for the last two and one-half weeks. While he has told me several times that he has broken off all communication with the other per-son, she always resurfaces.

I have now made the commitment to not talk with him anymore, since our conversations and discussions are not getting anywhere except for placing blame, defensiveness, and guilt. It seems like he wants our marriage to work but he cannot get away from the other person either. He needs to understand that he cannot have the best of both worlds.

I have been contemplating divorce but I do not want to be too hasty in throwing our marriage away. We went to a counselor at one point but I feel it did no good at all. Right now I have very little contact with him, not even by phone. The children are picked up from a nearby relative when it's his turn to have them, so I do not have to see him.

He just keeps lying to me all the time. He is not the man I once knew. I guess my only solution is just getting on with my life and putting as much distance as I can between us. He will probably lose me and his kids forever. If you have any insightful advice to give me, I would truly appreciate it.

C. M.

Dear C. M.,

Your husband probably has very little control over himself these days and does not have the willpower to stay away from his friend. You have done the right thing by having him move out until he gives her up, but how can you know when that is?

I often suggest moving far enough away from a lover to avoid easy access to her, even to another state if necessary. I am working with a couple right now who are moving from the Twin Cities to another state just to get away from an affair that has dogged them for the past two years. In their case it is a neighbor down the street from them, but in most cases it is someone at work.

Your husband probably loves both of you and cannot imagine leaving you or the other woman. He vacillates back and forth: When he's with you, he misses the other woman, and when he's with her, he misses you. Within two years, it is likely that his relationship with her will die out, but during those years, you will become emotionally distraught. You cannot wait for them to discover the foolishness of their relationship.

Suppose you and your husband move away from his lover. What's the likelihood of yet another affair? Unless you do something to improve your marriage, he is likely to get into one affair after another. There are three basic problems you should resolve:

1. *Dishonesty.* Most affairs develop under the cover of lies. They begin with casual friendship and develop into a very intimate and compelling bond. They usually surprise both people having the affair because of the intensity of it all. But if a married couple has learned to be honest with each other, any other relationship is broken off as soon as the friendship grows into an infatuation. As a husband and wife discuss the relationship, they decide together that the friendship is too dangerous to their marriage, and it is ended before it goes too far. If a cou-

ple follow my Rule of Honesty, it is almost impossible for an affair to take root and ruin a marriage.

2. *Need for mutual consideration.* In all of my writing and counseling I recommend the Policy of Joint Agreement to all married couples. When you follow the Policy, you make every decision together, taking each other's feelings into account. It's pretty obvious that your husband's affair would never have gotten off the ground if it had required your enthusiastic agreement.

3. *Meeting emotional needs.* Affairs develop because they usually meet emotional needs that are not being met in marriage. In my book *His Needs, Her Needs: Building an Affair-proof Marriage,* I introduce ten needs that, when unmet in marriage, can lead to an affair. Your husband can probably tell you what his lover is doing for him emotionally that you are not doing. I know that it's difficult to care for someone who has hurt you the way your husband has, but if you want to save your marriage, both you and your husband must learn to meet each other's most important emotional needs.

What to Do with an Unfaithful Wife

The last four letters were from wives whose husbands were unfaithful. The next four are from husbands who have unfaithful wives. The approach I recommend for the crisis of infidelity is similar for husbands and wives, but there is enough difference to consider the two problems separately.

I hope by reading these letters you can see the emotional turmoil that infidelity inflicts on the remaining spouse. It is without a doubt the most painful form of abuse that one spouse can inflict on another. Many have told me that they would rather have been permanently crippled than to have experienced the unfaithfulness of their spouse. And yet if love is to be restored to the marriage, the response to this suffering must be kindness, patience, and understanding. It goes against all of our instincts to respond this way but it works.

Dear Dr. Harley,

My wife and I have been together for sixteen years, married for eleven. We have two children, seven and nine. We've never fought much, always got along pretty well. I own and operate a successful business and we are doing well financially. My wife is a sales representative and enjoys her work. We are also making love about twice a week, in spite of our most recent crisis. Five years ago her mother, father, and disabled sister moved into our home, and three years ago her father died. Her mom and sister still live with us.

44

We've been through quite a bit together but have always been there for each other, until recently. A few months ago I found out she was having an affair. She says she loves us both and can't make a choice. If forced to, she says she will give up both of us. I love my wife very much and want to work it out. We are both in counseling, but she is spending quite a bit of her time with him. They even go on out-of-town business trips together. He is married and has offered to leave his wife for her. My wife says she is very confused and needs time. She will not tell me when she sees him or talks to him. I don't ask so as not to pressure her. I have always done everything for her to allow her to pursue her career. I am trying to be patient but how long should I wait?

A. W.

Dear A. W.,

People usually have affairs because their unmet emotional needs are met by their lover. There is probably something that your wife's lover is doing for her that makes her feel so good that she is willing to sacrifice the happiness of her children, her mother, her sister, and you just to get it. What is it? What does her lover do for her that is so important? What does he give her that you have not given her? Can you change so that you can meet that need?

The reason she is having trouble deciding between you and her lover is that you both meet different emotional needs. She says she still loves you and that may be the case, particularly since she still makes love to you twice a week. She loves you because you are meeting some of her important needs. Since she says she would leave you both if she had to decide between you, there's a good chance that neither of you meets enough of her needs for her to settle on one of you. But if you could do for her what this other man is doing, the conflict would be ended and your family would be secure. You would have learned to meet all of her most important emotional needs, ending her affair—and the risk of others.

With her mother, sister, and your two children living at home, I imagine that there is little privacy. It could be that when she is with

45

her lover, they have the privacy that is needed to meet important emotional needs. Maybe it's not so much him as it is the environment that she and her lover share that makes him so attractive. She spends time each week alone with him when they give each other their undivided attention. That kind of time and privacy is essential in meeting most of the important emotional needs. It could be that you have not given her enough of your undivided attention in a stress-free and private environment.

If possible, have a nonthreatening discussion with her about what her friend does for her that you don't. Ask her to complete the Emotional Needs Questionnaire (appendix B) so that you can see which of her most important emotional needs you are meeting and which of them you are not meeting. It's a pretty safe guess that her lover is meeting the ones you are missing.

When you have this discussion, the Taker in you will tell you to express your resentment over how much she has hurt you. Your Taker may even encourage you to let her lover have this ungrateful woman so that you can find someone who will love you the way you are (see The Giver and the Taker on page 18). You will be tempted to lose your temper, to say disrespectful things, try to straighten her out, and give her ultimatums. If you do any of these things, she will find you repulsive and withdraw from you more than she already has. It will get you nowhere.

On the other hand, if you can show her that her feelings are important to you and you are dedicated to making decisions that are in her best interest, it will add greatly to your credibility. Right now she doesn't think that you have put her first in your life. Convince her otherwise.

After you have established what her lover does for her that you don't do, ask her to give you a chance to prove to her that you can do it too. She probably wants a soul mate, someone to whom she feels emotionally connected. Over the past few years, she has lost her connection with you. Give yourself about six months and go all out to try your best to meet her needs and reconnect. Be sure you do not wreck it all by being thoughtless or disrespectful. If she is willing, take her with you on short vacations to places she would enjoy. Make her an integral part of your life without making her feel that you are trying to smother her and take control. Never make any demands on her time; just offer her opportunities to become a part of you and express your willingness to become a part of her.

Don't tell her that your plan is only for six months because that would constitute a threat. Besides, you cannot be sure how long you will last. But at the end of six months, evaluate your progress. If your relationship is improving, you may be encouraged to continue for another six months. Remember that her state of mind will improve if you are depositing love units and not withdrawing them. She may become less defensive and less secretive about her lifestyle. She may also tell you that she has completely abandoned her lover and is giving you a solid chance to work things out.

If, however, at the end of six months, she refuses to stop seeing her lover and doesn't seem to be responding to your efforts, tell her that you can't take the pain any longer and move out of your house. You will not be able to compete head-to-head with her lover indefinitely. Your Taker will finally convince you that your happiness lies elsewhere. So leave while you still have the ability to express your care for her and before you say or do things that upset her. Don't say a harsh word to her. The last thing she will remember of you is how kind you were to her and how hard you tried to make her happy.

When you leave, gently tell her that you do not wish to talk to her again. Then don't talk to her or see her. Do whatever the law requires but no more. It will be tough to carry out, with two children, but if possible, have your friends or family mediate so that you don't talk to her when you see your children.

When you are meeting some of her needs, and her lover is meeting others, she has the best of both worlds at your expense. Your total disengagement from her will break the deadlock and will give her lover a chance to win her over. If he succeeds in meeting all of her needs, your marriage will be over. But if he fails, which is the usual outcome, she will realize her relationship with him isn't as fulfilling as she thought it would be.

If after your separation she comes to you asking to give your marriage another try, you will need to determine if she is still attracted to her lover. If there is evidence that her lover really blew it with her, is completely out of her life, moved out of state, returned to his wife, or has done something else that convinces you they will never see each other again, go back to your original plan and learn to meet her needs.

If she is still tempted to see her lover behind your back, I suggest that you and your wife leave the area. Even if your marriage improves, your wife may want to remain "friends" with this man. It is an arrangement that few husbands can or should tolerate. There's a good chance that she is addicted to the man, and he is addicted to her. The only way to overcome the addiction is to have a period of abstinence. Moving away would be difficult but it is the only way to prevent your wife from having easy access to her lover.

Dear Dr. Harley,

I first want to thank you for your valuable web site. Through it and the concepts that I found in "His Needs, Her Needs." I have tried to save my marriage. At this point, I am encouraged but I have some questions for you. First, let me describe my situation.

My wife and I have been married for six years and had our first child about a year ago. I thought we had a solid marriage, but shortly after my wife returned to work—after having the baby—she started crying a lot and said that she did not want to be married anymore. I thought it was post-partum blues and that she would eventually snap out of it. But she didn't. She quit working out and slept more. Our sex life became nonexistent. She also spent more and more time at work and with a male subordinate. When I questioned her about the time she spent with her friend, she said it was nothing and did not want to discuss it.

As winter turned to spring she seemed to withdraw into herself. Any attempt to break through to her met with resistance, and I also withdrew. I thought about leaving her but I love her and my new daughter too much to go through with it. By summer she seemed to warm up a bit and we seemed to be moving on the right track. It was during a business trip of hers that she revealed on the phone that she was on antidepressant medication. She started taking it in late May and was feeling much better. But I was upset that she kept this from me, and she withdrew from me again.

In the middle of the summer my wife's friend from work called in a drunken state and revealed quite a bit about his relationship with her. She admitted that she had had an affair with him around Christmas and had broken it off because she decided he was not what she wanted. We seemed to resolve some things that weekend and it looked like we were headed back in the right direction. Even though I was hurt, I realized my failings and tried to change my behavior to meet her needs.

But one day after one of her therapy sessions, she informed me that she had decided that the best thing for her to do was to take the baby and leave me. I was devastated but was more committed than ever to learning to meet her emotional needs. I exercised more and lost some weight because my lack of conditioning was one of her complaints. I was willing to do whatever I could to improve myself and provide for her better than before.

Over Labor Day weekend we were able to get away without our baby. She warned me not to expect any miracles. It was our first getaway in several years. We had a great time. We talked a lot and I got to know her better than I ever had. We relaxed in the sun, danced, and talked into the evening. When I suggested to her that we spend more time together, I got the biggest hug I've had in over a year. We held hands during a tour we took and she wanted me to take her picture in front of the bar "where we had so much fun."

When we came home, things continued to improve. She started to thank me for the household tasks I have been doing and she's been kissing me on the lips as I leave for work. She also has started wearing her wedding ring again.

But she is still committed to leaving me. When I try to discuss it with her, she tells me that I am not respecting her decision. I told her I respect it; I just don't agree with it. I feel that if she leaves me, she will create far bigger

49

problems than she has now. But she insists that everyone else breaks marriage commitments so she can also.

Last night, for the first time, she told me why she has been so angry with me. Four years ago I was underemployed and decided to go back to school to upgrade my skills and better my employment chances. I was doing it for both of us, but she felt I abandoned her. I was in school from 4 P.M. to midnight and worked from midnight to 8 A.M. We rarely saw each other. After I finished school, when she was pregnant, I worked hard to get a higher paying job so I could take better care of my family. But in doing that, I spent very little time with her, and she felt ignored. Even though she felt very hurt and lonely, she kept her feelings from me.

I know I am not perfect but I think I have come a long way. She says she feels independent of me and can leave whenever she wants, but I think I do a lot for her that she would miss. She seems to enjoy the affection I give her and she likes talking to me, as long as we don't talk about our relationship. This morning we agreed to take it one day at a time. I asked her to give me pointers on what she likes and dislikes and she agreed to do that.

I am concerned with her therapy. Her therapist is having her read books on co-dependency as a way to help her overcome depression. We both have read these books and neither of us really buys this theory, but she continues to see the same therapist anyway.

Here are my questions:

1. How do you think I'm doing? Would you make any changes in the way I am trying to work things out?
2. I feel that my wife has changed from the withdrawal state to the conflict state. Do you agree?
3. Do I encourage her to find a different therapist or do I leave that one alone?
4. Should I just try to back off and "be normal" as she sometimes says?

Thank you for reading this long letter. I love my wife and daughter and want my marriage to work out more than anything else. I await your reply.

P. T.

Dear P. T.,

There are many who would have given up on your marriage, but you have shown that perseverance can pay off. You're still not out of the woods and you will have discouraging moments but you are certainly on the right track.

It's instructive to see how your neglect was inspired by good intentions: trying to improve your income for your family. I've quoted the saying many times: "The road to hell is paved with good intentions." The truth is this: If you neglect your wife, she'll find someone who doesn't neglect her, even if he's an alcoholic. It may help you to read my article, Why Women Leave Men (appendix F). The reason is neglect.

I'll answer each of your questions in order:

1. How do you think I'm doing? You seem to be following a plan that will restore love to your relationship. There will be ups and downs, but you have been doing all the right things so far. Your one weakness may be disrespectful judgments (see The Five Love Busters, appendix C). Stop trying to straighten your wife out. It drives her nuts. She brings the problem of your disrespect to your attention on a regular basis, but you insist on directing her to your enlightened perspective. Stop doing it or she will retreat into withdrawal.

2. I feel that my wife has changed from the withdrawal state to the conflict state. Do you agree? Your wife has definitely changed her state of mind from withdrawal to conflict. That means she sees hope in her relationship with you and she is letting you try to meet her emotional needs. Keep it up and before long she will be in the state of intimacy. The reason her state of mind changed from withdrawal to conflict is that you went out of your way to show her that you are safe. You tried very hard to avoid being angry or judgmental, and even though you were hurt by her affair, you did not try to make her pay for her indiscretion. Eventually you will deposit enough love units so that every once in a while she will enter the intimacy stage. That's when she will reach out to meet your needs too.

3. Do I encourage her to find a different therapist or do I leave that one alone? Leave the therapy issue alone, even though I agree with you that the advice she is getting may be counterproductive. Co-dependency-type counseling tries to help people learn to become independent in their relationships. It makes sense when you're married to an alcoholic, and perhaps your marriage was so bad that she could see some wisdom in it. But when your marriage becomes great, your wife will see that co-dependency principles don't apply to your marriage. This is another area where you must not try to straighten her out.

4. Should I just try to back off and "be normal"? Yes, you should back off and "be normal," if by that your wife means you are to stop spending so much time talking to her about how she feels about you. Your wife is trying to help you become the husband she needs, and what she needs is for you to help her, not annoy her. As time goes by and she falls in love with you again, you may be tempted to talk to her about what was going on in her mind. But if she just wants to put it all behind her, let it pass. Use my Policy of Joint Agreement—*never do anything without an enthusiastic agreement between you and your spouse.* It applies to what you talk about and how you talk about it.

All you need to do is deposit enough love units in your wife's Love Bank for her to reach the state of intimacy. But remember, people vacillate from state to state, so once she's there, she will probably fall back to conflict once in a while, or even withdrawal. But hang on, because the more love units you deposit, the longer she will be in the state of intimacy.

One last thought: You may be tempted to address the "power" issue. She may be feeling that you try to meet her needs in an effort to make her dependent on you. Her occasional statements that she intends to be independent makes me think that she does not trust your motives. She may also be convinced that being married to you somehow robs her of her identity, your very presence overpowers her, and only a divorce can allow her to return to her own self. It's a tough argument to counter because the issue is so emotional, and there are many women these days who believe that sort of thing. They feel they are the victim of men's emotional control over them, robbing them of their very essence. My warning to you: Don't argue with her about it. Let her sort it out for herself. Any effort you make to convince her otherwise will be interpreted as disrespectful.

The marital crisis inspired her consideration of these philosophies, and the restoration of a loving marriage will help them disappear. You will ultimately drown out the "power" issues when you are her best friend and she loves you again.

Dear Dr. Harley,

My wife of nineteen years recently had an affair with a coworker for at least two months. She has admitted to spending long hours with the man and, in effect, making him instead of me the focus of her emotional being. She claims that the two have not had sex, but I am convinced that they have because of phrases in letters of hers that she wrote him. She denies this.

He has ended the affair with my wife for fear of losing his children. She has left the state for a few weeks (the trip was planned long before I found out about the affair), and I am left alone with the images.

I want to forgive her but I feel that she has not revealed the full depth of her betrayal and that I would not be able to completely forgive her as long as there is still some doubt.

Is it possible to forgive what you fear, without confirmation?

C. S.

Dear C. S.,

The question you need to ask yourself is, Do I want my wife to love me? Or even, Do I want to be married to her? If the answer to these questions is no, then I don't have much advice for you. But if the answer is yes, you have a lot of work ahead of you, and forgiveness is about the last thing I'd be worried about. Your wife almost left you, and if you're not careful, she eventually will. What you just experienced was a wake-up call.

The reason her relationship didn't go anywhere was that her friend wanted his own marriage to survive, not that she wanted hers to survive. As a marriage counselor, I am always hoping that the lover will go back to his or her spouse so I can help the couple rebuild their marriage without interference. But don't think for a minute that their relationship is over or that she will ever be really sorry for what she did.

You have a chance right now to save your marriage, and what you do in the next few months will be crucial. First, let's analyze the problem. Over the past few years, you and your wife have grown apart. You have become incompatible and you are not meeting her emotional needs. She probably isn't meeting yours either. She found someone who meets her needs and she was willing to give up her relationship with you to be with him. She comes back to you reluctantly, because she has no choice. But it gives you an opportunity.

You must take this opportunity to prove to her that you can do something you haven't been doing for some time: meet her most important emotional needs. First, you need to discover them. What was her friend doing that she found so irresistible? He probably talked to her, showed an interest in her, was respectful and encouraging, and demonstrated his care by being there for her when she needed him. And maybe, most important, he didn't criticize her or try to straighten her out.

Call her, send her flowers, and tell her how much you love her, how much you miss her. Don't smother her but let her know in no uncertain terms that you value your relationship with her.

Even though you have been very hurt by her affair, don't blame her for it. Don't expect her to apologize and don't ask her to explain the gory details. She is probably suffering depression because the relationship didn't work out. It's a common symptom of withdrawal. She will want to talk to someone about how bad she feels. Try to be the one she confides in, even if what she says is how much she misses this other man. *Don't judge her!* If you do, she simply won't open up to you. If you can't handle it, she should talk to a friend or a counselor, but don't risk losing her by venting your anger or your judgment on her.

You're in a tough situation, but I've seen couples work out problems like this a vast majority of the time. It may take six months to two years to recover your wife's love, but when that's accomplished, you will have the relationship with each other that you have both needed throughout your married life.

What to Do with an Unfaithful Wife

Dear Dr. Harley,

My marriage lasted eleven years. My wife and I were involved in many different things, some together, many apart. We were restoring a house together and having children at the same time that I was working full-time and finishing my education. She was also working full-time. By the time the second child was born, we had both grown neglectful of the romantic aspect of our relationship.

It was like we had both fallen asleep—but she woke up first. Eight years into the marriage, she had an affair with a man that worked with her. Instead of telling me that she was attracted to someone she knew, she kept it from me and got involved with him. She eventually told me about it, and we went to a counselor, but for three years we struggled. The counselor suggested that, because her lover was important to her career, if I insisted on my wife's not seeing him, I would risk losing her. I reluctantly complied, but he continued to pursue her, and eventually she got reinvolved with him and the marriage was over.

I regret now having spent those three years struggling with an unfaithful wife who could never close the door on her infidelity. I feel demeaned by it and I feel that I did myself harm by doing everything I could to put the genie back in the bottle when it was already too late.

Is there anything I could have done that would have saved my marriage? And now, how can I ever trust another woman? I have become deathly afraid that I will fail again, that whomever I would marry will eventually tire of me, and that I will not be able to meet her needs. After three years of tilting at windmills with my wife, I almost expect to be betrayed.

B. R.

Dear B. R.,

Your fear comes from an incomplete understanding of why your wife had an affair and how you could have overcome it to restore your love for each other (and save your marriage).

We marry because we are in love and we fall in love with the one who meets our most important emotional needs. When the one we marry stops meeting those needs, we become vulnerable to others who are willing and able to meet them. If we let someone else meet our needs, we fall in love with that person, and an affair is off and running.

What about future relationships? How can you ever trust anyone again? Before you marry, try to follow my Policy of Joint Agreement—*never do anything without an enthusiastic agreement between you and your spouse*—try to meet each other's most important emotional needs, and follow my Rule of Honesty. If you and your future spouse are comfortable following these principles, you have nothing to fear in marriage. You will also be convinced that your first marriage would have been affair free if you had done the same in that marriage.

No woman will marry you unless you meet at least some of her emotional needs. And after you marry, if you don't continue to meet her needs, she will be vulnerable to an affair.

I should leave you with another important point. The most commonly stated reason that women divorce men is neglect. Unless you make your wife an integral part of each area of your life, she will not be bonded with you emotionally, an essential condition for her love for you. I explain this in greater detail in "Why Women Leave Men" in appendix F.

Escaping the Jaws of Infidelity:
How to Avoid an Affair

*M*ost of the letters I receive are from people whose spouses are having affairs. Affairs destroy families and often the innocent spouse doesn't know how to respond to the unfolding tragedy he or she witnesses. But once in a while I receive a letter from someone who is about to have an affair and wants help avoiding it. Quite frankly, the only one who can avoid an affair is the one who is about to have one. While his or her spouse can make the job easier or more difficult, the spouse can't do the avoiding. So these letters from those who are tempted get to the heart of the issue, how to avoid an affair.

Dear Dr. Harley,

I have been married almost seven years to a wonderful man who treats me like a queen. I was pregnant when my husband and I got married but I never experienced the passion for him that I know I can feel for a man. We now have four children and he has been a solid foundation for our relationship and our family. He has done whatever he can do to make me happy. I do not deserve him.

I am a very aggressive woman in my mid-thirties. I love to party, dance, and laugh. My husband, on the other hand, is very passive and serious. He's just not much fun. The problem: I am gravitating toward an older man in his late forties. A man with a tremendous zest for life, who too is married and in the same business as I am. I have not had sex with this man but I feel as though I am falling in love.

I am overwhelmed with guilt. I know that I am a horrible wife for feeling this way. Please help!!

N. S.

Dear N. S.,

The man you are attracted to is meeting one or more of your emotional needs much better than your husband does. From your description he seems to be meeting your needs for conversation and recreational companionship. You have such a good time when you're with him that his account in your Love Bank has reached the threshold that triggers the feeling of romantic love.

It's not uncommon to find a person other than your spouse, who could meet your needs, but it's dangerous when, at the same time, your spouse is doing a bad job of it. At first, you simply find yourself in love with this person. If you also love your spouse, you shake it off and move on. But if you are not in love with your spouse, as you are not, you feel confused as to why you feel more love for the other person than for your spouse. Then, in an effort to make sense of it all, you think you are being cheated by your spouse out of what's rightfully yours—a fulfilling life. You think, if your spouse can't do the job, you have the right to find someone else who can and you should grab the opportunity while it exists. It may be a once-in-a-lifetime chance.

Many faced with this dilemma are not in your position, with a spouse who has dedicated himself to your happiness. They find themselves married to a spouse who has ignored them or even abused them. It's much easier to justify an affair under those conditions. But since your husband has tried very hard to give you the best he has, and you have four children who need you to stay together, your feelings of guilt are quite understandable.

Although your husband has put a great deal of effort into making you happy, he has missed the target, apparently right from the beginning. His efforts have been misdirected. Your husband's lack of dedication or good intentions is not the problem. It is his lack of knowledge and skill. He *can* learn to meet your needs as well as anyone, and you can be more in love with him than you've ever been. When that happens, your marriage will be secure.

You are on the brink of an affair and once you jump in, you may not be able to get yourself out before you have done untold damage to your family. Sooner or later most affairs die out, but in their wake they leave indescribable pain. Your husband would rather have his hand cut off than go through the agony of your unfaithfulness to him. It is the most cruel decision you could possibly make. Avoid that choice at all costs. Instead, dedicate yourself to teaching your husband to become the man you've always needed.

First, tell your husband what has happened to you. Explain your feelings to him just as you've explained them to me. Honesty is one of the most important ingredients in a successful marriage and without it your husband will not be able to understand you. Besides, honesty will help prevent you from hurting him. The reason your relationship with the other man has gone this far is that you have not talked to your husband about it.

Second, you should avoid seeing the man at work altogether, and it will mean quitting your job. You are already addicted to him, and your emotions will control your decisions whenever you see each other. It won't be long before you have thought through a justification for your behavior, and then there will be no stopping you. You will lose all perspective and ruin your marriage and family, to say nothing about intentionally hurting a man who cares a great deal for you. Six months after your affair has started, you will be up to your eyeballs in guilt and you will be contemplating suicide. Get this man out of your life at all costs!

Finally, you should try to discover what it is this man does for you that you need so much you'd risk giving up everything to have it. After you identify what it is about the other man that you find so attractive, try to teach your husband to do whatever it is. I understand personality limitations—your husband is more passive, while this man is more aggressive, like you. But you should be able to identify your needs, such as for conversation and recreational companionship, that can be met regardless of the personality type of the person you are with. I have seen remarkable recoveries of couples just like you with seemingly incompatible personalities. It turned out that their personalities were not incompatible; it was their habits and activities that were incompatible. Once their lifestyle changed, their marriage was terrific.

Four children can do a lot to change your lifestyle and your ability to meet each other's needs. You and your husband should set aside time to be alone so that you can have privacy and meet each other's most important needs. Your husband should be your favorite recreational companion. To give him a fair chance to succeed, make him your *only* recreational companion for a while. Get him involved in the activities you enjoy the most.

Dear Dr. Harley,

My husband and J have been married for two years (but have been a couple for the last ten years). Neither of us had a very stable family and both of us had a chaotic childhood. Our relationship has brought much stability to both of our lives.

We have a wonderful relationship, better than most J know. But there is one lurking problem that constantly seems to resurface in our relationship. J am very attracted to men who give me attention. J constantly seek other men's attention to the point that J am afraid that J am going to have an affair at some time.

J have done a lot of soul-searching and looking into different aspects of my marriage to see if J am unhappy with something or if one of my needs is not being met, but J just can't identify what it is. My husband is very attentive and caring and we have a wonderful sex life.

What is wrong with me and how do J take care of this problem? J want nothing more than to have a very long, happy marriage and J don't want to destroy my marriage by my own selfish desires. Help, please.

C. W.

Dear C. W.,

One subject I do not spend much time writing about is people who are prone to affairs even when their spouse seems to be meeting their needs.

It is an important subject, though, because a small percentage of marriages end, not because needs are not being met, but because one of the spouses simply refuses to be faithful to the other.

Whenever I counsel someone who seems incurably attracted to the opposite sex, I give that person the following rules to avoid temptation: (1) Spend all your recreational time either alone or with your spouse; (2) No meals alone with someone of the opposite sex; (3) No rides in cars alone with someone of the opposite sex; (4) Never tell someone of the opposite sex that you find him or her attractive or that you like him or her; and (5) If someone of the opposite sex ever tells you that he or she finds you attractive, start talking about how much you love your spouse. Many people have followed my advice and have spared their spouse the pain of an affair.

If you are attracted to other men, you have a responsibility to your husband to prevent yourself from forming romantic relationships with them. You should follow the rules I suggest (altering them to fit your situation). If you ever find yourself infatuated with another man, have nothing to do with him, even if it means quitting your job, leaving your church, or moving from your neighborhood. And for sure, don't ever tell him how you feel about him.

Your fears are well founded. You can do something now to protect your marriage for the rest of your life. We are all selfish in many ways, but some of our self-centered predispositions can be a real threat to those we love. Protect your husband from your self-centered tendencies by making it difficult to act on them.

Infidelity on the Internet

The Internet has opened a world of adventure and discovery to most of us who use it regularly. But for some it has opened a can of worms. A growing problem is the development of marital infidelity through the Internet.

The first letter is not about Internet infidelity but rather about falling in love over the Internet. It should give you an understanding of how easy it is to do. Then the next five letters are about Internet infidelity and my analysis of the problem and its solution.

Dear Dr. Harley,

I met a woman and have fallen in love on the net. We began the relationship on the precept that we would take a chance on falling in love with mind and soul. With that in mind we decided to not discuss appearances, hair color, employment, any of a hundred sundry details neither felt were germane to a good and lasting relationship.

Our efforts concentrated on the things we felt were important—values and morals. Spirituality was a strong consideration. We pray together often.

Three days ago we both made the commitment to be married. No date set, left it open. I feel this will be soon. She too feels the "urge to merge." Are we foolish in choosing this route? Is the brief duration of courtship a consideration?

The process of falling in love took us about six weeks. We then exchanged photographs and job descriptions, etc. In about one month I am to go spend a week with her at

her home over the Thanksgiving holidays—Thanksgiving
. . . appropriate holiday to meet a soul mate.

Is this as odd a place to begin a relationship as it seems
to me? How do you perceive the chances for a relationship
based on this scenario?

D. D.

Dear D. D.,

There are a host of people doing what you've just done. They fall
in love because they meet each other's emotional needs over the
Internet, needs of honesty and openness, conversation, admiration,
and affection. These are powerful needs and when they're met,
people usually fall in love.

But when Internet lovers try to live together, they find themselves
faced with a problem they did not anticipate. The vehicle of emotional bonding and need fulfillment, the Internet, is replaced by face-
to-face conversation. The replacement does not work as well. Most
people find that they are not nearly as good at meeting each other's
needs when they try to talk to each other face-to-face. And when
they marry, they discover that the countless adjustments that must
be made in daily living turn out to be bigger challenges than they
had ever imagined.

Internet romance has many advantages and few disadvantages,
compared to face-to-face romance. It's similar to telephone romance,
where lovers can talk for hours with each other, meeting some of each
other's most important emotional needs. Undivided attention is the
key advantage of the Internet and the telephone. There are very
few distractions. Undivided attention helps you meet most emotional
needs.

Dating also limits distractions, especially when just you and your
date go out to dinner or go for a walk, but even an evening of conversation in front of the fireplace is often not quite as effective in
meeting emotional needs as an evening on the Internet. That's
because there are more potential distractions in a face-to-face
encounter than over the Internet.

For years now I've encouraged couples to spend a minimum of
fifteen hours a week giving each other their undivided attention,

because it takes time to meet emotional needs. It's what you did when you decided "to take a chance on falling in love with mind and soul." I'm sure you spent fifteen hours a week or more doing it. I did it myself when I dated my wife, Joyce. We talked for hours each week, even though I was a full-time student and worked part-time. If I had dated her one evening a week and checked in with her occasionally, she'd be married to someone else right now.

I encourage you to pursue your relationship in person, but you will need to find effective ways to compensate for your loss of the Internet as a way to communicate. Will you be able to share your deepest feelings with each other when you sit face-to-face? It will probably be more difficult but it can be done, and you can do it.

Begin by trying to see your friend every day and giving her at least fifteen hours of your undivided attention each week. Discuss face-to-face the same topics you discussed over the Internet, because it's that conversation that met your emotional needs. Develop good habits of conversation that will be used when you marry and live together.

When you finally marry, it will be tempting to stop setting aside time to just talk to each other. You will be so busy with the pressures of life and raising a family that you will feel you do not have the luxury of taking fifteen hours from your busy schedules just to be alone and talk. But I guarantee you, if you forget what it was that gave you your love and emotional bond, you will lose it, like so many others do. You will find yourselves no longer in love and no longer emotionally bonded.

I suggest that you not marry for at least a year to give yourselves a chance to learn to meet each other's needs without the use of the Internet. You will also need to adjust to a new lifestyle that takes the feelings of both of you into account simultaneously. If you are still in love at the end of the year, you can thank the Internet for bringing you together. But your ultimate success will depend on your willingness and ability to continue to meet the needs you met over the Internet.

Dear Dr. Harley,

I've been married for two years and have known my wife for almost ten years total. Several months ago I met a woman online. What started out as an interesting and casual correspondence has now become a highly emotional, rewarding, and sexual relationship. We exchange as many as fifteen e-mails a day and have spoken on the phone several times. This woman lives in another country, so ordinarily the chances of meeting her would be quite slim. But she will be traveling to my area quite soon, and we have discussed getting together.

J know it's wrong and J know it could destroy my marriage, which J feel is a good one—J love my wife and would never want to do anything to hurt her. Yet J feel absolutely compelled to meet this woman—J simply have to see her. J'm completely torn at this point and emotionally frayed at the edges. Any suggestions?

S. R.

Dear S. R.,

You're right when you say, "It could destroy my marriage." E-mail romances are common and have ruined many marriages. As with most affairs, once the relationship gets real, it falls apart, but many marriages are already lost by the time that happens.

The bottom line is that you must completely sever your relationship with this woman, as difficult as it will be for you to do. Even though you feel compelled to meet her, don't let the relationship go any further than it already has.

Affairs are addictions, both in real life and on the Internet. You are addicted to this Internet woman because she meets your most important emotional needs. You're still in love with your wife because she meets some of your emotional needs, but the other woman meets other needs. That's why you love them both. It's important for you to understand what the Internet woman is doing that your wife should do for you.

The solution to your problem is simple: Have your wife meet the needs now met by the Internet woman. My book *His Needs, Her Needs: Building an Affair-proof Marriage* explains how.

As soon as you sever ties with your Internet lover, you will probably feel an overwhelming sense of loss. You may want to consider asking your doctor to prescribe an antidepressant. It may seem extreme for me to suggest medication, but it will help you not to wreck what you and your wife have and will have for the future. The depression will last only a few weeks, and an antidepressant helps relieve the symptoms of withdrawal.

You are certainly on the right track to recognize your Internet relationship as a compulsion. It is a compulsion, and the sooner you can get out of it, the better. Then learn to find in your marriage what you are currently finding on the Internet. It will help prevent you from getting into a mess like this in the future.

Dear Dr. Harley,

My wife and I have been married for nine years. We were very happy for a long time until our first son was born. At least that's when I can remember that everything started to go downhill. We now have another child. We have had lots of ups and downs. But lately it has been more down than up.

About a year ago I was really stupid and started an affair with a woman online. My wife found out about it, and I have cut all connections with the other woman. But now my wife is doing the same thing. She spends most of her day on the computer talking to the guys in the sex rooms on the IRC.

It's really starting to drive me crazy. I confronted her about it, and she told me she was sorry and that she would stop. Well that was about three months ago; she didn't stop. The only thing she did was try to prevent me from finding out. Now she will get online and talk until just before I come home for lunch, then turn off the computer. After I leave to go back to work, she gets online again until just before I get home and she turns off the computer again.

I don't know how to deal with this situation. What should I do?

C. G.

Dear C. G.,

You and your wife are not meeting each other's emotional needs. And it probably started right after your first child was born. All the pressures of life have prevented you from taking the time to reach each other emotionally and bond with each other. With that vacuum, you are both vulnerable to others who *will* meet your needs.

The Internet is a great place to find people who are willing to help you with almost anything. If your emotional needs are not being met, there are literally thousands of people on the Internet who are willing to try to meet them for you. Both you and your wife have figured that out by now.

To inoculate yourselves from Internet affairs, you must simply meet each other's emotional needs. Take the same amount of time that brought you together in the first place, about fifteen hours each week, to give each other your undivided attention. Get out of the house away from your children and away from friends. Spend time together that gives you distraction-free opportunities to be honest, loving, and caring toward each other, the way people are on the Internet. It's not just sex that your wife enjoys on the Internet. It's the attention she receives. Don't give her an excuse to go to the Internet to get the attention she should be getting from you.

Dear Dr. Harley,

I am so happy to have found your web site; sometimes I get into such a state of despair regarding my marriage. I do not want to lose my wife. We have five daughters and I love my wife with all my heart.

Here is my problem: My wife escapes into this world of chats to receive fulfillment. And I found out that she has an "online lover," for the lack of a better term. She has never met him or seen him, she doesn't even know what he looks like, but she needs to talk with him. She doesn't have cybersex or anything like that—they just talk.

I am so torn on what to do. My first instincts are of course to ask her to give us a chance and stop her relationship with him. In your terminology it seems that he is the one who's getting to stick credits into her Love Bank, not me. One of the things she expresses is that she doesn't know if she believes in marriage anymore—the idea that two people can live in love for a lifetime. She basically uses the argument, "Who do we know that are happily married?"

To be honest, I don't have a good answer for that. All I can tell her is that there are millions of couples who love and cherish each other for a lifetime.

Can you give me some insight or suggestions on how to handle this situation? I am not fighting with her and I am not withdrawn. I try to support her and tell her how much I love her.

I am so sad. I love her so much.

H. B.

Dear H. B.,

Love on the Internet is becoming an epidemic. The bottom line in your case is that you were not your wife's best friend before she began using the chatline. A cyberfriend has taken your place, and you can be grateful that it's not the man next door.

The state of withdrawal that your wife is in is not permanent. She will slip into the state of conflict once in a while (see The Three States of Marriage, pages 20–27), and when she does, she will explain to you how you've failed to meet her emotional needs—for conversation, affection, honesty and openness, and other needs. She will also give you a chance to meet those needs. That's when you can start depositing love units.

What is it about her Internet friend that she finds so captivating? What does she talk to him about that she can't talk to you about? Perhaps it's as simple as being there whenever she wants to talk. Perhaps she feels he admires her, respects her, and finds her interesting.

He gives her his undivided attention for hours each week. You need to learn as much as you can about what this friend does for her and see if you can meet the same needs yourself.

The thoughts she has about divorce are more like brainstorming than plans for the future. She does not have much to look forward to in her relationship with you and she is thinking of alternatives. Make sure that her future with you will be just as fulfilling as her future would be with her fantasy friend. Learn how to make it turn out that way. Encourage her to teach you what you can do to meet her needs. And when you've figured it out, keep it up for the rest of your lives together.

Dear Dr. Harley,

I met my wife on a BBS chatline. We hit it off, fell in love, and got married about a year after we met. A couple of months after we got married, I found out that my wife was still sending love letters on the BBS, but they were not to me. They were to someone else. I asked my wife about it. She said she would never cheat on me and that this was just a pretend game. I told her to knock it off, and she apologized and stopped the game.

I got bored with the BBS shortly after our marriage, but my wife has refused to quit and still communicates with the same guy. I'm having a problem with it. I know my wife is not unfaithful but I am still upset about it.

I have lost a lot of respect and love I had for her and she's mad at me because I have been cool to her. At first, we had a great sex life, but now she feels it is the least important part of a relationship. Do you have any advice?

S. E.

Dear S. E.,

People fall in love with those who meet their most important emotional needs. The way you communicated with your wife on a BBS chatline met her emotional needs, and she fell in love with you because of it. You probably revealed some of your deepest feelings, and she did the same. You communicated emotional interest and support for each other. If you had continued sending each other love letters on the chatline, I suppose you would have continued to meet her emotional needs.

Your problem arose when you stopped sending her love letters. The reason she kept right on corresponding (with someone else) was that it was extremely important to her to receive the affection she got from those letters and she missed it terribly. She found someone else to take your place when you quit.

You mention how upset you were when you found her writing love letters to someone else. That would upset anyone, but if you remain cool and unforgiving to your wife, you may as well kiss your marriage good-bye. She married you because she thought you cared about her, but if you distance yourself from her, she'll find someone else on the Internet who's easy to get along with. Don't risk it.

Sex isn't as important for your wife as it is for you. That's the way it is for most women. The reason you had such great sex at first was that she was in love with you. Women in love like sex with the one they love but they usually don't need it. When they're out of love, they generally don't like it anymore. Most women are repulsed when they make love to a man they don't love. She probably was more turned on with the affection you gave her in your letters than she was lying next to you in bed.

You and I and most other men I know don't feel the same way. Real sex with a live person in the same room is usually much more fulfilling to men than love letters. That's probably why you stopped writing to her. You now have her in person, so why write her any letters?

The solution to your problem is to find some way to meet her need for affection and conversation without having to use the Internet. You live together now but you probably communicated your affection for each other a thousand times more effectively when you were using the chatline. Perhaps you haven't known how to do it any other way.

Now's the time to learn, before you and your wife lose everything you felt for each other. You simply must take the time and be as creative as you were when you were using the chatline. You may even want to look at some of the letters you wrote each other to understand what you did then that's now missing in your conversations.

Your wife may never be as interested in sex as you but she'll like it as much as she did when your sexual relationship was the hottest, if you meet her needs for affection and conversation the way you once did. She can't meet your needs if you don't meet hers.

The questionnaires in the appendix may help you. Ask your wife to complete the Love Busters Questionnaire (appendix D) to see if you're doing anything to turn her off (like being "cool" to her). Have her fill out the Emotional Needs Questionnaire (appendix B). I'll bet you'll find that she thinks what you were once doing on the Internet to meet her emotional needs of affection and conversation has vanished. Get to work!

Dear Dr. Harley,

I'm a thirty-three-year-old female, second marriage to a forty-year-old male, never married before. We met on Prodigy and he told me he was a Christian. We had a clean, value-based, long-distance relationship and were married eight months later. The first five months of marriage were okay, good sexually. After that, he started to lose his sex drive. We went from having sex every day to having it every once in a while.

Ten months after marrying, I caught him having computer sex (he was at work). I signed on to our computer at home, under his JD and got his screen. Not only was he having cybersex, he told the woman he was divorced. After I confronted him, he denied it, insisting it was a janitor or someone else on his computer. But eight months later he finally confessed, and I don't think he's doing computer sex anymore.

However, his sex drive is terrible. I've wanted sex only three times a week, or at least once, feeling it's important to connect this way for marital intimacy. But we've gone three weeks without making love, despite my advances, which he's rejected throughout that three-week period. I've asked him if he wants me to try new positions, what he likes, etc., etc. He always says everything's good the way it is.

He refuses to go to counseling. I've tried leaving him alone, not pressuring him, surprising him creatively, reinforcing his desirability (he's gained seventy-five pounds and says his weight makes him self-conscious). I don't know what else to do. We have no children, which allows for the pleasure of spontaneity, and yet he is never spontaneous. Sex is always preplanned by appointment, which I've been receptive to for the sake of having sex.

I am very attractive, long brown hair, size 8–10 range, and I always dress nice for him, looking my best when he comes home from work. He is physically affectionate, complimentary, and appreciative, so I am baffled by our sexual problems. I'd appreciate your perspective on my situation.

B. K.

Dear B. K.,

As you've already noticed, marriage has its surprises, and sex is usually one of them. You'd think two adults would be able to figure it out to each other's satisfaction, but actually in most marriages sexual incompatibility is the norm.

One of the problems with Internet romance is that there is an illusion of honesty and openness. People who e-mail each other assume that they are getting an unfiltered, even raw, glimpse into the lives of others. The truth is that there's a lot of role-playing going on, and when people fall in love on the Internet, they may be falling in love with an actor, or at least only part of a person.

I'm not suggesting that people should avoid meeting people on the Internet, or even avoid marrying people they meet. What I am saying is that Internet romance should lead to face-to-face relationships that last long enough to get to know the other person. I recommend two years before marriage is considered. Then there is time to strip the facade that one or both people may have created.

Getting to your problem, when you discuss your sexual frustration with your husband, he seems to be suggesting that it's not a problem for him. If that's the case, you should explain that it's your problem and you would like him to help you solve it.

The first step in solving your problem is to describe it to your husband as clearly as possible and then describe what a resolution of the problem would be like. How often and under what circumstances would you like to make love? It sounds to me that three times a week would work.

Then you should try to understand why your husband does not want to make love as often as he once did. He could have a low sex drive, but his adventure on the Internet after marriage suggests we look for other answers. What's more likely is that he has developed tried and proven ways to masturbate that he prefers over making love to you. Masturbation is simple and predictable. If his masturbation satisfies his sexual need, it could account for his reluctance to make love to you.

Most sexually experienced women who are in love can outlast the men they love. You mention that you and your husband made love every day for the first five months. You may also have made love for hours at a time. It's possible that you have worn out your husband. He may have decided that sex with you is too much work and has reverted to what he did before he married you, masturbation, which was less work and thus more satisfying.

Over the years I have come to the conclusion that married couples should try to avoid sexual experiences outside each other's company. My reasoning is that sex is so enjoyable that the pleasure people receive from it should not be squandered. My Love Bank concept says that whenever you have pleasure in each other's company, you deposit love units in each other's Love Bank, thereby increasing your feeling of romantic love for each other. If you limit your sexual experiences to times you are together (especially if they are often), the feeling of love will be enhanced.

On the other hand, if you have sexual experiences with others, even over the Internet where it is essentially a fantasy, you build feelings of love for those people instead of for your spouse. Even masturbation, with no one present and no object of fantasy, takes the place of times that love units could have been deposited in your spouse's Love Bank.

Your husband may be back to computer sex, only this time he's figured out a way to prevent you from seeing his screen. But whether he is just tired or has channeled his sexual energy elsewhere, his being honest and open is the key to discovering what it is that is inhibiting him. I discuss the Rule of Honesty for a successful marriage in appendix E. Perhaps you and he could read it together, and then see if he will agree to it. It may be that he has been keeping his sexual behavior from you because he knows you would be offended by it. Besides, he already knows what you will do when you discover it—you'll make him quit!

The problem may go beyond just sex. It may be some other aspect of your relationship that is turning him off, although you have said that he remains affectionate and complimentary toward you. He knows better than anyone else what the problem is and if he wants to, he can explain it to you.

After you know what it is that keeps him from making love to you more often and more spontaneously, create a plan together that addresses his concerns. The secret to success in this step is to brainstorm. Come up with as many ideas as you can think of and don't start filtering them until you have given your imaginations a chance.

Finally, select the plan that appeals to both of you. It may mean that he is more spontaneous in return for not having to do as much when you make love. He may want to limit sex to ten minutes. Whatever obstacle to lovemaking he identifies, it should be overcome in your final plan.

Above all, be sure that your negotiations are *safe* and *pleasant*. If your discussion becomes threatening or unpleasant to either of you, break it off and reschedule it before you hurt each other. (Men should follow the same procedures when their wives do not make love to them as often as they want. Safe and pleasant negotiations offer effective and lasting solutions.)

The Lover's Perspective

*I*n most affairs, there are three players: the wayward spouse, the wayward spouse's lover, and the wayward spouse's spouse. My goal as a marriage counselor has been to help the wayward person leave the lover and reconcile with his or her spouse. That goal is achieved in most cases. The husband and wife learn to meet each other's emotional needs, ending the risk of divorce and future unfaithfulness.

But what happens to the lover? My plan of reconciliation seems to give lovers the boot, entirely ignoring their feelings. In fact my plan does take the feelings of lovers into account, and there are important and positive steps they can take to come out of the situation emotionally healthy and happy.

My plan for the lover is explained in my answers to the following letters.

Dear Dr. Harley,

I have read many books, searching for solutions to my particular problem, but I have found nothing that helps me. I have been married for twenty-three years to a very unkind and abusive man. Even though I have tried very hard to be the wife he needs, he continues to be cruel to me and critical of whatever I do.

A year ago I found myself very much in love with my employer. His wife became suspicious and threatened to leave him, so we ended the working relationship. I am sorry to tell you we have resumed seeing each other, although the once every two or three weeks is a far cry from the five days a week we were seeing each other when I worked for him. We have tried to stay away from each other but it never lasts.

Very little is written to help the "other woman." There is lots out there for the tempted male and for the deceived wife but virtually nothing to help us "others" get free of the desire and weakness. I have prayed every prayer I know to pray, I have fasted several times, I have had religious counseling, but all fail when this man calls me, needing me. This is the first time I have ever felt truly loved. The pull is so strong. If I give him up, I will never have another warm, loving, passionate relationship as long as I live. What do you suggest?

R. D.

Dear R. D.,

I have counseled and received letters from quite a few "other women" expressing the same desperation that you feel. In many cases the woman's despair is so great that religious faith is either at risk or lost altogether because prayers don't seem to be answered. She sees no hope for herself in her present marriage. Her happiness seems to be found only in a life with her lover, and yet she feels guilty for trying to break up her lover's marriage and family.

Your feeling of love for your former employer comes from the fact that he met important emotional needs that your husband failed to meet. Your husband's failure has created an emotional vacuum that was filled by your employer's care for you. You were unable to resist the emotional impact it had on you and you fell in love with him.

Your employer also had emotional needs that his wife had failed to meet. You met those needs and that's why he fell in love with you. Once you both realized you were in love with each other, the commitment to your marriages was forgotten and you began to plan for a day that you would divorce your spouses and marry each other. The realities of how it would affect your spouses and children were ignored.

But, as is often the case, realities eventually wrecked your plan. Your employer's wife discovered the affair and did the right thing. She threatened to leave him if he did not get you out of the office. He made the right decision by not working with you.

At this point in your experience, you and your employer should have confronted your spouses with what was lacking in your marriages, and your spouses should have learned to meet your unfulfilled emotional needs. My impression from reading your letter is that your husband is still in the dark about the affair, and you have not explained your feelings of desperation to him. But it may be that your employer and his wife are working together to build a strong marriage by learning to meet each other's needs.

Because you are not following a similar plan, you continue to find yourself in a hopeless situation. Unlike your employer's wife, your husband is making no effort to improve his relationship with you because you have not insisted on it. As long as you do not confront your own problems, you will continue to find yourself in this hopeless blind alley. The solution is quite straightforward. There is a sequence of steps you should follow, after which you will no longer experience despair.

The first step is to completely undo what you have done. Step out of the mess you are in. The man you love is committed to his wife and children. To marry you would create untold pain and sorrow for these people he cares for. He is clearly out-of-bounds for you, and you will never be personally fulfilled as long as you are in any kind of a relationship with him. You should simply never see or talk to him again.

I know you have said in your letter that you have tried to break off the relationship but have failed. Let me suggest stronger measures. Begin by finding a friend or counselor who can provide emotional support while you go through withdrawal. It will last as long as six months, and during that time I suggest you consider an antidepressant and a minor tranquilizer to help you get through moments of utter despair. You may even feel like killing yourself at first but if you hang on and avoid seeing him at all costs, the intense feeling of attraction you have will subside.

Then the next step is to confront your husband with the inappropriateness of his behavior. Your marriage is less than nothing in its present state. You cannot save your marriage by yourself but you can give him the opportunity to save it with you.

Before you confront your husband, read one more book: *Give and Take*. Educate yourself in the best way to approach your husband with your ultimate bargain: "If you learn to meet my needs and stop hurting me, I will learn to meet your needs and not hurt you." If he responds with abuse or ignores you, separate from him. This may bring him to his senses. Then offer the same bargain again. If he still doesn't respond, don't return to him until he is willing to show you the care you are willing to show him. But don't have an affair that will ruin some poor woman's life and the lives of her children.

It's *very likely* that a firm and honest approach with your husband will work. It will not be easy. At this time you probably do not even want a good relationship with your husband, but it's the right way to get out of the mess you're in.

Dear Dr. Harley,

As I read your suggestions regarding affairs, I don't see any compassion for the lover. You suggest that the lover never be seen again, should just get out of the picture.

I have built a relationship with a man over a period of ten years and the last three have been sexual. I want to spend the rest of my life with him because being in love is such a beautiful experience, something I may never experience with anyone else.

I believe he is a gift from God. In all of its wrongness, there is so much right. I don't believe something so beautiful could not have been a gift from above. But he loves two women, and we can't live in this triangle forever. He has chosen to try to make it right at home. I cannot prevent him from trying, but we work together and neither of us can leave town. There's no chance of us escaping that way. And I can't stop loving him.

How can the lover stop this triangle? Tell me that even if he divorced his wife and we were to get together, it wouldn't work because it was built on such an ugly foundation. Ugh! How can two people with eyes wide open be so blind?

S. B.

Dear S. B.,

One of the most destructive and painful acts that one human can do to another is to have an affair with the other person's spouse. That's why I am so opposed to affairs and why I try so hard to help couples prevent them.

People try to justify their behavior by creating a belief system that supports it. In your case you try to believe that God had something to do with your affair. I've heard it expressed many times, but it can't possibly be true. God would never give you someone else's husband, because that would create so much pain for your lover's wife and children. God cares about them too, you know.

Married men are out-of-bounds for you. You must find love and happiness among those who are not married. Your affair may have been bliss for you but it was a nightmare for your lover's wife.

You are right when you suggest that even if he divorced his wife and married you, the relationship would not work. Most affairs don't lead to marriage and most of those that do, end in divorce. Affairs are definitely not the way to find a life partner.

My advice is for you to leave the job where you work with your lover. The longer you stay, the longer you will feel depressed and lonely if he reconciles with his wife. I know that you want to stay, out of hope that you and he can renew your affair, but that hope is terribly misguided.

You feel that you may never experience the same kind of love with anyone else. The love you developed with your coworker grew out of a long friendship, and you think you are running out of time. Not all great relationships take ten years to develop, and because of your experience, you can shorten that time considerably. What is most important is that you recognize how much you need a man who meets certain emotional needs. When you find that unmarried man, you will not only find fulfillment in your life but, most important, your happiness will not be the cause of someone else's sorrow.

How to Forgive

The matter of forgiveness often causes problems in marriage. Offenses are common, and the offender usually wants to be forgiven. But the offended is often reluctant to forgive, particularly if the offender hasn't learned anything from the ordeal.

I believe in forgiveness but I also believe that marriage should be fair. Since, in many cases, forgiveness is unfair, what should be done? As you will see in my responses to the three letters that follow, I support the concept of just compensation for some marital offenses, so I don't always recommend forgiveness. This should be an encouragement to those of you who have been feeling guilty about being unable to forgive. But, at the same time, it should also encourage offenders, because the compensation I propose will earn you a terrific marriage, and it won't hurt at all.

Dear Dr. Harley,

My husband had an affair a year ago and since then I have not felt the same toward him because of his betrayal and my loss of trust. I want to move forward in this relationship but I'm having a very difficult time forgiving him. I believe, as you do, that honesty is essential in marriage, but my husband does not. As a result, he continues to lie to me about his behavior, and I continue to discover "bombs" that further explain the absolute wretchedness of his affair.

I'd prefer for him to be honest and get it over with so I can begin the healing process, but after a year of emotional turmoil, my focus has changed somewhat. My inability to forgive is eating me up and I need to get better. I've read your columns and I don't find specific advice on how to forgive. Are there steps I can take to resolve this terrible pain?

H. L.

Dear H. L.,

Forgiveness is something I believe in with all my heart. I forgive others and have been forgiven many times. God wants us all to be forgiving just as he has forgiven us. When you don't forgive someone, it can eat you up, as you said. It's not healthy to keep resentment bottled up inside of you.

The vast majority of couples I counsel who have been through the horror of an affair have better marriages after the affair than before. It's because the affair jolts them into recognizing the need for building an affair-proof marriage, and the safety precautions they use help them create compatibility and love. But has the offended spouse forgiven the offender in these marriages? Yes and no.

First, let's try to understand what forgiveness is. One illustration of forgiveness is telling a person who owes you ten thousand dollars that he won't have to pay you back. You "forgive" the debt. In other words, forgiveness is eliminating an obligation of some sort.

But we generally don't think of money when we think of the need for forgiveness in marriage. Instead, we are concerned about inconsiderate behavior that has caused us pain and suffering—the pain that an affair causes, for example. Forgiveness in these situations means thinking about the person as if the offense never took place. That is extremely difficult to do. The offended spouse usually thinks, *What can he or she do to make it up to me? How can I be compensated for the pain I've suffered?*

To make matters worse, a spouse who has had an affair rarely regrets the offense and rarely is willing to compensate the offended spouse. The offender usually asks to be forgiven, but that doesn't mean he or she is deeply remorseful. It usually means that he or she doesn't want the subject to be brought up anymore. And he or she is also often unwilling to change the thoughtless behavior. In other words, the offender wants the pain suffered by the offended spouse to be ignored or forgotten. He or she wants the ten-thousand-dollar debt to be forgiven and then the offender wants to borrow another ten thousand dollars.

I'm in favor of forgiveness in many situations, but infidelity isn't one of them. In this case, compensation not only helps the offended spouse overcome the resentment he or she harbors, but the right kind of compensation helps restore the relationship and prevents the painful act from being repeated.

In most cases, an offended spouse would be stupid to forgive the wayward spouse. It's like forgiving a friend of a ten-thousand-dollar debt, when it would actually be in the friend's best interest to pay you in full because it would teach him how to be more responsible with money.

As it turns out, in every affair there is a way to adequately compensate the offended spouse that is good for the offender and good for the marriage. At first, the offended spouse may not want to be compensated. He or she may try to get as far away from the offender as possible to avoid further pain. But if the spouse asks for forgiveness *along with a willingness to compensate,* the offended spouse is usually willing to entertain the proposal.

So let's talk about adequate compensation. What could the offending spouse possibly do to compensate for an affair? After all, it's probably the most painful experience anyone could ever put his or her spouse through.

Spouses usually have affairs because their emotional needs are not being met in the marriage. The way to affair-proof a marriage is for couples to meet each other's most important emotional needs. So whenever one spouse has an affair, the other should try to learn to meet the unmet needs that led to the affair. I know. That doesn't sound like compensation at all. It sounds like blaming the offended spouse for the affair! But in most cases, neither spouse is meeting the other's needs prior to the affair. The reason that there were not two affairs is often a lack of opportunity for the offended spouse. And sometimes when there is that opportunity, there actually are two affairs.

The point I'm making is that both the offending and offended spouses' emotional needs are usually not being met by each other prior to the affair. One compensation for the affair, therefore, is for the offending spouse to learn to meet the emotional needs of the offended spouse. But this won't change the conditions (unmet emotional needs) that spawned the affair. If the offended spouse is willing to do something that should have been done all along—meet the offending spouse's emotional needs—then the adverse conditions are removed. There is not only compensation for the affair, but the arrangement seems more fair to the offending spouse and the marriage is restored and affair-proofed.

It is often easier for an offended spouse to forgive when there is a change of behavior in the offender that meets his or her spouse's needs. This helps to compensate for some of the pain that was suffered. Technically, accepting compensation isn't really forgiveness. It's a payment for the pain of the affair. But I don't quibble. If you want to call balancing the books forgiveness, that's fine with me.

Using this meaning of forgiveness (accepting just compensation), the person asking to be forgiven must first demonstrate an awareness of how inconsiderate the act was and how much pain his or her spouse was made to suffer. Second, he or she must express some plan to assure the forgiver that steps have been taken to avoid the painful act in the future.

Unlike the repayment of ten thousand dollars, when the debtor suffers a ten-thousand-dollar loss to provide compensation, in marriage the compensation does not lead to the debtor's loss. If the couple follow the Policy of Joint Agreement, they will meet each other's important emotional needs in ways that would not cause either to suffer. They learn to please each other in ways that are mutually enjoyable. I'd say that's reasonable compensation, wouldn't you?

Speaking of the Policy of Joint Agreement, there's another important point that I should make regarding forgiveness. When you discovered your husband's affair, you learned two things about him that you had not known before. You learned that he would make decisions that did not take your feelings into account (having the affair), and you learned that he would lie about his behavior to cover it up. In other words, you learned that he was not following the Policy of Joint Agreement or the Rule of Honesty. That discovery was undoubtedly very disillusioning to you. Who wants to be married to a man who is inconsiderate and dishonest?

Now you are trying to create a new understanding with your husband, where he will agree to follow the Policy of Joint Agreement and the Rule of Honesty. Good for you! Apparently, he has not yet agreed and that has a great deal to do with your reluctance to forgive him. I'm sure you will not find forgiveness in your heart until he agrees to be honest with you and to take your feelings into account in the future.

Forgiveness will be much easier after you are convinced that your husband considers your feelings whenever he makes a decision (he is following the Policy of Joint Agreement), is completely honest with you about everything (he abides by the Rule of Honesty), and is meeting your important emotional needs. For you to be convinced, he must not only agree to these changes, but he must also demonstrate his commitment by living them for a while. Forgiveness may still require a bit of generosity on your part, but if he makes these changes, I think you'll be able to handle it. When that happens, the burden of resentment you are carrying will be lifted, and the love you have for each other will be restored.

Dear Dr. Harley,

My wife of almost thirty years has filed for divorce. She is intending to move out next month and to another state this summer. Neither of us have ever had an affair nor have there been addictions, abuse, or financial problems.

She is hurt by my past decisions concerning where we lived (in Europe for a six-year period when she wanted to be elsewhere), how I treated the children, financial issues, and, in general, making decisions without considering her input. It caused her to feel unloved, unequal, unrespected, and unadmired by me. Now almost ten years later after Prozac and thirty therapy sessions, she wants out of the marriage.

When I made those decisions, I wasn't aware of the Policy of Joint Agreement or the effect of my decisions on her Love Bank. I thought I was doing the right thing and that she would appreciate my leadership in the family. But now I know I made terrible mistakes throughout our marriage. I've taken several marriage enrichment courses (alone since she won't go) and read several self-help books. I've also seen a therapist at least eight times to see what I can do to help her and myself. She went with me once but didn't like him because he was trying to save our marriage. I'm not trying to control her, but no one she talks to seems to feel that marriages can be saved even when a spouse (me) is willing to change his behavior.

I am on good terms with our children and love my wife, but her spirit is shut down. I am beginning to wonder if it is time to stop trying, or is there some hope or method yet that I have not considered? What do you suggest I do?

C. S.

Dear C. S.,

I suggest you keep trying to reconcile right up to the day she moves out, then up to the day you are divorced, and then continue on for about two years beyond your divorce. Your account in your wife's Love Bank is so far in the red that she probably can't remember when you had a positive balance. Each time you do something to make her feel good and avoid doing something that annoys her, you reduce the deficit. She probably hates you right now because her Love Bank balance is so negative, but eventually you will have deposited enough love units to break even. From then on, you will be depositing into the black, and she will like you again. With more deposits, she will eventually love you, and your marriage will be restored.

Your wife is suffering from deep resentment that developed over a lifetime. She does not want to forgive you for the mistakes you made during your marriage and she certainly can't forget. Her Taker reminds her of her lost years when she was forced to live according to your plans and your schedule. It reminds her of the times she begged you to consider her feelings and how you ignored her pleas. She is reminded of her overwhelming feeling of loneliness and hopelessness that she felt on numerous occasions. How could she ever forgive a man who put her through all of that?

It's no wonder your wife wants to make her own choices from now on, and her first choice is to leave the prison. She has probably been counting the days until your children would be on their own so she could be on her own. Every effort you are now making to keep her with you will be interpreted as the same oppressive control that she endured throughout your marriage.

Your wife is now in the state of emotional withdrawal, which makes it difficult for you to deposit love units into her Love Bank. She does not want you to try to meet her emotional needs because she does not believe you will ever be able to make her happy. She thinks that as soon as she drops her defenses, you will trap her, and she will be under your control again.

For a while she may want to regain total control of her life so that she knows what it feels like. Once she has regained control, however, she may miss what it was you did for her. After all, none of us can meet our own emotional needs. They can only be met by someone else. That's what marriage is all about. She may be willing to reenter a relationship with you on new terms. If you can meet her needs without it costing her control of her life, you will have made a deal that will compensate her for some of the pain she has suffered. From there her generosity toward you may carry her the rest of the way to forgiveness.

Interestingly enough, a sign of her beginning to trust you may take the form of an outward expression of her anger and resentment. If she changes from withdrawal to the state of conflict (which is an improvement), she will tell you how angry she is and blame you for her depression. Her Taker will release its storehouse of resentment. Her shaming of you and her disrespect will be hard for you to take but it will give you an opportunity to hear from her Taker what she wants from you. You will have an opportunity to make a deal with her to compensate her for all of the pain she has suffered. If you can get through her attack without losing too many of her love units from your Love Bank, you will gain valuable information and an opportunity from your wife to implement change.

Read The Three States of Marriage (see page 20) for more information about how states of mind affect your negotiating strategy.

You should also read *Give and Take*. If you read it now, you can start applying its principles while she is still with you and follow through on them after she has left. Pay close attention to the chapters on the Love Busters disrespectful judgments and selfish demands, because they will get you into a ton of trouble if you persist in them while she is still around.

Appendix F, Why Women Leave Men, may also be helpful to you. If possible, make a copy for your wife to read to see if she agrees with me.

The Policy of Joint Agreement is the ultimate equalizer in marriage. Your wife's stated reason for leaving you is that her feelings have not been taken into account whenever you have made decisions, and she feels like the caboose on your train. All her married life she has felt out of control. The Policy of Joint Agreement will change all of that for both of you, and if you try to reconcile with care and consideration for her feelings, you and your wife will have years to practice using it together.

Dear Dr. Harley,

How can I forgive and forget the past? Whenever my husband and I argue, the past comes back to haunt us. One of us is always guilty of this poor communication trait. Please help.

D. R.

Dear D. R.,

The Taker is in charge of arguing. And the Taker has a very good memory. As you and your husband debate an issue, your Taker is running back and forth through the files of your mind, finding every conceivable thing your husband ever did to hurt you. You not only use it as ammunition during a fight, but your Taker also uses it to remind you what a bum you married and how he isn't worth any of your respect. Of course your husband's Taker is doing the same thing for him.

The idea of fighting fair is an oxymoron in marriage. It's like jumbo shrimp or George Carlin's "military intelligence." A fight is simply unfair for both spouses and should be avoided at all costs.

Learn to stop arguing. The whole purpose of arguing is to impose your own views or wishes on your spouse. It not only doesn't work, but it gets you both upset. Instead, learn to make decisions by taking each other's feelings into account. Use the Policy of Joint Agreement to help you resolve every conflict.

Never talk about the past as part of an effort to resolve a conflict. Instead, talk about the conflict itself and brainstorm solutions to it. After you think of several possible solutions, try to find one that both of you can agree to enthusiastically.

As you learn to resolve conflicts thoughtfully, all of your memories of the past will represent the time in your marriage when you simply didn't know how to care for each other. You will open up a new era in your marriage, and the past will be just like a bad dream. Try it for a week. It will work!

Part 3
Sexual Adjustment

What to Do When You Are Not Meeting Your Spouse's Need for Sex

A husband and wife should do some very important things for each other: They should meet each other's emotional needs. As long as those needs are being met, their expectations for each other are fulfilled and there's very little to complain about. But when the most important emotional needs are unmet, a firestorm of protest is usually ignited.

Of all the emotional needs met in marriage, sex is usually the need that gets the most attention, particularly when it's *not* being met. This fact is reflected in the hundreds of letters I receive from frustrated spouses. Unlike the other emotional needs, sex cannot be ethically met by any person other than a spouse. So it is crucial that it be met in marriage.

The following letters are from women who know how important it is to meet their husband's sexual needs but for some reason just can't do it. How can they break down the barriers that are preventing them from having a fulfilling marriage?

Dear Dr. Harley,

Three weeks ago my husband of sixteen years said he wanted to separate. He said he felt that his emotional needs had not been met for a long time and he doesn't want to fight to have them met. We don't argue very much. We respect and truly like each other. I know that I have a difficult time meeting his emotional needs because of my childhood. J am presently in therapy to learn how to overcome my problems. Both of us deserve a chance to have our needs met, but J don't know if J will be able to meet his.

What do you think? J would appreciate any and all comments.

J. W.

Dear J. W.,

I would guess that the need you do not meet for your husband is sex. You mention in your letter that he doesn't want to fight with you about it and he wants a separation. Over the years he has probably tried numerous, useless tactics to improve your sexual interest, like arguing once in a while and threatening separation. Apparently your sessions in therapy aren't working very well either. Nothing has worked so far and I'm sure you think that nothing will.

You mention in your letter that experiences in your childhood have prevented you from meeting your husband's need for sex (I assume that this is the need you are referring to). Your husband is probably very frustrated with the progress that has been made toward resolving those childhood issues. Most men become frustrated with therapy, because it does not usually help their wives become better sex partners. My experience and the experience of many sex therapists I know have convinced me that trying to resolve childhood issues does not lead to great sex between a husband and wife. In many cases, it has actually led a couple to divorce.

On the other hand, sexual inhibitions are relatively easy to overcome using methods that do not require a rehash of the past. I believe you can learn to meet his emotional need for sex in spite of unpleasant experiences you may have had in your childhood.

One of the greatest sexual inhibitors is a bad relationship. If you and your husband are not getting along very well, and that seems to be the case if he is threatening to leave you, your first order of business is to resolve your marital conflicts by taking each other's feelings into account. I'm afraid that more or better sex will not accomplish that objective.

When a couple has a bad relationship, I do not begin by encouraging more sex. First, I fix the relationship, and nine times out of ten, sexual problems disappear, with or without unresolved childhood experiences. I spend very little time fixing sexual problems because most couples I counsel don't have sexual problems after they have learned to make decisions that take each other's feelings into account.

If I could be convinced that you do, in fact, have a loving and caring relationship with your husband and you still have sexual problems, then my advice for you can be found in my response to the next letter.

Dear Dr. Harley,

I am married to a very patient and understanding husband. The only major problem we have involves our sex life. I just seem to have no interest in sex whatsoever. I believe part of the problem is due to an episode from my childhood but am not sure. I have tried many things to help get me interested. I have bought stacks of books, magazines, and movies and I have even talked to my gynecologist. Nothing seems to help.

I got married the first time right after my eighteenth birthday and it was similar in that I had little interest in sex. But I also did not love my first husband the way I love my current husband. I knew my first marriage would never last but now I know my second will if I can get some help with this problem.

I know it is not fair for my husband. It has been two months now without our being intimate, and I can tell that it bothers him. I don't miss the sex but do feel bad that I am not giving him what most people consider something that comes naturally. I want my marriage to last forever, for I love my husband with all my heart and find him attractive. We have two children of our own and one from my first marriage.

I just don't know what to do. He is a kind and caring man, and I feel I may lose him if I can't change my attitude toward sex, even though he says he won't leave. I enjoy sex when I can get in the mood. It's the getting in the mood part that is the problem. I just don't see it as an expression of love the way my husband does. I just do it to make him happy and because I feel I am supposed to. I would love any comments you may have on our situation.

B. K.

Dear B. K.,

One of the most important reasons that husbands and wives fail to meet each other's emotional needs is that they don't share the same interest in them. Men want marriage to meet the needs they have, such as sex, and women want marriage to meet the needs that mean most to them, such as affection and conversation. The truth is couples *can* do it all. Marriage can meet a man's need for sex and a woman's need for affection and conversation, even when the wife has little interest in sex and the husband has little interest in affection and conversation.

The key to understanding how men can meet women's needs and vice versa is to understand that you don't have to share the need to meet that need in someone else. A man who has no need for affection can learn to be an affectionate husband, and a woman with no need for sex can learn to be a great sex partner.

Why don't you have more interest in sex? you may ask. Why should you? is my answer. It's like peanut butter. Some like it; some don't. There are a host of reasons why some people have very little sexual interest, but very few of those reasons need to prevent people from having a frequent and satisfying sexual experience.

What you describe is probably low sex drive. What that means is that as far back as you can remember, you did not find yourself easily aroused sexually. You may find it very difficult to climax, you rarely fantasize about sexually arousing experiences, and, for you, sex is more pleasurable as affection than it is for sex per se.

The solution to low sex drive is to make love only at the time of day that you have the most energy. Most of the women I've counseled report to me that the more often they make love, the stronger their sex drive becomes. It is usually the opposite for most men. One suggestion would be to try to make love to your husband every day for a few weeks, with you deciding the time. I recommend that you

94

take the superior position (top). Do it your way, making the experience as enjoyable for you as possible.

I wouldn't be compulsive about it. For example, if there are occasions that you simply don't have a good opportunity to make love, skip a day. But even if you make it three out of seven, you will be way ahead of anything your husband was expecting.

Don't ignore the problem. Start right away and don't worry about whether he is satisfied. Pay more attention to your own reactions to your lovemaking. Make it as pleasant for yourself as possible, but do it.

The most important thing to remember about marriage is that both you and your husband have a great opportunity and responsibility to meet each other's most important emotional needs. Learn to become experts in meeting those needs.

If you find yourself repelled by sex, you may have more than just a lack of interest. You may have a serious aversion to sex, and that may be what's keeping you from having sex with your husband. If that's the case, read the answer to the next letter on overcoming sexual aversion.

How to Overcome Sexual Aversion

$\mathcal{S}$exual compatibility is very important in most marriages. On rare occasions I find a happily married couple who don't have sex at all, but in most cases the quality of sex determines the quality of marriage. When a couple's sexual relationship begins to suffer, the marriage is usually suffering. When a sexual relationship is thriving, the marriage is also thriving.

The husband often has the greatest need for sex, but that isn't always true. I am finding more and more wives who need sexual fulfillment more than their husbands. However, whether it's the husband or the wife with the greater need for sex, the one with lesser need is at risk for sexual aversion.

In an effort to satisfy the spouse with the greater need for sex, the spouse with the lesser need often sacrifices his or her own emotional reactions. Instead of sex being an experience that they both enjoy together, sex becomes enjoyable only for the one with the greatest need. It can become a nightmare for the other spouse. In all too many marriages, sacrifice leads to a sexual aversion, which in turn leads to no sex at all.

My answers to the following questions will help you overcome a sexual aversion if you suffer from it. But even if you don't, it may help prevent you or your spouse from becoming its victim.

Dear Dr. Harley,

I have been married for nine years and have two children. I have no interest in having sex. In fact the thought of it is repulsive to me. J shudder when my husband reaches over and touches me when we are in bed together. Earlier in our marriage J had sex with my husband because J knew it was important to him, even though J was not interested. Sex was not disgusting to me then, just not enjoyable. Over time, however, J began to refuse him more and more often, and the thought of having sex became more and more unpleasant.

J finally told my husband that J no longer would have sex with him and asked him to please stop trying. J feel guilty about not meeting his need for sex but J feel so much better. J can finally go to bed and relax. J feel like a terrible burden has been lifted from me. J feel safe. But J am afraid for my marriage. J don't believe we can go on like this forever. Do you have any advice?

C. R.

Dear C. R.,

You and your husband fell in love with each other and were married because you were successful in meeting some of each other's most important emotional needs. You deposited so many love units into each other's Love Bank that the love threshold was shattered and you found each other irresistible.

You were not necessarily meeting the same emotional needs. He may have met your need for conversation, and you may have met his needs for recreational companionship. He may not have needed to talk with you nearly as much as you needed to talk with him but he may have spent hours at a time talking with you anyway. And you may have watched football with him on television, not because you enjoy violence on TV, but because you wanted to join him in his favorite recreational activities.

The reason you met your husband's emotional needs is that you loved him and wanted to make him happy. He was willing to do the same for you. You were both in the state of intimacy (see page 21) and in that state of mind you were both willing to do whatever it took to meet each other's emotional needs.

But, as is the case in many marriages, you are now no longer meeting those needs. Your neglect of each other has probably already taken its toll, and you are probably no longer in love with each other.

The Importance of Meeting Emotional Needs

It's common sense to believe that spouses should try to meet each other's emotional needs. No one has ever seriously argued with me that we *shouldn't* meet those needs in marriage. And yet in marriages that are failing, spouses are usually not meeting each other's needs. Sometimes it's intentional and sometimes it's unintentional. They know that they should meet each other's emotional needs and yet they don't or can't do it.

The most common reason that spouses don't meet each other's needs is that they fall out of the state of intimacy and into the states of conflict or withdrawal. In either state of mind, people do not feel like making their spouses happy because of the way they have been treated. Love Busters, such as angry outbursts, disrespectful judgments, and selfish demands quickly destroy the state of intimacy.

If your husband is angry, disrespectful, or demanding, do you want to watch football with him? If you treat him the same way, will he want to talk with you for hours? You may watch football with your husband simply because you want to see the game with someone, and he happens to be the only one around. He may talk with you for hours because he needs to talk to someone, and you are there to talk. But if you don't have the same needs and you're in the state of conflict or withdrawal, he watches football all by himself and you read a book instead of talking to him.

In most marriages the husband and wife don't have the same emotional needs, or at least they are not prioritized in the same order. Your marriage is that way too. Sex has probably always been a very low priority for you and a very high priority for your husband. When you were in the state of intimacy, you were willing to make love to him as often as he wanted, just to make him happy, even though sex wasn't what you needed. Your husband may also have been willing to meet your needs, even though they may not have been important needs of his.

You would probably still be making love with him today, and cheerfully, if you could have remained in the state of intimacy for the past nine years. But there's no marriage in existence that has achieved that kind of record, and sooner or later your husband was bound to make a mistake that drove you from the state of intimacy into conflict. He withdrew just enough love units for you to fall out of love, and at that moment, he wanted to make love.

You may remember the first time you tried to make love to your husband in the state of conflict and you probably realized then that it was an experience you would not want to repeat. You never had enjoyed sex that much, but then you were trying to do it after your husband had hurt your feelings. You had taken your first step toward sexual aversion.

What Is an Aversive Reaction?

An aversion is a negative emotional reaction that's been conditioned to a behavior. In other words, when you have a bad experience doing something, you are likely to feel bad when you try to do it the next time. If you have many bad experiences doing something, the very thought of it will create anxiety and unhappiness, and doing it will make matters even worse.

If your boss yells at you occasionally when you go to the water cooler, you will find yourself very tense whenever you drink from it. Your boss's yelling, which gives you a negative emotional reaction, becomes conditioned to your drinking from the water cooler. It's not the drinking itself that's unpleasant; it's the association with your boss's yelling.

Aversions can be created in association with anything we do. Unpleasant classroom experiences can create "school phobia," something many children have great difficulty overcoming. An automobile accident can leave people with a fear of driving and the very thought of getting into a car puts them into a panic. Even shopping for groceries can raise anxiety in people who have had a bad grocery shopping experience.

Aversions can be created when spouses try to meet each other's emotional needs if the effort is associated with an unpleasant experience. There can be an aversion to meeting the needs of admiration,

affection, physical attractiveness, domestic support, family commitment, financial support, honesty and openness, recreational companionship, conversation, and sex. These aversions can be created in
a number of ways, but the most common is when a frustrated spouse
becomes abusive if a need is not met to his or her satisfaction.

When one spouse tries to earn enough money to support the family and the other spouse becomes angry with a paycheck that's
judged too small, an aversive reaction to bringing home a paycheck
can be created. When a spouse tries to be affectionate and is angrily
rebuffed because it isn't done "right" for some reason, an aversion
to affection can be created. When a spouse tries to join in recreational activities but has a miserable time, an aversion to recreational
companionship can be created.

In other words, whenever someone tries to meet an emotional
need and finds the experience particularly unpleasant, there's a great
possibility that future efforts to meet that need will be associated
with unpleasant feelings—an aversive reaction.

That's one of the reasons it's so important to meet your spouse's
needs in a way that you find enjoyable and that's why I put so much
emphasis on the Policy of Joint Agreement. If you ever develop an
aversion to meeting one of the needs of your spouse, you'll find it
impossible to meet. You will first have to overcome the aversion
before you can ever learn to meet the need again.

Sexual Aversion

Aversion to sex is not unusual in marriage. Suppose a husband is
upset with the frequency and manner in which his wife makes love
to him. Instead of solving the problem with thoughtfulness and
understanding, he becomes verbally and physically abusive whenever sex isn't to his liking. He may not be abusive every time she
objects and his abuse may actually be rather infrequent. But whether
it is frequent or infrequent, she associates the unpleasantness of his
abuse with the sex act itself. After a while, she becomes afraid to
make love to him, finding the act extremely unpleasant, and she tries
to avoid it if she can. She has developed a sexual aversion.

C. R., you may not have developed your sexual aversion the way
most women do, as a result of your husband's pressuring you to have

sex with him when you didn't feel like it. In most cases of sexual aversion, a husband is the source of the unpleasant experiences, but it is not always that way, and you may be one of these exceptions.

You probably began your marriage not knowing how to enjoy sex and made love to your husband out of a spirit of generosity. You may not have known how to become sexually aroused or how to climax. But as long as you were in the state of intimacy, the experience was somewhat pleasant for you because the sex act made you feel more emotionally connected to him.

Eventually your husband did something that made you feel less than generous. He hurt your feelings. It may have been something he said to you that was angry or judgmental, and you didn't confront him with your resentment. Out of obligation, you made love to him anyway. That experience was downright unpleasant because you had absolutely no interest in being emotionally connected to him at the time. You probably wanted him to get it over as quickly as possible. Your husband may have had no idea that you were suffering.

From that point on your sexual experiences became unpleasant. You made love because he expected it, not because you were willing, and you did whatever you could to avoid it or to make each experience brief. You eventually hated him to touch you and you may have told him how much it bothered you. But he did it anyway. There was no way to stop him. Eventually you developed an aversion to sex.

The same thing could have happened around football. In the state of intimacy you would have enjoyed watching games with your husband because you felt emotionally bonded to him. But if he had hurt your feelings and then expected you to watch football with him, it would have put you on the path of a football aversion. If you had felt obligated to watch football with him, week after week, with no natural interest of your own and no feeling of intimacy, it would have felt like torture to you. Eventually you would have felt disgust and revulsion whenever football was mentioned.

Had you started your marriage with an agreement that you would only make love to your husband when and in a way that you would enjoy and to which you could respond sexually, you would never have had an aversion. On the contrary, your sexual interest would have increased over the years.

You are wired physiologically to enjoy sex. If you had made love to your husband on your terms and for your pleasure, it would only have been a matter of time before all the connections were discovered. Then you may have realized you need sex as much or more than he does. But because you did not understand how important your emotional reaction was, you not only didn't try to enjoy the experience sexually but also put yourself through emotional pain in your effort to meet your husband's need for sex. Your effort to unconditionally meet his need did you in and now you're not meeting it at all.

Most sexual aversions are poorly understood by the ones who have them. These people commonly report that engaging in sex is unpleasant, something they want to avoid. They may find that sexual arousal and even a climax is unpleasant. There isn't anything they like about sex, and some actually experience a panic attack in the sex act itself. When they're asked to explain why they feel the way they do, few have a clear understanding of their reaction. They often blame themselves.

Their ignorance comes from a poor understanding of where their feelings come from. People often have the mistaken belief that they can decide to feel any way they want. They can decide to feel depressed or they can decide to feel cheerful. But those who suffer from chronic depression know it's not that simple. And when people have a sexual aversion, they cannot simply decide to feel good about sex.

Emotional reactions are not based on our decisions and an emotional aversion is no exception. An aversion is an unconscious, physiological association of a particular behavior with an extremely unpleasant emotional experience. Those who have that association have no control over the aversive reaction that is inevitable.

As in your case, sexual aversion is a disaster of major proportions for couples that experience it. Sex is a need that should be met in marriage, but if a spouse has an aversion to meeting it, it becomes almost impossible as long as the aversion exists.

To avoid aversions in the first place, keep unpleasant experiences to a minimum. That's why I am so adamant about couples learning to follow the Policy of Joint Agreement. If they apply the Policy to their sexual relationship, making love will never be unpleasant for either partner. Not only does the Policy help them create a lifestyle of compatibility, but it also eliminates the possibility of developing any aversion to meeting each other's needs.

Overcoming Aversion to Sex

The symptoms of aversion to sex with your husband may include the following: fear of engaging in sex, trying to make the sex act as short as possible, finding that you need to build up your confidence and resolve before sex just to get through it, thinking of excuses to avoid or postpone sex, and feeling ill just prior to sex and somewhat depressed afterward. It is common for people to experience their symptoms of revulsion at the very thought of having sex.

One symptom that is not due to sexual aversion is vaginal pain. It can *cause* a sexual aversion but it is not a symptom of aversion itself. If you experience vaginal pain or discomfort when you make love, it is probably due to an infection or a reflex called vaginismus (see page 113 for a discussion of this condition).

Any of the symptoms of sexual aversion will interfere with your ability to meet your husband's need. You can't meet his need for sex if you have one of these reactions. You must overcome the aversion if you ever hope to enjoy a sexual experience with your husband. And he will be sexually fulfilled only if you enjoy lovemaking with him.

There are many methods that help people overcome an aversion but they all are based on a simple psychological principle, the principle of "extinction." Remember how you got the aversion in the first place? You associated a certain behavior, having sex, with an unpleasant emotional reaction. Eventually the unpleasant reaction was triggered whenever you even thought about the behavior, and certainly when you engaged in it.

To overcome the aversion, you must break the association you have made between sex with your husband and the unpleasant emotional reaction. The easiest way to do that is to associate sex with the state of relaxation.

Those without a sexual aversion may suggest that you take the direct route: Try to relax next time you make love. However, you and all of the others experiencing this hardship know that the direct route is impossible to follow. The very thought of having sex with your husband probably puts you in a state of near panic.

So that's where we will begin—with your thoughts.

103

Step 1: Learn to relax when you think about sex. The exercises that I am recommending to you will require about fifteen minutes of your time every day. It is very important that you not miss a day because the process will not work as well if you allow time gaps in the procedure. It is also important to reflect on what you experience during the exercise. Having a journal in which you can record your thoughts will be helpful.

Sit in a comfortable chair with your eyes closed in a room by yourself. If possible, play relaxing music in the background. Think of various experiences that you have had. Some of them will help you relax and others will make you feel tense. If you have an aversion to sex, whenever you think about making love, you will probably feel your tension rise and it will definitely feel unpleasant to you.

Stop thinking about sex and redirect your thoughts to the relaxing experiences. Then focus on relaxing each muscle in your body. Begin with your feet and move all the way up to your head, focusing your attention on relaxing every muscle along the way. It may take you five minutes or more before you know that all of your muscles are fully relaxed.

When you are completely relaxed, think about making love again, but this time try to remain completely relaxed. Be aware of muscles that begin to tense—perhaps in your stomach or your legs. Try to relax those muscles. As you think about sex, you will notice that some thoughts don't bother you at all, but others, like making love to your husband, may make it almost impossible to remain relaxed.

Don't think about making love to your husband just yet. Think only about sex in general. Leave your husband out of your thoughts altogether. Investigate your own reactions to sex by imagining various aspects of sex. If you have any sexual fantasies, think about them and what it is that makes them appealing to you. Then, without thinking of your husband, think about other aspects of sex that are less appealing or downright unappealing. Try to keep your muscles relaxed while you are thinking of all of these things.

When your first fifteen-minute relaxation exercise is over, take notes of what you learned about yourself. What sexual thoughts were appealing to you and what thoughts were unappealing? What thoughts made you feel relaxed and what thoughts made it difficult for you to relax? Don't share your journal with your husband until your sexual aversion is completely overcome and you have a mutually fulfilling sexual relationship with him.

If there were certain sexual thoughts (not related to your husband) that made your muscles feel tense or made your stomach feel tight, repeat this fifteen-minute exercise each day until you can think about those things without feeling tense. Write about your feelings after each session to help you think through the reactions you are experiencing.

I have helped rape victims overcome nightmares and sexual aversion with this technique. It was so successful in one case that a lawsuit based on the assumption of permanent disability was dropped because all of the aversive reactions created by the rape were eliminated.

Step 2: Learn to relax when you think about having sex with your husband. If you have an aversion to sex with your husband, you will feel an unpleasant tension whenever you think of making love to him. So in this step the goal is to be able to think about having sex with your husband without feeling tension or experiencing an unpleasant reaction.

As I've already explained, an aversive reaction is created when an unpleasant emotional reaction is associated with a situation or behavior. The way to reverse the aversive association is to try to stop the unpleasant reaction from occurring when the situation or behavior is present. If you can feel relaxed just thinking about sex with your husband, that will tend to extinguish the aversive association that was previously made.

Close your eyes, sit back, and relax. Be certain you are alone and without anything or anyone to distract you. Relax all your muscles from head to toe as you did before. Then think about making love with your husband.

You will notice that certain thoughts are more upsetting than others. It could be that one of the ways your husband wants to make love is particularly upsetting to you. The thought of him forcing his hand over your body, particularly putting it between your legs may raise your anxiety level. Eventually as you practice relaxing, you will find that even thoughts of the sex acts that were most upsetting will no longer elicit an unpleasant reaction. That's because with proper relaxation, you can extinguish your emotional reactions to almost anything.

You may be wondering how long this will take. Each step will take from one or two sessions to thirty or forty sessions, depending on the intensity of your aversive reaction. You move to the next step when you can be completely relaxed in the current one.

The information you learn about yourself in this step will help you in the next step, so be sure to continue taking notes in your journal after each fifteen-minute session. You should document the aspects of lovemaking with your husband that create the greatest stress for you. Even though you will learn to be relaxed when you think about them, they should be avoided when you get back to making love to him again.

Step 3: Learn to relax when your husband is in the same room and you think about having sex with him. As soon as you have learned to relax when thinking about making love to your husband, you are ready for the next step, inviting him to join you in the same room.

At first, he should simply sit somewhere else in the room and read a book. Even though he is not paying much attention to you, you may need to start practicing relaxation all over again. His very presence may make you tense. But if you relax all of your muscles from head to toe, you will eventually find yourself comfortable once again. Then, as you think about making love to him, continue to relax.

Continue these exercises every day until you are completely relaxed thinking about making love to your husband with him in the same room. And don't forget to describe your experience in your journal.

At this stage, your husband should not say or do anything but sit and read a book. If he cannot follow that simple instruction, you have serious problems. The reason you have a sexual aversion is that he has tried to make love to you in a way that is enjoyable for him but unpleasant for you. To overcome your sexual aversion, he will need to learn to take your feelings into account when he makes love to you in the future.

In this step if he refuses to follow the assignment, and instead of quietly reading he starts talking to you or walks over and touches you, stop the procedure entirely. There is no hope for a successful transition to sex with your husband if he cannot follow your simplest requests.

It is essential for your husband to understand that you, not he, must be in complete control of your recovery process or it will not work. If he cannot or will not agree to that, it not only explains why you have the aversion to begin with but also explains how his lack of cooperation has prevented your recovery.

Step 4: Learn to relax when you talk to your husband about having sex with him. Now you are ready to tell your husband what you are thinking. Sit back in your comfortable chair and close your eyes. At first, limit your description to sexual situations that you find easy to talk about and avoid talking about those sex acts that you find particularly disturbing. When you first start talking about sex, you may find your tension rising again. If that happens, stop talking and concentrate on relaxing the muscles that are tense. After a little practice, you will learn to relax as you describe your feelings. He should say nothing to you as you talk to him. All he should do is listen.

If your husband decides to take charge and tries to talk you into making love to him after you describe your thoughts, tell him that it is that very thing that created the aversion in the first place. If he cannot follow the program, end it.

Eventually you should describe as many sexual situations to your husband as you can think of. You may want to refer to your journal to help you remember what some of them were. Whenever you talk about them, try to remain completely relaxed and you will eventually find that even your most disturbing sexual memories will no longer elicit a tense or anxious response. You're ready to move on when you feel relaxed talking about sex with your husband.

Step 5: Learn to relax when you make love to your husband. You should ease into a sexual relationship with your husband very slowly and comfortably. Continue to spend fifteen minutes each day on this step so that you do not lose momentum.

First, you should learn to become comfortable with affection, being able to hug, kiss, and hold hands without any fear that it will lead to sex. Then have your husband rub your arms, feet, lower legs, back, and other nonerogenous areas (avoid breast, stomach, and genital areas), again without it leading to sex. Do the same for him. When you are comfortable being touched by your husband in nonerogenous areas and you are comfortable touching him, you are ready to begin the first stages of making love.

I have not discussed feelings of sexual arousal with you because our goal was to overcome aversive reactions. But by the time you are able to talk to your husband about having sex with him while feeling completely relaxed, you may have already started to experience feelings of sexual arousal. The affection you experienced through touching may also have led to feelings of sexual arousal. That is your signal to begin making love to your husband. Don't ever try to have intercourse without first feeling sexually aroused.

Remember, if any aspect of lovemaking is unpleasant to you, figure out a way of making it enjoyable. Have your husband rub your back in a way that you enjoy, not just in a way that he enjoys. Resist the temptation to go ahead and make love just to make your husband happy because it is likely to set you back. Remember, if this program is not successful, you will probably go back to not making love at all!

When you are ready for intercourse, have your husband lie entirely motionless on his back at first. Sit or lie on top of him so that you are in complete control of the situation. Experiment with different positions and methods of intercourse so that you can learn how your body works to create the most enjoyable feelings. Only relinquish control to him after he has become educated in what it is that enables you to enjoy the experience with him.

Because your habits will all be very new, you may experience what behaviorists call "spontaneous recovery." That's when you suddenly feel the old aversive reactions without any warning. When that happens, relax your muscles just as you did before. It just means that there are residual effects still present that crop up from time to time. You'll find that these unexpected intrusions will decrease over time until they hardly ever occur.

How to Overcome Pain during Intercourse

*T*he three letters that follow are a sampling of the experiences of women who suffer from painful intercourse. My answer covers all three of their situations. The fourth letter describes a woman who has overcome the pain but has not made a good sexual adjustment after the symptoms ended. My answer to that letter explains how to overcome the effect of having tried to have sex under conditions of extreme pain.

Dear Dr. Harley,

In one of your Q&A columns, you say that failing to meet your spouse's needs opens the door for an affair. I hate to hear you say that! I have been having problems for several months now and my doctor believes I may have endometriosis. One of the problems I have been having is very, very painful intercourse. Therefore my husband's needs are very hard for me to meet. We have tried outlets other than intercourse, but they don't seem to be enough for him. How can I get him to understand that intercourse really does hurt a lot!!! He thinks I am faking or that I am having an affair because I don't want sex with him. It just plain hurts and I don't want to do it very often. Our marriage is deteriorating fast because of this and also a few other factors. He's making it very hard for me to love him! Any suggestions?

R. D.

Dear Dr. Harley,

My husband and I have been married for almost two years. We are very much in love, we enjoy each other's company, and we have a solid commitment to our marriage. The problem has been our sex life. Both of us were virgins when we got married. Although my husband has been an extremely patient lover, from the very first night of our honeymoon, sex has been an ordeal for us. Sometimes it works and other times it doesn't. Almost every time we attempt to make love, I get very nervous and it is painful for me. A very few times in the last two years, we have had wonderful, spontaneous sex. I have switched birth control pills and tried relaxing before sex, but it seems that arousal is difficult because I anticipate the pain. I have no history of abuse (of any kind) and I very much want to have sex that will drive my husband wild! What can I do?

A. P.

Dear Dr. Harley,

I have a problem. Whenever I have sex, it hurts. Sometimes, after we are finished, blood shows up in my underwear. Do you have any idea what could be causing the problem? I am going to a doctor but I would like to prepare myself before I get there.

C. D.

Dear R. D., A. P., and C. D.,

A good sexual rule of thumb is *Don't have intercourse if it's painful.* If you ever experience pain during intercourse, stop. Then, see a doctor to help you determine the cause of the pain and overcome the problem. If there is a physical cause, you will be able to go back to having intercourse painlessly and enjoyably when the pain is eliminated. Trying to have intercourse while there is still pain invites disaster.

It's true that when important emotional needs, such as sexual fulfillment, are unmet, there is a risk for an affair, but having sex at all costs is not the solution. In fact if you follow my Policy of Joint Agreement—*never do anything without an enthusiastic agreement*

110

between you and your spouse—you would never have sex in a way that's painful to you. Instead, you would pursue painless sexual options until you have resolved the problem.

Most women throughout most of their lives experience no pain whatsoever when they have intercourse. The vagina is designed for intercourse and works very well for that purpose under most conditions. But once in a while most women do experience pain during intercourse. And when they do, they should identify and treat the problem before having intercourse again.

There are *primary* and *secondary* causes of vaginal pain during intercourse. The primary causes are those that are responsible for the initial pain or discomfort. Secondary causes are those that are created by the pain itself if intercourse continues, and they can trigger vaginal pain long after the primary causes have been overcome.

Primary Causes of Vaginal Pain

One of the most common primary causes of vaginal pain during intercourse is a dry vagina. Usually when a woman is sexually aroused, fluids are secreted in the vagina that keep the lining well lubricated. But if a woman is not sexually aroused or if fluids are not secreted for some other reason, intercourse can cause very painful damage to the vaginal lining. In some cases, the vaginal lining can actually tear, resulting in post-intercourse bleeding.

There are two ways to avoid a dry vagina during intercourse. The first is to avoid intercourse until you are sexually aroused. The second is to use an artificial water-based vaginal lubricant, such as K-Y jelly, Vagisil Intimate Moisturizer, or Replens Vaginal Moisturizer, as a substitute or backup for natural lubricant.

Since vaginal secretion is usually an indication of a woman's sexual interest, I usually recommend that intercourse wait until she experiences sexual arousal and natural lubrication. I want couples to avoid getting into the habit of sex that's passionless for her. But if natural secretion is an unreliable indicator of her sexual arousal, I would certainly recommend an artificial lubricant.

If you're not sure if a dry vagina is the cause of your pain, use an artificial lubricant once. If there is no pain under those conditions, then you have proof that it's the cause of your distress.

Another common cause of vaginal discomfort during intercourse is bacterial infection. This occurs frequently in women, and an antibiotic will generally cure the problem within a week or so. A related problem is bladder infections. While the problem may be in the bladder or urethra, not in the vagina, it often causes discomfort during intercourse.

A visit to your doctor will identify and treat a bacterial infection so that you will have minimal interruption in your sexual fulfillment. But be sure to make the appointment as soon as intercourse is uncomfortable. Otherwise it can develop into a secondary cause of vaginal pain that I will explain later.

There are other diseases that can cause pain or discomfort during intercourse. Vaginal endometriosis is one of them. When your doctor examines you for possible bacterial infection, be sure to ask him or her about endometriosis, because it is often overlooked during an examination. Your doctor will also be able to check for any vaginal tumors or venereal diseases that may be causing your discomfort.

If you have experienced vaginal bleeding after intercourse, your doctor should also be able to identify its source and treat it. Sometimes a scratch or tear in the lining caused by something other than intercourse can be the cause of your problem.

It is very important for you to be comfortable with regular pelvic examinations. Otherwise you may let a medical problem become so far advanced that it causes you permanent injury. If you are embarrassed to see a male doctor, find a female doctor. But whatever you do, don't let your inhibitions prevent you from receiving treatment and experiencing painless intercourse.

If your doctor can identify the source of your vaginal discomfort, don't have intercourse until the problem is treated and overcome to his or her satisfaction. Some problems can be treated in a week or less, while others, like endometriosis, may take months to overcome.

During treatment for a vaginal disease, you may be unable to have intercourse, but that doesn't mean you'll be forcing your husband to rush off to have sex with someone else. I suggest that your doctor inform your husband of what it is you are going through and how you will be treated. A major problem you may face is your husband's failure to see your sexual reluctance for what it is: vaginal pain brought on by a physical cause. If he doesn't believe you when you explain that it's the pain that makes you reluctant, his ignorance puts your sexual relationship, and probably your marriage as well, at risk. But once he understands the nature of the problem and knows that it isn't an affair or some other emotional cause that's keeping you from sex, he will be happier with alternatives to intercourse while you wait for your treatment to take effect.

In some cases a husband's thoughtlessness is remembered long after the painful symptoms are gone. If your husband tries to force you to have painful intercourse with him and threatens you if you do not cooperate, your memories of his insensitivity will be a far greater barrier to your future sexual relationship than your disease ever could have been. Don't let him create those barriers to your future happiness. Insist that there be no sex unless you enjoy the experience with him. It's not only in your best interest but in his too. If you try to make love when it's painful for you, you may have a very difficult time making love to him in the future.

A Secondary Cause of Vaginal Pain

But what should you do if you eliminate the primary causes and you still experience vaginal pain? Or what if your doctor finds no physical cause for your discomfort during intercourse? That can be very discouraging to most women, who begin to think that it's all in their heads.

Most cases of persistent vaginal discomfort are not due to primary causes at all but rather to a reflex called vaginismus. It's not psychological or emotional; it's very physical. Vaginismus is a painful reflex that is created in association with a primary cause of vaginal pain. In other words, if you experience vaginal pain from any one of the primary causes I've mentioned, vaginismus can develop secondarily. And long after the primary cause is gone, the vaginismus can persist.

This reflex responds to stimulation of the vaginal opening. If you suffer from vaginismus, you will notice it most whenever you first try to insert something into your vagina. The opening involuntarily contracts and pain is immediately felt. In extreme cases, the contraction is so tight that nothing can penetrate it.

From this description you can see how it would interfere with intercourse. Regardless of how sexually aroused you may be or how well lubricated your vagina may be, as soon as you try to insert your husband's penis, you will experience excruciating pain. Inserting his penis may be difficult, because the vaginal opening is constricted. In some cases it's impossible to insert the penis.

Naive couples often don't know what to make of vaginismus. Some of my clients believed it was God's punishment for their having sex before marriage. Others have blamed it on the sins of their parents. But whatever its cause, it certainly feels like punishment for something. Only after I am able to explain the cause of the reflex and help them eliminate it, do they realize that sin has nothing to do with it.

There is a tried and proven way to overcome the vaginismus reflex, and if you follow this procedure, I guarantee your success. I recommend that you do these exercises in the privacy of your bathroom or when you are alone in the house. Your husband should not be included until the later sessions.

First, you determine how strong the reflex is and what triggers it. The way to determine its strength is to insert your finger into the vaginal opening to see what happens. If there is no reaction to your finger, insert objects increasingly wider, like candles, until you can trigger the reflex. There will be an involuntary contraction of the opening as you try to insert the object and it will be painful.

Notice how large the object must be before the reflex is triggered and how tight the opening gets. The smaller the triggering object and the tighter the opening, the more difficult it will be to extinguish the reflex. If you can't get your finger into the opening without extreme pain, you have a very well developed case of vaginismus. But regardless of its intensity, it can be eliminated.

The way to eliminate the reflex is to set aside a few minutes each day, preferably several times a day, to expose the opening of your vagina to penetration without triggering the reflex. If you can associate vaginal penetration with no pain or discomfort, the reflex will be extinguished. But remember, even an occasional triggering of the reflex can strengthen the reflex.

Begin each session by covering your finger with water-based lubrication (K-Y jelly), which is easy to clean off when you are done. Very slowly lubricate the opening of the vagina with your finger; then slowly insert your finger about an inch. Even in the worst cases of vaginismus, a finger can be inserted so slowly into a lubricated vaginal opening that the reflex is not triggered. In a slow, circular motion, gently rub the vaginal opening with your finger in ever-increasing circles. Remember to go slowly enough not to trigger the reflex or experience any discomfort. After you have rubbed the opening for about a minute without any pain or discomfort, slowly insert your finger into the vagina and in a circular motion gently rub the inside of the vagina as far as your finger will go. Then remove your finger and do the same thing all over again. Do it about five times before you end the session.

You will notice that after the first insertion of your finger, the opening is much less sensitive, and you will be able to penetrate more quickly without triggering a reflex. Move your finger slowly enough so that you avoid any discomfort. But after a while, you will find that you can move it very freely without pain.

You may end the first session thinking that you have overcome the reflex, only to discover at the beginning of the next session that it is back. So start the next session very slowly and carefully, doing again what you did during the first session. When you think you are ready, use a larger object than your finger, such as a candle, and increase the diameter of the object until it is about the size of a penis. Be sure to lubricate whatever you insert and go slowly to avoid the reflex.

The number of sessions needed to completely eliminate the reflex will depend on the severity of the vaginismus. But when it is eliminated, you should be able to insert an object the size of a penis, with lubrication, fairly rapidly without any pain or discomfort.

There are some women who are not comfortable touching themselves and would prefer having their husband carry out these exercises. While it can work, the problem with anyone else doing them is that no one but you knows precisely how much pressure to use, and your husband would inadvertently trigger the reflex far more often than you would. That means that it would take much longer for you to overcome vaginismus with his help.

His turn should come after you are convinced that the reflex is extinguished. Up to this point you should have avoided intercourse because it would have brought the reflex back. But when you think the reflex is gone, it's time to start having intercourse again. Unfortunately you will find that after you have learned to insert a penis-size object into your vagina without incident, the reflex may suddenly reappear the first time your husband tries to insert his penis.

To prepare for that common outcome, the first time you have intercourse you should insert his penis yourself. Use plenty of lubricating fluid and lie on top of him when you do have intercourse so you can control the penetration. He should lie motionless so that the penetration and thrusting is done only by you and you can stop whenever you experience the least amount of discomfort. Eventually you will be able to insert his penis without any pain, thrust as fast and deep as you want, and experience no discomfort whatsoever. The vaginismus reflex will have been eliminated.

If it ever comes back, it will be in a much milder form, and you will be able to eliminate it in a day or so by going back to inserting your husband's penis yourself and controlling the thrusting motion during intercourse.

To repeat what I have already said numerous times, *whenever you experience any pain during intercourse, stop immediately.* And then solve the problem before resuming intercourse.

Dear Dr. Harley,

My wife and I have been married for about two and one-half years. Before our marriage and for a short time afterward, our sexual relationship was fantastic. Two or three months after we got married, she was diagnosed with endometriosis and went into the hospital for a laparoscopy to remove the endometriosis. She was still having quite a bit of pain a couple of months after the surgery and the doctor put her on Zolodex [a drug that makes a woman go through a temporary "menopause" while she is on it]. She was on the Zolodex for about five months, and our sex life has never been the same. We rarely had sex while she was on the Zolodex, and it's been that way since then.

She has spoken to her doctor who put her on the medication. He says it's all in her head (which of course did not hit home very well at all). She has told me that she is still very attracted to me but she just can't raise those emotions anymore.

It has now gone on for well over two years and I am really getting frustrated about not being able to resolve it.

116

My greatest desire is to get our sexual relationship back to the point it was when we got married. She wanted me as bad as I wanted her. I am willing to do whatever it takes to get us back to where our relationship was and build on that, but her response is "If I don't have any desire, how can I fix the problem?"

At this stage of the endometriosis, she does not have pain during intercourse (though at the beginning of this fiasco she did). We are now at a point where we are fighting a battle over desire. She is very willing to do what it takes to solve the problem, so if I can find any possible solutions, she is willing to try them. She thinks it's a hormonal problem, but she's already asked her doctor and he doesn't agree with her.

She has this fear that everyone we talk to about this is going to tell her she has a mental problem and that bothers her. This may be a reason why she hasn't pursued a solution to this herself. She wants this to be a physical thing, such as a low estrogen level, but her doctor assures her it's something else.

What started with a small, outpatient surgical routine, has turned into a full-blown problem, which has led to some very stressful evenings and conversations (mostly for me). I am more than willing to do anything you might suggest to get to the bottom of this. I would love to have the girl I married back.

M. H.

Dear M. H.,

From what you have told me, I would agree with your wife's doctor that the problem is not physical, but rather emotional. She is probably now as physically capable of passionate sex as she ever was. Her loss of desire can be explained by the experiences she had with you while she endured the symptoms of endometriosis. Those experiences not only included painful intercourse but could have also included your insensitivity to her predicament. And since then apparently you have been arguing with her about it, perhaps being disrespectful and demanding. Those Love Busters really do a number on sexual desire!

Sexual desire for most women is considerably more fragile than for most men. For men, physiological factors (testosterone) tend to dominate, while for women, emotional attachment and past sexual encounters have more influence.

I imagine that her endometriosis turned her terrific sexual experience with you into a nightmare, and she came to view lovemaking as a very unpleasant necessity. For a while she endured the pain just to please you but eventually she could not bear it any longer. She may have even been brought to tears while making love to you.

To compound the problem, your sex drive may have made you insensitive to her pain. Even though you knew that she was suffering, you may have charged ahead to meet your need. Then she would have seen you in an entirely new light—a man who cared more about sex than about her. When the endometriosis was discovered and treated, your months of celibacy may have made you less affectionate and thoughtful.

In the beginning of your marriage you were meeting your wife's emotional needs and avoiding Love Busters. She wanted to make love to the man who loved and cared for her, and each sexual experience was a treat. She was emotionally connected to you and she had memories of many enjoyable sexual experiences. That's why she had sexual desire—she expected each sexual experience with you to be terrific because every past experience had been that way.

But when your wife contracted endometriosis, it may have marked the beginning of a downward slide in your relationship. Perhaps a few Love Busters were unleashed, and perhaps you were not as thoughtful or affectionate as you had been in the past. By the time the disease was under control, she couldn't even remember what it had been like to enjoy sex and she was no longer emotionally connected to you. Result: no sexual desire.

You and your wife are at a point in your marriage where you can recreate the enjoyable experience you once had, but to do it, you will need to begin at the beginning. First, you must make sure that your wife reconnects with you emotionally. Have you eliminated Love Busters that may have been created during the months of her endometriosis? Are you meeting the emotional needs you once met?

You may want to encourage her to complete my Love Busters Questionnaire (appendix D) and Emotional Needs Questionnaire (appendix B) to help identify the obstacles to your relationship.

Then if she still gets a knot in her stomach whenever she thinks about having sex, I suggest that she follow the advice I offer in the chapter How to Overcome Sexual Aversion. These procedures may seem to be long and technical but they work. Once you have a willing sex partner again, you will appreciate what you have even more than you did before and you will know how to protect your relationship so that you don't lose your passion for each other again.

Your wife went through sexual hell when she had endometriosis, so it's no surprise that she just doesn't feel the same about sex. But if you treat her with the love and thoughtfulness she deserves, and she learns to overcome the aversive reactions she has developed, those bad experiences will be replaced with good experiences, and sexual desire will return to her.

What to Do When Your Spouse Has an Addiction to Pornography

*A*ddiction to pornography makes compliance with the Policy of Joint Agreement almost impossible. And for that reason alone, it ruins marriages.

There are as many forms of sexual addiction as there are ways to have sex. They range all the way from masturbating while looking at pornographic magazines and videos to breaking into apartments and raping unsuspecting residents. But they all have one thing in common—in each case, sex is more important than the feelings of others.

For a few years I treated some people with illegal but nonviolent forms of sexual addiction, such as peeping toms, flashers (men who expose their genitals in public), and people who make obscene telephone calls (several were women). It was not too difficult to prove that these forms of sexual pleasure were inappropriate, since the victims would come forward and have the perpetrators arrested.

But it's more difficult to demonstrate the inappropriateness of some of the private forms of sexual addiction, such as masturbating to pornography. After all, who could possibly be hurt by such a private and unobtrusive act? No one, if you're single. But if you're married, your spouse could be, and usually is, very offended by such behavior.

The first letter is a good representative of scores of others I've received from women who want their husband to stop masturbating to pornography. The second letter is on a related subject, pornography as an aid to marital sex.

120

Dear Dr. Harley,

I am thirty-seven years old and my husband of six years is forty-five. We have two preschool children. This is my second marriage, his fourth.

Two days ago I came home to his surprise and discovered him watching a porn video. This is something he has engaged in from time to time since before our marriage. In the past I have encouraged him to share this facet of his sexual life with me, but he has chosen not to.

Over the life of our marriage I have seen a steady decrease in the frequency of our sexual activity until now when we only make love once or twice a month. His enthusiasm for sex has decreased as well.

Although he always watches the movies in secret, I suspect he has been engaging in this activity at least once a week for the past year. I have discovered him a couple of times before and told him that it hurts my feelings for him to prefer this activity over taking an opportunity to make love with me. He assured me that watching the movies was no big deal to him and if it hurt my feelings, he would stop but he didn't. I have told him that I would like to have sex more often and am willing to do just about anything, but our sex life remains unchanged.

This last incident is "the straw that broke the camel's back"—I feel totally undesirable, depressed, and unwilling to share myself with him sexually and emotionally. I am sure he resents my infringing on his right to privacy, but it's something I cannot tolerate. His assurance of my attractiveness and his love for me mean nothing after he does these things.

He put the tapes in the attic and vowed again to make a change, but I do not trust him. I need a deeper explanation of what is going on and he cannot or will not provide one. It hurts that he would continue to engage in an activity that hurts me and detracts from our relationship and I can't help but wonder that if this outlet is taken away from him, he would resort to something more devastating, like having an affair or utilizing the Internet to meet his sexual needs.

By the way, out of curiosity I have seen some of the tapes he watches and I don't find anything perverse or unusual about them. It just seems that he needs something other than me. I would be most grateful for any help you could provide.

J. S.

Dear J. S.,

When you were first married and before you had your children, sex was rather uncomplicated. You had privacy and a great deal of energy. It isn't surprising that you and your husband enjoyed a mutually enjoyable sexual relationship.

But now that you have two children, sex probably requires more planning and you have less energy. Your husband's use of videos is his way of having his sexual needs met while avoiding all the hassle. His strategy is somewhat effective, since it does lower his sex drive, and it is certainly convenient. But it is at your expense.

The two rules I encourage couples to follow—the Rule of Honesty and the Policy of Joint Agreement (see the chapter on my basic concepts)—can help couples resolve almost every marital conflict. Your husband, however, in his effort to solve his sexual problem, has not followed either of these rules, and that's why you are so upset with him.

He has followed the Rule of Honesty to a point. He has let you know about his interest in pornographic videos and has shared them with you, but he has not let you know how much he uses them to fulfill his sexual need. You would not have known about his use of videos if you had not come home unexpectedly. He has agreed not to use them in the future, but that's something he had agreed to do several times in the past. He has placed the pornographic videos in a convenient location—in your attic. If he had no intention of using them again, he would have thrown them out.

He has been dishonest with you in the past regarding these videos and he will probably continue to be dishonest with you. It's possible that he doesn't believe in the Rule of Honesty. After four marriages, he may have decided that honesty has done nothing but get him into trouble.

He has also violated the Policy of Joint Agreement by watching the videos when he knows you are offended by them. From your description, he seems to agree with the Policy when you confront him—he agrees to not watch them in the future because it upsets you. But as soon as you leave the house, he doesn't follow through with his agreement. It could be that he tells you whatever you want to hear so he can get you off his back. He may not really feel that the Policy of Joint Agreement works in marriage, because it prevents him from doing what he wants to do.

There's another explanation for all of this. It could be that he is addicted to pornographic videos.

If you have found that your husband follows the Rule of Honesty and the Policy of Joint Agreement in every area of his life except sex, he probably has a sexual addiction. A test of this premise is to simply ask him how he feels about these two rules. If he knows that he should be completely honest with you and wants to consider your feelings in every decision he makes, then he could have an addiction that overrides his willingness to follow these rules. In other words, he can't use the rules to guide his sexual conduct because he is addicted.

Quite frankly, if he doesn't believe in the Rule of Honesty or the Policy of Joint Agreement, there is no point in discovering whether or not his problem is an addiction. If he will not be honest or take your feelings into account, your marriage will end up being his fourth in a long list of failed marriages. In that case, your only hope of saving your marriage is trying to convince him that both rules are essential to your future as husband and wife.

I will assume that your husband really does want to be honest with you and he does want to take your feelings into account when he makes decisions. He knows that his behavior upsets you and he wants to stop doing it but he can't, regardless of how unhappy it makes you feel. In other words, I will assume he is a sex addict.

Your husband probably masturbates a lot more than you think. It may be several times a week. That would account for his decreasing sexual interest in you. If he were not to masturbate at all, I'm certain he would want to have sex with you more often. But he has become so addicted to pornographic videos that he can't resist them and uses them whenever he gets a chance.

You are considering the possibility of trying to adjust to his addiction because, if you don't, he may choose something even worse, like infidelity or cybersex. And you also offer to do "just about anything" to motivate him to have sex exclusively with you. That probably means that, just to have him all to yourself, you are willing to engage in sex acts with him that would be unpleasant for you.

Neither of those two alternatives will work. The alternative of adjustment won't work because his masturbating to videos has always upset you and will continue to upset you. The truth is that you will continue to be upset until so many love units are withdrawn that you will not love him anymore. It's already happening to you. You admit that you no longer feel like sharing yourself with him emotionally or physically. That's just the beginning.

Your second alternative—giving him whatever he wants whenever he has sex with you—won't work either. His sexual activity with you must meet your standards of enjoyment, or you won't want to make love to him for long. Suppose he confesses to you that the only way he could have enjoyable sex with you is anal penetration. If you're like most women, you'd regret the day you took him away from his videos.

The only reasonable solution to your problem is for your husband to abandon his offensive use of videos, and any other forms of sex apart from you, and have sex with you in ways that are fulfilling for both of you.

The procedure for overcoming an addiction can begin when the addictive material is inaccessible. Those addicted to alcohol must be completely separated from alcohol. They must get it out of their houses and they must avoid situations where alcoholic beverages are present.

The same principle applies to sexual addiction. For your husband to overcome his addiction, all of his pornographic videos and any other sexual material he uses when he masturbates should be destroyed. While it's possible for him to purchase more, if they aren't readily available in your home, he won't be easily able to renew his habit during a momentary lapse.

If your husband were to avoid masturbation for a week, he would find his normal sex drive returning and he would be more sexually attracted to you. The longer he avoids the pornographic videos and any other sexual material and focuses all of his sexual interest on you, the more completely your sexual relationship will return to the way it was when you were first married.

It won't be easy for him to give up his tapes or whatever else he uses for sexual release. Over the years, his methods of self-arousal have probably become very sophisticated and work extremely well—much better in fact than his sex with you.

As with any other addiction, at first, he will crave what he has left behind. He will go through the same withdrawal that alcoholics experience. He may become depressed and frustrated, and it will be quite an adjustment for both of you. But if he can do it, if he can stop having sex in any context that does not include you, he will eventually find complete sexual fulfillment in his relationship with you.

Don't forget that the way you make love together should be with your enthusiastic agreement. If he says that you must make love to him in a way that upsets you or is at all uncomfortable, he's back to his sexual addiction again—where having sex is more important to him than your feelings.

It is very important that sex be exclusively reserved for the marital relationship. There are important reasons for this. Sex is one of the easiest ways to deposit love units in marriage. To waste its pleasure apart from each other is to miss an opportunity to build romantic love.

Another important reason to make sex exclusive to the marriage relationship is that when one spouse has sex outside of marriage, the other spouse is usually offended. And as you've seen, it doesn't have to be a spouse having sex with someone else to be offensive. You are offended whenever he has sex that doesn't include you.

Your reaction is quite normal. It's appropriate for you to want your husband's exclusive sexual interest. I encourage you to do what I recommend to resolve this conflict with your husband because once it's resolved, you will have learned the lessons that will make this marriage your best and last.

Dear Dr. Harley,
    I read in a book about marriage and sex that a study showed women become as sexually aroused as men when

showed an explicit pornographic movie. The book also had some quotes from several wives saying that these movies got them "jump started" for lovemaking, even if they weren't in the mood. Do you think pornography can be useful in a marriage and if so, how much is too much?

W. C.

Dear W. C.,

Actually, explicit sexual movies or photographs rarely turn women on. That's why men are far and away the primary customers of pornography. Once in a while I come across a woman who finds them helpful sexually, but these women usually don't have much of a problem to begin with. And in many cases, it isn't the nude men they like to see; it's the nude women.

To answer your questions: A woman who watches pornographic movies with her husband usually does so because he wants her to. He seems to like it, so she goes along. Just sitting with him watching a movie, any movie, can be enough to turn her on, particularly if he is amorous at the same time.

Before you run out to buy pornographic videos, ask your wife how enthusiastic she is about the idea. Unless you have her enthusiastic agreement (Policy of Joint Agreement), I'd forget about it. Springing it on her one night when you are alone together has all the makings of a gigantic blunder.

To test my theory, watch a romantic movie with your arm around your wife and see where it leads. Most women are much more comfortable with that approach to lovemaking than to watch naked actors doing their thing.

Part 4

How to Negotiate in Marriage

Negotiating with the Policy
of Joint Agreement

Almost every day I receive letters from people who are having difficulty implementing the Policy of Joint Agreement—*never do anything without an enthusiastic agreement between you and your spouse.* In most cases they don't quite understand how the Policy is supposed to work, but once the misunderstanding is cleared up, they usually find that it helps them resolve their marital conflicts.

My letters in this section will answer some common misconceptions about the Policy of Joint Agreement, an essential rule for marital negotiation.

Dear Dr. Harley,

My girlfriend and I are both divorced and want this relationship to turn out better than our previous relationships, but we are in total disagreement with each other regarding the value of your Policy of Joint Agreement.

My girlfriend has read and believes in Dr. Wayne Dyer's "Your Erroneous Zones" and holds the position that her "right to independence and personal space" means that she can do whatever she wants without considering its effect on me and our relationship.

As an example, she feels it is her right, according to Dr. Dyer, to take a vacation with her girlfriend instead of with me. We have limited resources, and she plans to spend what little money she has on a trip to Northern California, seeing plays and visiting wineries. This is a trip that J would like to share with her.

J feel strongly that the principles expressed in Dr. Dyer's book prevent the development of intimacy, because while they promote independence and space, they fail to take into consideration the feelings, desires, and reactions of one's partner. J agree with your Policy of Joint Agreement and feel that if we do not follow it, our relationship will suffer.

Js it reasonable to ask for limitations or constraints in being "independent" or in "preserving personal space"? That is, can one respect his or her partner's feelings and desires while maintaining independence?

A. J.

Dear A. J.,

You have managed to do something that very few unmarried couples do: Discuss the rules you would live by if you were to marry. Perhaps your own divorce has helped you understand that rules can make a difference in marriage.

After years of experience helping couples avoid divorce, I have found the Policy of Joint Agreement to be essential in preserving marriage because it's a rule that guarantees marital adjustment. But as you have witnessed, there are many popular philosophies that conflict with my Policy and lead married couples to lifestyles that create incompatibility and result in divorce. Your girlfriend may have followed one of these philosophies of independence during her first marriage and still doesn't realize that it's the philosophy, and not her husband, that led to divorce.

On the other hand, people like you and your girlfriend cannot be expected to follow the Policy of Joint Agreement just yet. The rules of dating and the rules of marriage are quite different because dating couples have not made a commitment to "love and cherish until death do us part." Your girlfriend certainly has the right to go on a vacation with her friend because you and she have not yet made a commitment of marriage to each other.

If your wife chooses to vacation without you after marriage, however, it would violate your commitment to love and cherish each other. The Policy of Joint Agreement is nothing more than a rule that says you will care for each other with every decision you make, and taking separate vacations does not usually reflect such care.

Your girlfriend may not feel like committing her life to anyone right now. Her first marriage may have convinced her that men cannot be trusted, and if she tries to accommodate them, they will take advantage of her generosity. She may like the theories of Dyer and others because they give her permission to take care of herself, even if she must ignore the feelings of the men in her life.

If your girlfriend decides to marry you, her decision may depend on how well you can adjust to the lifestyle she enjoys, so she does what she pleases to see how you react. Any effort you make to force her to live according to your wishes may remind her of the way her husband treated her and discourage her from marrying you.

On the other hand, if you and she agree to marry and make a commitment to each other, then, during your engagement, try following the Policy of Joint Agreement, because it's the rule you should live by for the rest of your married lives. When you are engaged, try it on for size to see if it fits. It will help you determine your compatibility, because every time both of you can't enthusiastically agree to a decision, you have identified an area of weakness to overcome.

But until you are engaged, your girlfriend can make up her own rules, and you can make up yours. Neither of you is obliged to keep the other's rules because it's a time for you to determine whether or not the person you're dating is worth accommodating for the rest of your life. But once you make the decision to "cherish and care for" each other, then there is one rule you will need to follow to fulfill your commitment: the Policy of Joint Agreement.

Dear Dr. Harley,

I feel like I'm a victim of the Policy of Joint Agreement! I've been married five years to a woman with whom I am very incompatible. She tries to control everything about me, and we often fight.

Our first conflict was about when to have children. She wanted children right away, and I wanted to wait. We had children right away. Then there was golf, the game that I love. She wanted me to give it up, along with all my previous friendships. As a result, I have played golf about four times in the past five years, and I've given up all of my friends. I feel like I've completely lost my identity.

But I do have a total commitment to my marriage. At first, I lied to her about what I was doing in an effort to enjoy myself and yet make her happy too. But I was caught too many times and eventually I promised that I would be honest and also that I wouldn't do anything without her prior approval. I've been miserable ever since.

How do you comply with the Policy of Joint Agreement if your spouse will never agree to anything? I'm afraid I am destined to rot away if I follow it much longer.

More specifically, how can I comply with the Policy of Joint Agreement if it's over matters as important as attending church, setting a financial budget together, and having friends?

J. R.

Dear J. R.,

I'm not sure you have actually been following the Policy of Joint Agreement. You must do more than just give something up; you must also try to negotiate a solution that meets with the enthusiastic agreement of both you and your wife.

Remember, the Policy of Joint Agreement says you can't do anything until you both agree enthusiastically—that includes you! You have stopped doing some things that have bothered your wife but you have not learned to follow a procedure that leads to a solution to your conflicts. That's a very important part of the Policy. The procedure I recommend to help couples come to an enthusiastic agreement is as follows:

1. Set ground rules to make negotiations pleasant and safe. Before you start to negotiate, agree with each other that you will both follow these rules: (a) be pleasant and cheerful throughout your discussion of the issue; (b) put safety first—do not threaten to cause pain or suffering when you negotiate, even

if your spouse makes threatening remarks or if the negotiations fail; and (c) if you reach an impasse, stop for a while and come back to the issue later.

Under no circumstances should you be disrespectful or judgmental of your spouse's opinions or desires. Your negotiations should accept and respect your differences. Otherwise, you will fail to make them pleasant and safe.

2. *Identify the problem from the perspectives of both you and your spouse.* Be able to state your spouse's position, and be sure he or she can state your position before you go on to find a solution to the conflict.
3. *Brainstorm solutions with abandon.* Spend some time thinking of all sorts of ways to handle the problem and don't correct each other when you hear of a plan that you don't like. If you use your imagination, you will have a long list of possible solutions.
4. *Choose the solution that is appealing to both of you.* From your list of solutions, some will satisfy only one of you but not both. However, scattered within the list will be solutions that both of you would find attractive. Among those solutions that are mutually satisfactory, select the one that you both like the most.

Your wife may be in the state of withdrawal or conflict much of the time, making it difficult for you to negotiate with her at all. But if you keep your conversations with her safe and pleasant, you will find her to be increasingly flexible and willing to consider solutions that benefit you. After all, she wants a good marriage too and when she sees you caring for her, it will encourage her to care for you.

I applaud your decision to give up golf and friends that upset your wife, but that was only the first step toward creating compatibility. The next and crucial step is to agree to alternative activities and friends that your wife will enjoy with you. Until you take that step, you have not followed the Policy of Joint Agreement.

The Policy of Joint Agreement identifies issues that create incompatibility in marriage. When you can't enthusiastically agree on a decision, it is an issue that has come between you. If you brainstorm solutions, you give your mind a chance to break the barrier, and create compatibility. Regardless of the importance of the issue—church, finances, friends—you should not make any decisions without your wife's enthusiastic agreement. In fact the more important the issue, the more essential it is to have agreement.

Dear Dr. Harley,

The Policy of Joint Agreement is a puzzle to me. It occurs to me that when it is first implemented, no progress is possible. In attempting to get enthusiastic agreement, paralysis is likely.

Are we talking about things that are as mundane as a trip to the store? If one is less than enthusiastic, we just don't go? Am I being too dense?

S. A.

Dear S. A.,

The reason I insist on enthusiasm is to make sure that the self-centered Taker (see The Giver and the Taker, page 18) in each spouse is a willing participant in each decision that the couple make. I want people to stop making either sacrificial or self-centered living a habit, and instead, develop a lifestyle of win-win decisions.

It's true that paralysis may occur at first, especially if both spouses are not used to giving each other their enthusiastic agreement about decisions. But once you get the hang of it, it is much easier.

So you be the judge. If your trip to the store is something that would in any way be a problem for your wife, you shouldn't go until you have resolved the issue. Then when you go, she will wave good-bye with a smile on her face.

Dear Dr. Harley,

I have read your book "Give and Take" and found that the Policy of Joint Agreement has worked wonderfully for us. It has also helped us with our teenage children, since now we present a unified front to them. Our son has had to deal with his drug problem, since we are no longer divided on what we say and do with him.

I have one question about an issue that has not come up yet but may in the future. Let's say that I want to do something and my wife doesn't want me to do it. And let's say that what I want to do is so black and white that there are no gray areas to negotiate. According to the Policy of Joint Agreement we would do nothing. Since it can't be negotiated, my wife would have her way by default, since doing nothing is what she wanted. I can see my doing the same thing to her concerning some other issue. Maybe it will never happen, but I would like to know how you suggest handling such a situation.

D. R.

Dear D. R.,

The Policy of Joint Agreement achieves two important objectives in marriage. First, it helps eliminate behavior that benefits one spouse at the expense of the other; and second, it helps create substitute behavior that benefits both spouses.

What you are proposing is a situation where the first objective is achieved, but the second one isn't. You have eliminated incompatible behavior but have failed to create a compatible replacement.

You've noticed that in your own experience, you have not found such a situation. That is the experience of most people who have learned to follow the Policy correctly. As it turns out, when couples are incompatible and have not been following the Policy of Joint Agreement, almost everything is "black and white." Decisions are often made intentionally to punish the other spouse for the last insensitive decision.

But when a couple learn how to negotiate in good faith, these areas of black and white fade into shades of gray. Spouses learn to respect the other's conflicting point of view and they also learn how to persuade each other without recrimination. They see each other's perspective in a new and compelling light.

If you hit one of these "black and white" issues, let me know about it and I will try to help you get through it. But as you and your wife learn to follow the Policy of Joint Agreement in all the decisions you make, I don't think that situation will ever arise.

How to Follow the Policy of Joint Agreement When You Seem VERY Incompatible

*I*n many of my answers to letters I receive, you'll find some reference to the Policy of Joint Agreement. I've found the Policy of Joint Agreement to be the most important concept in marriage counseling, because through it most of the problems a couple face can be eliminated. However, everybody that's tried to implement it knows that it's easier said than done. And the more incompatible a couple is, the more difficult it is to follow, particularly at first.

These letters deal directly with problems of implementing the Policy of Joint Agreement. My answers provide some encouragement and suggestions to those who have decided to use it to create compatibility but have found serious obstacles.

Dear Dr. Harley,

I can see how a couple will develop a more compatible relationship if they follow your Policy of Joint Agreement for a while. But as you warn, the first few weeks can be particularly difficult due to giving up the things we have done that please ourselves.

If both spouses are not in agreement on an issue, according to the Policy, they are not to do anything until they can agree. One of them will not be able to do what he or she wants, and that will make that person very unhappy.

The more important the issue is to one of them, the more unhappy that one will be if he or she is forced to do nothing. Do you have any advice on how to deal with these disappointments during the beginning stages of following the Policy?

R. B.

Dear R. B.,

You're absolutely right. The first few weeks of following the Policy of Joint Agreement are definitely the hardest, because that's when incompatible habits and activities are first identified for termination and that's when the termination begins. As a couple takes a critical look at their entire lifestyle, evaluating which elements of it are not acceptable to both of them, they may find fifty or more problem areas. Sometimes the results of that early analysis seem so overwhelming that couples don't know where to begin. And then, when they tackle the very first item on the list, the resentment you speak about rears its ugly head. You're right, when couples first tackle their incompatibility head-on, it can seem very discouraging.

First, let me review how incompatibility is created. It begins when one spouse does something in his or her own best interest that's not in the other spouse's best interest. An example is having an affair. People have an affair because it meets their emotional needs and makes them feel good. The fact that the affair hurts their spouse does not deter them. An affair creates instant incompatibility because as long as it's tolerated, there's no way that a couple can live together in harmony.

All other acts of self-interest at the other's expense also create incompatibility in various degrees. Incompatibility, therefore, is simply the accumulation of thoughtless habits and activities. The more of them a couple try to tolerate, the more incompatible they are.

Most marriages start off with very few thoughtless habits because successful courting usually gets rid of them. Couples who are considering marriage go to great pains to behave thoughtfully because if they don't, they won't get to the altar.

But after marriage thoughtless behavior usually starts to grow. In the name of personal freedom, private interests, and expanding horizons, spouses develop habits and activities that do not take each other's feelings into account. Before long they are no longer compatible.

The bottom line is that couples need to eliminate behavior that is good for one and bad for the other, even if it makes the one eliminating it feel bad. Truth is it should never have been there in the first place, and all you're doing is eliminating a bad habit. It's like telling a child molester to stop molesting children. It may make him feel bad to stop but he should never have gotten started in the first place.

The Policy of Joint Agreement compels you and your spouse to stop doing anything that bothers the other person. The one who gives something up to follow the Policy is sure to be unhappy at first.

So now I'll get to your question: How should people deal with the disappointments of giving up thoughtless behavior?

The more pleasure a spouse gets from his or her thoughtless behavior, the more difficult it is to eliminate. Affairs, which are usually intensely pleasurable, are very difficult to eliminate because the withdrawal symptoms are so severe. But even everyday pleasurable activities, such as watching *Monday Night Football*, can leave a husband depressed if his wife puts it on her termination list. Whenever we try to stop doing something we like, we miss it and experience some sadness.

Having spent some of my life helping people overcome addiction (when I operated chemical dependency treatment clinics), I am very aware of how difficult it is to give up something that gives a person considerable pleasure. The procedure we used was to provide emotional support in helping people keep the commitment they made. The worst of it was during the first few weeks of sobriety, but as time passed, it was easier and easier for them to remain sober.

I believe that the same principle applies to overcoming very enjoyable but thoughtless behaviors in marriage. At first, you may need support from someone who can not only provide emotional encouragement but can also provide accountability. Sometimes a pastor or good same-sex friend can fill the bill. If none of those people are available, a marriage counselor will provide support and accountability as part of his or her job.

As time separates a person from the enjoyable habit, the depression and resentment subside. But if a slip occurs, and the person returns to the habit, in many cases the process of withdrawal must begin all over again. This is most obvious when working with alcoholics and with those having an affair. One drink or one phone call to the lover is all it takes to plunge the person back into the captivity of the addiction.

In your letter you were probably not referring to alcoholism or affairs. You were probably referring to simpler but nonetheless troublesome behavior that you can avoid, but when you do, you are left feeling somewhat depressed and resentful. My advice in such situations is to give yourself three weeks to adjust to giving up the behavior. At the end of that time most people find their negative feelings turning around. Besides, if both spouses are abandoning thoughtless behavior, their improved lifestyle more than makes up for trivial losses of selfish pleasure.

As a couple identify and eliminate thoughtless behavior, the withdrawal they experience causes some unhappiness at first. But it doesn't leave a void—couples are not left with nothing to do. They replace their thoughtless behavior with new thoughtful activities that give them a solid marriage, love for each other, and much greater happiness than they ever could have had while engaging in their thoughtless activities.

Dear Dr. Harley,

My husband and I have been married for almost two years, and we are eleven years apart in age. Naturally we do things differently but we usually are trying to meet similar goals. Nevertheless, we are very incompatible on all levels.

He is a mathematics professor and I am a mental health tech on a psych unit. He thinks things through logically, but I look at them from an emotional perspective. From the time we were married, my husband has wanted us to make all decisions together so that we will develop, over time, a compatible lifestyle. But it's not working.

We married spontaneously, not knowing what kind of a couple we would make. After three unhappy months of marriage, I had an affair with my ex-boyfriend. My husband and I eventually reconciled, but he never forgave me. Since then, I have been faithful, honest, and apologetic for the bad decision I made two years ago. I talk when he needs to talk; I am silent when he wants to be distant; I hold him all night long when he feels insecure; I tell him every place I go and every dime I spend without exception. But he still feels resentful.

To complicate matters, my husband is jealous of another male friend I've known for years. To please my husband, I have had very little to do with my friend since I've been married so that I can dedicate all of my time to the relationship with my husband. The times I have contacted my friend, my husband has been with me. My husband insists that my friend is romantically interested in me. I have expressed my wish to maintain the friendship but have agreed to only visit in his company and with his blessings.

My friend sensed tension from my husband when we talked several months ago and suggested stepping out of the picture for my marriage's sake. I said no, but if this is necessary, I will end my friendship. I do not want to because in the end I am sure I will resent my husband for this request.

I feel that the sharing of decision making with my husband puts him in control of me. I wonder if this will ever change. If it will not, I may not be able to live here and stay sane. Some days I feel like leaving just for another taste of freedom. I crave independence. I know this relationship has to be unhealthy for us both.

At present my husband does not respect me and often refuses to talk to me. I wonder if actions wouldn't speak louder. Should I leave him for a while to force him to treat me better?

G. D.

Dear G. D.,

Your husband had the right idea when you were first married—he encouraged you to agree before either of you did anything. Your first reaction to mutual agreement may have been so negative that you did what he feared the most—you had an affair. It was a blatant and cruel violation of the agreement.

Maybe, prior to marriage, you and he had not practiced mutual agreement. You may have done whatever you pleased, and he may have accepted it. So when he proposed mutual agreement at the time of your marriage, you may have felt trapped by it. As is the experience of many that try it for the first time, you may have felt deep resentment and depression. But whatever it was that drew you to your old boyfriend right after you were married, it certainly could not have justified what it was you did to your husband. It undoubtedly hit him like a bomb.

In spite of your bad start, however, the Policy of Joint Agreement is what you need. It was created just for your situation. It's for people who don't feel like being thoughtful. If you had followed it faithfully when you were first married, you would not have had the affair and by now you would be sharing many common interests, mutual love, and respect for each other. It would have forced you to consider your husband's feelings, even when you thought you'd go crazy if you did.

There are two kinds of resentment: resentment due to something one of you *did* to the other that was hurtful, and resentment due to something you *didn't* do for yourself that you would have liked but that would have hurt your spouse. Your husband has the first kind of resentment because you had an affair three months into your marriage. What you did, hurt him. You have the second kind of resentment because you now feel obligated to avoid seeing a friend who is a threat to your husband.

I think you would agree with me that the first kind of resentment is the most difficult, because your husband knows you deliberately hurt him. It's no wonder he's having trouble recovering from the experience. Your poor communication may be partly due to the fact that he is still trying to recover from the shock.

The second kind of resentment, the kind you are experiencing, may be uncomfortable, but life is full of instances where we need to control ourselves for the protection of others. In other words, I'm saying that whatever resentment you may feel about avoiding your friend is nothing compared to the resentment your husband probably feels because of your affair.

You may be right about your incompatibility, but from what you've told me so far, what is separating you is not incompatibility, but his emotional withdrawal, which is a different matter entirely. He started out on the right track, wanting to settle all decisions on a mutually agreeable basis. But I think his best intentions are being overwhelmed by the grief he is feeling because of your affair a year ago. He may have been over it by now, but your effort to see another friend from your past is keeping his grief fresh. Why torment your husband with needless pain?

From your husband's perspective, if you cared about his feelings, you wouldn't see your friend. The fact that he has made his wishes clear, and you still want to see your friend, is proof to him that you care more about seeing your friend than you care about your husband. My advice to you is simple: Don't have friends who make your husband uncomfortable. Remember, incompatibility is a present condition, not necessarily a future condition. I'm in the business of helping incompatible couples learn to become compatible and I see it happen almost every day. Once you both learn to behave in ways that do not hurt each other—and I think I'm talking more to you than to your husband—your husband will have little trouble becoming emotionally reunited with you and will work with you to create a life that is enjoyable for both of you.

The fact that you hurt him with your affair does not mean that it will burden your relationship for the rest of your marriage, unless you keep bringing new men into your life who threaten your husband. It doesn't mean that you will have to live your life in a closet. It means you will develop friendships with men whom your husband knows and trusts. Develop friendships that are good for both you and your husband.

The Policy of Joint Agreement may make you uncomfortable at first. After all, it means you must give up everything you enjoy that hurts your spouse. But it doesn't take very long until all those self-centered pleasures are replaced with a mutually enjoyable lifestyle. And when that happens, you're compatible.

Can a Marriage Be Saved by One Spouse?

*C*an one spouse save a marriage? One spouse can set a good example and encourage the other to work together on a solution, but can one spouse actually save the marriage?

When a couple has a conflict, one spouse is usually hurt more than the other and that spouse is usually the most vocal about getting the conflict resolved. It's usually the wife who brings home books on marriage and suggests seeing a marriage counselor to resolve problems, because it's usually the wife who is most adversely affected by marital conflict. After years of being the only one who seems to care about the marriage, many wives eventually give up and file for divorce. Then the husband becomes the only one trying to save the marriage. Is that what it takes to get his attention—a divorce?

Many of the letters I receive are from women who realize that they cannot save their marriage by themselves. The loneliness and desperation are apparent in their letters. I'm including one of these letters, but the rest of the letters are from husbands whose wife has either left or is threatening to leave. They are wondering if they can save their marriage by themselves.

Dear Dr. Harley,

I have just read your book "His Needs, Her Needs," but my husband is not interested in reading the book or going to counseling. His theory is that things will get better on their own. After twelve years they are not getting *better—they are getting worse. I feel very alone in this marriage but will not give up on it just yet.*

Can counseling and self-help books help a marriage when only one of the partners is willing to try these resources?

N. R.

Dear N. R.,

I'll answer your question at the end of this letter but first, allow me to make a few observations about your situation. While your letter is short, the answer is long. Please bear with me as I try to be as concise as possible.

It is very likely that your husband is not suffering as much as you are. In fact the marriage from his perspective may be downright enjoyable. That would explain why he seems to have the patience of Job.

You and your husband may be in disagreement over how to spend money, how to raise your children, what to do on weekends, or any of a host of other issues. You may find that he tends to get his way on these issues and you have had to put up with it.

Or you may not be getting your emotional needs met. Perhaps he does not talk to you the way he did when you fell in love with him. He may have stopped being affectionate years ago and yet wants you to submit to his sexual advances. He may not even be home very often, leaving you to care for your children alone.

Or you may be suffering from ridicule, demands, dishonesty, or even abuse by your spouse. He may have become rude and insensitive or he may have become a tyrant, someone whom you have come to fear.

Whatever it is that is making you unhappy in your marriage, you are probably more unhappy about it than your husband is. That's the key to why he doesn't seem as interested as you in resolving your marital problems.

People in your position try, usually for years, to get their spouse's attention. Those that complain often feel guilty about complaining, and the spouse often reminds them that they should be grateful for what he or she does instead of being critical of what *isn't* done. So these people learn to say less and less as the problems become greater and greater. Some people never do complain because they don't want to be perceived as critical and unappreciative. But in the end the marital conflicts take their toll; the feeling of love for their spouse is lost.

When that happens, the person gives up. He or she comes to the conclusion that the spouse will not change. The one who is suffering decides to get used to the idea of living without care or consideration. Some of these people remain married for the sake of their values or children but they remain emotionally distant from their spouses to minimize their pain. Others leave their spouses for someone else who has offered to meet their needs. Still others simply leave because they find it less painful to be alone and out of the marriage than alone in the marriage.

When a person comes to me asking, "Can one spouse save a marriage?" my answer is a qualified yes. I see one spouse saving a marriage almost every week. The way it's done is that the one spouse teaches the other spouse how to negotiate fairly. It takes patience and understanding to get to the point where the couple learn enough about marital negotiation to resolve their conflicts, and many of the people I counsel lack the patience. They have lost their love for their spouse and have very little motivation to save the marriage.

N. R., you can still save your marriage but you don't seem to have much motivation left. Before long you will have lost your love for your husband and will have convinced yourself that your marriage is not worth saving. Then you will probably leave your husband for good.

Before your marriage gets to that point, there is something you can do. Your husband may not be willing to read books or see counselors but he may be willing to learn from you how to resolve marital problems. If you can figure it out, he may let you teach him.

The second chapter of this book will acquaint you with my basic concepts and give you many of the tools you'll need to resolve your conflicts. Your husband doesn't need to read the chapter if you can explain the concepts to him. When trying to reach an enthusiastic agreement over any conflict, you will need to follow the guidelines for negotiation found on pages 132–33.

Try to get your husband to fill out the Love Busters Questionnaire (appendix D) and the Emotional Needs Questionnaire (appendix B). Make two copies of these questionnaires so that you can fill them out too. Then if your husband agrees, read each other's answers. Agree to avoid certain Love Busters that he has identified if he avoids some that you've identified. Agree to do a better job meeting his needs in exchange for his doing a better job meeting your needs.

Even if he doesn't respond to your suggestions, you will have explained clearly what it is you want. If you are like most wives in your situation, you will eventually give up on him and perhaps file for divorce. But you will have left him with the knowledge of what it would have taken to make your marriage work. The day may come when he sees the importance of making some changes. He may come to you enthusiastically willing to put the things you've suggested to work in your marriage. I hope that day comes before you are divorced.

Dear Dr. Harley,

I am currently having marital problems. I am twenty-nine and my wife for seven years is twenty-eight. We have two girls, two and five. The day before Mother's Day, my wife told me she was not in love with me any longer. She has been feeling this way for some time but has never revealed her true feelings to me until now. To her, our marriage is over and there is no chance for recovery.

She is determined to find her "happiness" somewhere else. All this time I thought I was providing her with all the happiness she wanted—emotionally, mentally, and physically. I don't drink or smoke and I'm not abusive to her or the children. But for some reason I'm not worth a second chance.

She wants to continue to stay here until we can financially afford to separate, but I'm living on an emotional roller coaster. I never thought she would stop loving me. What can I do to save my marriage when she is so determined to be by herself? She tells me she wants to find her happiness with herself. What can I do? Any advice for what feels to me a hopeless case? I will always love her and do not want to lose her.

T. C.

I am not giving my answer to T. C.'s question. His letter shows what happens when marital problems are confronted too late. T. C.'s wife did not tell him what was bothering her because she did not want to be a complainer. Little by little her love for him diminished until it had completely disappeared.

T. C. is asking, "Can one spouse save a marriage when the other spouse has walked out the door?" It's a very different question from the question that N. R. is asking. In N. R.'s case, her husband loves her but he doesn't want to put any effort into his marriage because his needs are already being met. If he waits much longer, however, he'll be asking me T. C.'s question because N. R. will have walked out.

Don't let your marriage get so bad that your spouse finally gives up on you. Those marriages can be turned around, too, but it's much more difficult and the process is more painful. If your spouse tells you that there is a problem, fix it now, while you both still love each other. And if, like T. C., your spouse never complains but may be harboring resentment, fill out my Love Busters Questionnaire and Emotional Needs Questionnaire and ask him or her to do the same. It will help you uncover problems in the early stages when they are much easier to solve.

Dear Dr. Harley,

I am in exactly the same position that T. C. describes in his letter. My wife wants to leave me but I am still very much in love with her. We have a twenty-one-month-old son, whom I adore. She is an educated woman with a very responsible career. Now, even after a year of marriage counseling, she wants a divorce. My wife is in total lock-down; she refuses to discuss the situation with me. I thought the counseling sessions were working, but she says she was just pretending so as to avoid conflict.

How can I save this marriage? I gave her a book, but she refuses to read it. The only people she talks to want her to divorce me so they are driving a bigger wedge between us. I know I have changed over the last year and I know I can be the loving and supporting man I was at the start of our relationship ten years ago. I realize I've made too many large withdrawals from her Love Bank but J've been trying hard to make deposits for some time now. Js there any way J can break through her shell and get past the influence of her friends? J want to save my family.

A. J.

Dear A. J.,

The truth is you are in a better position to be your wife's husband than anyone on earth. You are married to her and you are the father of her child. The reason she wants a divorce is that the disadvantages have far outweighed the advantages for so long that she has made this very painful decision—for her it *is* painful! But it is even more painful for her to remain married to you.

The solution is for you to see to it that her relationship with you is painless and clearly in her best interest. You must eliminate every situation where she has been uncomfortable (including your trying to get her to stop talking to her friends) and replace your insensitive behavior with things you do that meet her emotional needs. Since she is in the state of withdrawal, at first she will not want you to meet her needs, so she may not give you much opportunity. But the reason she is in withdrawal is that you are doing and saying things that cause her to raise her defenses. Stop trying to straighten her out and start making her life enjoyable! Then she will lower her defenses, emerge from the state of withdrawal, and allow you to meet her needs.

You've been to marriage counseling for a year, and yet she is divorcing you. Was the counselor as surprised as you? He or she should be able to help you discover what it is your wife is running away from. Perhaps she thinks you are responsible for her loss of self-esteem, her loss of identity, or her being depressed all the time. If so, what does she think you could have done that would have prevented that from happening? Are you disrespectful toward her? Do you threaten her? Do you make demands? What do you do that makes her unhappy? Whatever it is, learn to overcome it.

You need to understand what she is going through and try to help her overcome it. Be her best friend, not her adversary. The child you have in common is an undeniable and lifelong link to her heart that will bring you back together again if you demonstrate your care for her in the respect you show for her. Perhaps you could talk to her on the telephone instead of in person. It is sometimes easier to communicate that way. When she is comfortable talking to you on the telephone, you may then suggest talking face-to-face, but don't push. Let her take her time. Prove to her that you care more about her feelings than your own and that you will not do anything to hurt her again.

Dear Dr. Harley,

My wife has already given up on our marriage and left. I love my wife more than anything and do not want to lose her. I have come to realize by reading your book "His Needs, Her Needs" and through personal reflection that I have not met her emotional needs. So she had an affair with someone she works with and she wants a divorce. Since this has all happened over the last few weeks, I have tried to show her how much I love and miss her through cards, flowers, and notes left in her car. I know that these things will not change the past, or me, or even remove all the resentment she feels toward me but these are all I can do to show her how much I love her. I am seeking counseling for myself to deal with childhood abuse issues that quite frankly prevented me from loving myself, let alone meeting my wife's needs.

If only she were here!! I would be very interested in your advice.

H. S.

Dear H. S.,

At this time, your wife believes that her friend can offer her more than you can. It's a very self-centered time in her life, and there's nothing you can do to change that. The most constructive thing you can do is to prove to her that you can run circles around her friend. You can't prove it in an hour, a day, a week, or even a month. But you will have your chance sometime within the next six months to two years, because most affairs fall apart in that period of time. You want to be there to catch her when it happens. You want to be the man who cares enough about her to be there for her even after she has left you for someone else.

Don't do anything to upset her, don't try to make her feel guilty, and don't expect her to apologize if she ever returns. Instead, let her know that you want her to be happy and you are upset with yourself for having failed to make her comfortable when you were together. All you want is a chance to prove that you can learn to meet her emotional needs. If it turns out that you can't do it at this time, wish her the very best in life and tell her you will always care for her and that you may be able to meet her needs at some point in the future.

I know this approach to your problem is difficult. After all, you may think, don't your feelings count for anything? But remember, right now you are in no position to bargain. Her friend has done a pretty good job proving that he cares about her. She is in the state of intimacy with him and in the state of withdrawal with you. The question is can he keep caring for her until she emerges from withdrawal to give you a chance to meet her needs?

If you are kind and considerate to her during that period of time, and she feels she can return to you without fear of judgment or anger, she will turn to you when her friend slips, and I'm sure he will slip many times. You must remember that anyone who pursues someone else's wife has quite a few character flaws that eventually show up. Your wife will see them sooner than you think.

Incidentally, I don't think that childhood abuse issues have much to do with your problem or its solution. I've helped thousands of couples save their marriages without ever "resolving" any of those issues. We always get right to the heart of the matter: Stop hurting each other and start helping each other. It's simple but it works. You need a counselor who can help you change whatever it was that drove your wife away and help you learn to meet her emotional needs. Each of us can choose how we want to treat other people without spending much time agonizing over our past.

You may want to speak to your physician about the possibility of taking an antidepressant to help get you through this period of unprecedented grief, anxiety, and anger. It will help calm you down at a time when your whole life seems to be falling apart.

Remember, every self-centered act on your part at this time will make it more difficult for your wife to return to you. Be sure to lay out the welcome mat.

Can You Negotiate
with an Angry or Violent Spouse?

*A*ngry outbursts are a primitive and ineffective form of negotiation. In an effort to solve a problem, anger is used to bully a spouse into submission, rather than seeking a mutually acceptable solution. It doesn't work but that doesn't keep people from trying it.

These letters reflect the suffering that anger and violence create in marriage. How can a marriage survive this destructive problem-solving strategy? It can't. Anger and violence must be eliminated to make room for the Policy of Joint Agreement.

Dear Dr. Harley,

My husband and I were high school sweethearts and married shortly after we graduated. Our first child was born a year later and I went through a period of depression. I felt neglected and unattractive and in a moment of despair I had sex with another man, just once, after which I felt terrible. My husband was terribly hurt, but we stayed together and eventually had two more children.

Fifteen years have passed, but my husband has never let me forget about my mistake. Anytime we fight with each other, he always brings it up. I have had to live with the memory of my past infidelity many, many times in the past fifteen years. He says I can never be trusted again and he has never forgiven me.

We have also had many loving, close moments during our marriage and we have been strong, loving parents to our children.

Last week my husband and I went on a week-long vacation, without the children. The first five nights were incredibly romantic. We both agreed it was our best vacation ever. Then on the sixth day, a man at a nearby table stared at me while we were having dinner. When my husband and I went to our room for the night, he accused me of enjoying the other man's looking at me. I was so angry with him that I just climbed in bed with my clothes on. And for the rest of the vacation our romantic moments were over. We tried discussing the incident many times before coming home, but it always ended up a stalemate.

On the way home from the airport, my husband called me some awful names and we had a heated argument, both saying hurtful things to each other. He then took our bags to the front door, ran to the car, and sped off, even before the children could say hello. He left a note in view for the whole family, describing my infidelity of fifteen years ago and the lack of my love and support. I wrote him a letter letting him know, once again, how sorry I am for all of my mistakes and that we all love and need him.

My husband is my best friend, and in his letter he stated that I am his. I know that our love for each other and for the family runs deep. What should I do?

R. K.

Dear R. K.,

I'm certain that this is a time of crisis for you, but you can also look at it as a time to resolve a conflict that you and your husband have had for fifteen years. Let me give you a few opinions and observations and then I will offer some suggestions.

First, I guarantee you that your affair is not the problem that you think it is. Instead, it is an issue that your husband has used over the years to get the upper hand whenever you and he have an argument. It may show up especially whenever you have been reluctant to have sex with him. It throws you off balance whenever he mentions it and makes you feel guilty, wanting to make it up to him somehow. He may also bring it up whenever you are winning in a power struggle he is having with you.

Prior to the incident where a man was staring at you, you may not have seemed to be as sexually interested in your husband as he would have liked. At the dinner you may have looked particularly appealing to your husband, and he may have felt inadequate. His intimidation may have sparked his argument with you, which was his attempt to put himself back into a position of control. But instead, you became angry with him and rejected him sexually by going to bed with your clothes on. That made him feel even more inadequate, and he felt he had to increase his abuse to try to regain control. He may have thought he needed to teach you a lesson so you would think twice about refusing him sex again.

But his abuse did not work this time. You met his aggression with your own aggression. By the time you got home, he had not yet won the battle and the fight continued to escalate. He decided to raise the stakes a notch and left you and the children. He also told the children about your affair to punish you for not giving in to him. Again, he was using your act of infidelity as a way of regaining control.

I think your husband wants to come back to his family but he wants to come back with pride, with his head high, and with you begging his forgiveness. He wants the children to believe it was all your fault, that he had every reason to leave. And he wants to regain his position of control. He also wants you to assure him that you will never again hold out on him sexually.

Your husband's behavior is abuse, pure and simple. I'm sure you have retaliated with your own abuse of him, and that's something you should learn to avoid too. But there is no excuse for the way your husband left you and the children. There is no excuse for him bringing up the moment of weakness you experienced years ago. There is no excuse for his accusing you of wanting to go to bed with a man that looked at you. He is being disrespectful and abusive.

There's another side to the story, of course. His side. He would explain to me that you do and say things that hurt his feelings, and whenever you do, he doesn't believe you love him or ever did love him. He thinks you do not agree with him enough and that proves

153

you don't support him. He may think that whenever you prefer not to make love to him, it's evidence that you don't love him enough.

I would point out to him that your lack of love for him is *his* problem, not yours. You love him to the extent that he is meeting your needs and not hurting you. There are times that he has done an excellent job of meeting your needs, but there are other times when he's been awful.

In your letter you say you love him and you want him to return home. He probably loves you too and wants to be home. He has just shot himself in the foot and doesn't really know what to do next.

Those are my opinions and observations about your situation. Now, what do you do about it?

I would look him right in the eye and say to him, "Listen, Buster, do you love me? Do you care at all about how I feel? If you do, you sure have a funny way of showing it! I love you and want to spend the rest of my life with you. But it sure will be unpleasant for both of us if you keep treating me this way. You are not doing things that I admire; you're doing things that I find disgusting!"

What if he says, "Fine, then let's just get a divorce and end it all"? To that I would say, "It's up to you. I married you for life, but if you want a divorce, it's your call. If you want to be in a love relationship with me, however, you're going to have to treat me much better than you have been treating me. From this moment on you will never again bring up my affair and if you are upset with me, you will have to treat me with respect until we can solve the problem. I will agree to do the same with you. If you are upset with our sexual relationship, I want us to discuss it as adults and solve it with mutual respect. I refuse to be treated like this, even by the man I love."

It may take him a while to digest what you say, and he may leave in a huff. But once it sinks in, he will probably agree with you that at least some of the problem is his.

Pay close attention to my Love Busters concept. You both need to work on avoiding angry outbursts. You probably need to work on avoiding disrespectful judgments and selfish demands as well. While you're at it, you may want to complete my Emotional Needs Questionnaire (appendix B) to see if you are failing to meet any of each other's important emotional needs.

I think your marriage is secure, at least for the short run. Your husband, to his credit, still has your love. But he won't have it for long if he gets away with this one. The most encouraging part of this crisis is that it may provide the catalyst to help you straighten your marriage out once and for all.

Dear Dr. Harley,

My husband and I cannot communicate! When I try to talk to him about a problem I have (and not necessarily a problem about him), he seems to get angry and I end up crying. I wish he could try to understand what I'm having a problem with, instead of defending himself.

For example, I told him that I didn't think his family treated me very well and that it was hard on me when we were together. He became angry (even though he's complained about them himself). I ended up in tears. I wish he could just say something like, "I'm sorry and I appreciate all that you put up with from them," but it never happens. I know this must be a common problem among men and women but when you can't talk to each other about anything, it makes life real hard. Please help!

R. L.

Dear R. L.,

You've done a good job describing a problem that exists in a host of marriages. When you want to talk to your husband about something that's bothering you, he gets angry with you. It's a serious problem, indeed, because when you ask for his help, you're already feeling bad. But when his response to your appeal for help is anger, you're devastated.

There's no good excuse for bursting out in anger in marriage, although everyone does it, thinking they have good reason for it. As far as I'm concerned, it is a mistake that damages a relationship.

In your case, I would guess that your husband's anger has a lot to do with the responsibility he feels about solving your problems. He wants you to be happy and, when he isn't angry, he wants to help you with any problems you bring to him. When he's successful, and you appreciate his help, he feels terrific. But when he can't help you with your problems, he becomes frustrated. One approach he may take is to try to convince you that your problem is not all that serious and you shouldn't feel bad about it. If that works, he's off the hook. But you may respond to this approach by feeling that he is not taking the problem seriously enough.

Or he may try another approach. He may try to convince you that there's nothing that can be done about your problem. If you can adjust to the problem, he doesn't have to solve it. Again you may feel that he does not understand the pain you are suffering, and this approach may also make matters worse.

If he can't help you solve the problem and he can't convince you that it's not serious or that nothing can be done about it, he will then recognize that he's failed to do something very important to him, and he will be frustrated. Then he will make the mistake that leaves you devastated: He will become angry with *you*. It makes no sense, of course, but that's what people do when they're frustrated—they lash out at the nearest thing, and you're it.

Whatever the cause of his anger, I'm sure it has something to do with your being unhappy, and his feeling responsible for fixing it.

The solution is to tell him that whenever you are unhappy, you want him to help you, but the way he can help you the most is to avoid getting angry. He may deny being angry, so you may have to call it "frustration."

Your husband is probably quite helpful to you in most matters, and it's only when he can't think of a solution that he gets frustrated (like what to do about his family). If he knows how to control his temper, I think the solution to your problem is quite possible.

In a sense, the solution is simple, but if he has a serious problem controlling his temper, its implementation may be quite difficult. In that case, he should seek professional help.

However, if he knows how to control his anger, he should learn to calmly help you when something bothers you. He should discuss alternatives with you and offer assistance in solving the problem. He should understand that even if he cannot help you or cannot think of any solutions, you appreciate just talking with him about it.

What follows is a series of three letters from one person and my answers. The letters begin with her concern for her own safety and end with her in a shelter for battered women. It is at this point in her nightmare that her decisions may mean the difference between life and death.

Domestic violence is not as common as people think. Most of the troubled couples I've counseled have never experienced domestic violence, and most couples in general go through life without having had a single physical altercation. If your spouse has ever hit you or if you have ever hit your spouse in anger, you're in a tragic minority and in a dangerous situation.

If you have ever pushed, slapped, grabbed, or hit your spouse in anger, you are a perpetrator of domestic violence and you're likely to do it again. You need to take extraordinary steps to protect your spouse from yourself. Most violent spouses are deeply remorseful after sending their husband or wife to the hospital and sometimes to death, but remorse does not make up for the pain. Violence cannot be a part of any relationship.

Whenever domestic violence occurs, people are shocked and confused as to what to do about it. My perspective as a professional who has counseled hundreds of violent clients is that these couples should be separated until there is assurance of safety. In many cases that assurance can never be given. Throughout my career as a marriage counselor, I have done whatever I can to save marriages, but when it comes to domestic violence I draw the line. Unless a spouse can guarantee the other's safety from his or her own anger, I don't believe they should live with each other.

I hope G. S.'s letter and my advice can offer perspective to you if you find yourself in her situation. And if you are a perpetrator of violence, get help immediately.

Dear Dr. Harley,

It is hard to know where to begin. I met my husband on the internet. We "talked" for a while that way, then exchanged phone numbers, and finally met face-to-face.

It seemed we had so much in common; I guess we still do. But now things have gone very wrong for us. He is often depressed and becomes extremely angry with me if I question him in any way. Only lately has there been a hint of violence. In anger he put a dent in my car and some bruises on my arm.

I know that I have been moody. I am pregnant and I am finding it hard to adjust to all the hormonal changes in my body. Sometimes I think I am being very reasonable when in fact I am not. Later I am sorry and apologize. Even so, I don't think that my bad behavior gives my husband the right to be violent toward me.

I am finding it extremely difficult to be intimate with him in any sense of that word. If I tell him a confidence or admit to a fault, he throws it up in my face every time we fight.

In bed I just can't get aroused at all, which I don't think is totally due to my pregnancy. I try to please my husband in that way anyway because I know that is very important to him. He knows that I am not enjoying myself and that makes him even angrier at me. It seems to be a cycle that feeds on itself. I need to get back to emotional and intellectual intimacy before I can really enjoy the other.

I am becoming increasingly frightened and I need some good advice. Please help me.

G. S.

Dear G. S.,

Angry outbursts are the most destructive of the five Love Busters and disrespectful judgments comes a close second. What is happening to your marriage is that your husband's anger, not his depression, is destroying your love for him, and with it goes any sexual desire you may have had. I'm sure you are doing your best to try to control your reactions, but your emotions will dominate you, as they should in your situation.

Your husband's anger has gotten the best of him. He can't quietly discuss your problems without blowing up, so he avoids talking about them at all. From your description, you need professional help to guide you through this crisis, but it may not be solved even with professional help. The anger that you are describing is very difficult to control.

What, specifically, has gone wrong, and how are you approaching your problems? I gather that you are going to him for solutions, possibly even blaming him for the problems, and he can't handle it. He may have tried to solve the problems in the beginning but has given up trying. His depression may be due to his failure to provide solutions, or maybe he feels *he* is the problem. Perhaps he has a long history of having failed and thought that marrying you would give him a fresh start. Now he finds himself in the same mess he has been in before. When you try to talk to him, he may be angrier with himself than he is with you. Your pregnancy may have given him a sense of overwhelming responsibility. Perhaps he is reacting to that feeling with alternating expressions of anger and depression.

These ideas are pure speculation on my part. Your husband probably knows what is depressing him and what makes him feel so angry. Ask him what is bothering him but don't be critical of his answers or suggest that he is not seeing things correctly.

E-mail to me these details, and I will try to help you through this but at this point I feel very uneasy about your marriage.

Dear Dr. Harley,

Thank you so much for getting back to me! We really need help, both of us. I know you must be very busy and do greatly appreciate your time.

I'm not sure what details to give you but here goes!

Things got out of hand about a month and a half ago. Jim would come home and blow up at me about insignificant or imagined issues. We both agreed that he needed to see a counselor about his depression, but his insurance paid for only four sessions, and he is already through those. Things got a little better while he was seeing the counselor. Instead of his coming home from work and yelling about stupid stuff, he would come home and yell about things that were really bothering him.

About what bothers him, he seems to feel that people don't respect him and are trying to take advantage of him. The situations he describes to me don't seem to be so extreme. I don't understand why he gets so furious. Last week his supervisor corrected him. He was furious. He came home and spent the whole evening raving about how rude his supervisor is. I have been corrected many times in my profession but I see no reason to take it personally. I did not tell Jim that I felt he was overreacting to situations because I didn't think he could handle it.

As long as I have known Jim, he has told me he wants to be a lawyer. He has always said that it is his dream and he won't be happy until he is one. He says it is what he has wanted all his life. He certainly is smart and hardworking enough to do it, so I have supported him in it. If that is what he needs to be happy, then that is what he ought to do.

Last Thursday he called me at work to tell me that he wants to be a teacher. He has never expressed an interest in teaching to me before this and what scared and upset me is that Jim denied ever having wanted to be a lawyer. It's as if he has forgotten all of our conversations about his dream. Now being a teacher is his lifelong dream. He also has forgotten things I have told him about myself. I've told him just about my whole life story, but he doesn't remember anything about me.

I don't think my husband has really been bad tempered all his life, unless he has suppressed it very well (which may be a possibility). He does suppress a lot. He gets mad at people at work all day and just smiles at them like he doesn't care. But when he comes home he lets me have it all. That is what makes me think he could have been hiding a bad temper.

This evening he told me that he thinks I've been stealing his money and sending it to my parents. This is not the case. Our combined incomes would barely make pocket change for my parents. In fact my mother has on occasion sent us money. He says his parents have me figured out. They are the ones who told him I'm stealing his money to send to my parents! They, apparently, have been telling him a lot of bad things about me.

I used to be able to bounce things off Jim, and he used to help me work through my own issues. However, now he uses my problems against me. I am afraid I will never be able to trust him enough again to be that transparent. I guess

J am mourning the loss of intimacy; it makes me very sad. Jt was something J really treasured about our relationship!

J call my mom to tell her my problems, but Jim won't let me use the phone when he is around. Thank you for listening to me because J really feel alone these days. J guess we are in a lot of trouble. J believe in staying married to one person all your life but J am so unhappy!

G. S.

Dear G. S.,

In my first letter, I suggested that you find out from your husband what's bothering him, not to be critical about his answers or suggest that he is not seeing things correctly. The purpose of this investigation is to discover the causes and nature of his anger and depression.

What you told me in your last letter is very alarming. Your husband appears to have a very serious emotional problem that may be getting progressively worse. The behavior you describe—emotional outbursts, paranoid thinking, forgetfulness, and distortion of past events—point to a possible progressive organic neurological disorder, such as a brain tumor. Even if it's not a tumor, he seems to be suffering from a serious mental disorder.

A very nonconfrontational and nonjudgmental approach will tend to support my diagnosis. The safer he feels telling you his inner thoughts, the more he will reveal of himself to you and hopefully to a mental health specialist. He will probably reveal fragmented and distorted thinking, confirming his underlying mental disorder. Don't tell him he is wrong about his feelings and judgments because it will only infuriate him.

But there is a possibility he may not have a mental disorder at all. His forgetfulness may be due to his not listening to you when you talk to him. He may simply be very self-centered and may have had a very bad temper throughout most of his life when he didn't get his way. I wish it could be that simple for you but I suspect that he is battling quite a bit more than self-centeredness.

Your fear of him is well founded and you should consider him dangerous. I understand how panicked you must feel, and under the circumstances you may wish to visit your parents to have the support and protection you need.

Dear Dr. Harley,

I tried to learn about how Jim thinks, like you suggested, and he eventually agreed to counseling together as a couple. At first, things seemed to be going quite well. He seemed much more caring and expressed a willingness to control his temper.

But on Friday night Jim beat me up. He grabbed me by the hair and threw me around for about twenty minutes, yelling the whole time. My whole body aches, especially my neck and scalp. He also tried to crush my head with his hands and tried to strangle me. He relented before I passed out. I am terrified that next time he won't relent in time, which would kill not only me but our unborn baby.

Like the last time he hit me, he called his parents to come over. The last time, they tried to convince me that I was the one who drove him to violence, so this time, I managed to get out just as they were arriving. The three of them insist that what Jim does is not violence and that it is my fault for provoking him, not his. They say I deserve this kind of treatment.

I am now staying at a shelter for battered women. I am terrified for my life, terrified that if he and his parents have a part in the raising of this child, they will impart these warped values to my child. I don't believe in divorce but see no alternative. When I first wrote you, I thought he was incapable of hurting me to the point of death. Now I see that it is only a matter of time before he kills me and/or the baby.

G. S.

Dear G. S.,

I'm so very sorry to hear about what you've been through. Throughout my professional career, I've tried very hard to keep marriages together. But short of providing your husband with a cure for his mental disorder, I don't think your marriage can be saved. My original guess that he has a serious mental disorder, perhaps organically caused, is probably correct. The fact that his parents are so supportive doesn't necessarily negate my opinion. Many parents blindly support their children in the face of overwhelmingly damning evidence.

I don't believe that in his more rational moments he really wants to hurt you, but that's not the point—he did hurt you when he was not rational, and that makes him too dangerous to be married to. At this point no one knows how to prevent him from becoming irrational in the future, and therefore your safety cannot be guaranteed.

He will probably want you to return to him and will probably agree to anything to get you back, even counseling. But his problem may be so serious that no treatment would guarantee your safety with him.

You are now faced with one of the most important decisions of your life: What will you do next? The fact that you and he will share a child throughout life makes the rest of your life dangerous for you, and you should take special precautions to avoid a sudden attempt on your life.

I suggest that you file a criminal complaint for assault and insist on his being given a neurological examination and a mental health exam. The best thing that could happen to him would be for him to be incarcerated and evaluated for a mental disorder. Perhaps a mental health specialist would be able to find a solution to his problem. At the very least you want his violent behavior to be on record. Quite frankly, he didn't do enough damage to convince most judges that he is a threat to you, but I'd file your complaints anyway. The people who work at your shelter should be able to help you follow through on that plan.

I believe that everyone who is ever hit by a spouse should file a criminal complaint for assault. That person should also tell all his or her friends and family about it. Those who are able to control their temper will control it pretty quickly when they are faced with incarceration and public scrutiny. In your case, G. S., I don't believe your husband has control over his anger, but you should file the report just the same.

Most cases of domestic abuse that I've witnessed have involved productive citizens. This is true in your case as well. Your husband has not spent his life in a mental hospital nor does he have a history of violence. Moreover, he is gainfully employed and has been reasonably successful. When you first met him, he seemed perfect to you, and you fell in love with him. And yet the fact is that he is capable of killing you.

I'm sure you have a great deal of compassion toward your husband and you probably still love him, but your love and compassion could be dangerous for you. I suggest that you move to where you can be surrounded by your friends and family, for emotional support and protection. Moving may make your life even more chaotic at first—losing your job and moving your things while you're pregnant—but in the end your life will be much more peaceful and secure.

Domestic violence comes unexpectedly. While it's progressive in most cases, it's often excused as something other than what it is—until it's too late. Now that you know that your husband is violent, you have no choice but to protect yourself and your unborn child from him.

G. S.'s ordeal has not ended. She is trying to reconcile with her husband, in spite of my warning. It is my experience as a counselor that most women do not leave their abusive husbands, even if their life is in grave danger. G. S. is no exception.

How to Resolve Conflicts of Faith

*W*hen one spouse converts to a new faith, it can be very much like an affair. The attraction can be so strong that the believer is willing to abandon everything, including his or her spouse, to follow the religious teaching.

A conversion experience can be not only *like* an affair, it can *be* an affair. The messenger of the faith is often the lover of the new believer, which can confuse the issues dramatically.

The first two letters in this section reflect religious conversions that are in each case actually an escape from a bad marriage and also an affair in disguise. In these cases, to save the marriage, I don't recommend challenging differences in faith. Instead, I recommend focusing attention on unmet emotional needs and Love Busters. It's been my experience that conflicts of faith in these situations usually melt away once love is restored between spouses.

Dear Dr. Harley,

My wife is spending an increasing amount of time meeting with people who have developed a passion for "Celestine Prophecy" (Redfield's best-selling book) and similar New Age musings. She has embraced consciousness-raising therapies where she reads, experiences, and hears about spirituality ideas that she does not, nor can not, properly analyze. When I question the nature of her beliefs, the deceptive information, and pseudoscience, she says that one can't analyze feelings and what she's doing "feels right."

Bit by bit, my wife moved into her present state over a period of several years but it's really become intensive this past year. After nine years of what I thought was a happy marriage, she now says she feels "disconnected" from me and is not able to commit to our marriage in the way she did when she felt connected. She has also withdrawn from me physically.

She decided to move into an apartment last year for a three-month period. Although she's now back home, she says that she has a "knowing" that her destiny in life is to do New Age–type "healing" work with others, which she envisions as requiring travel to other countries. Now she goes off to "do her work" and to local meetings with like-minded souls for several hours, several times a week, plus one or two weekend sessions each month of three to six hours each. Additionally she frequently spends an inordinate amount of time on the phone speaking in fascination about "harmonizations," "energies," "vibration levels," "synchronicities," etc. It seems like she is addicted; she is obsessed with this activity.

She does much of her "energy work" in the company of a like-minded man. I've told her that I'm uncomfortable with her being in his presence so often; she assures me that nothing is going on between them. I resent that she is spending so much time with him—which is certainly promoting emotional intimacy—and very little time working with me to resolve our marriage problems.

We have children, eighteen, sixteen, and eight, and she is a loving mother. She says she doesn't want to end our marriage but she cannot commit to our marriage as a priority over "finding herself." I cannot understand how our once romantic relationship has fallen into such disrepair.

For the sake of our kids and our marriage, what constructive action do you suggest that I take?

D. R.

Dear D. R.,

Over the past ten years, you and your wife have drifted into incompatibility. Her conversion to New Age philosophy may be a symptom of how far you've drifted apart but it's not necessarily the cause.

If I were to talk to your wife about her transformation, she would probably explain how she tried to stay emotionally connected to you and that her efforts were rebuffed. She would probably complain of Love Busters such as angry outbursts, disrespectful judgments, and selfish demands. She would also tell me how much she needs someone to talk to, but talking to you had become an exercise in futility and frustration.

So she did what she had to do; she withdrew from you and found others that would meet her emotional needs. These people who met her needs happened to believe in New Age philosophy but they could have believed in almost anything. As a result of her relationship with them, she has adopted their system of belief. One of them, the man you refer to in your letter, probably did more than the rest to meet your wife's emotional needs, so it's likely that she has fallen in love with him.

As long as her emotional needs are being met by these friends, she will continue to share their beliefs, and it will be impossible for you to dissuade her. Notice how she tells you that it feels right. What feels right is that her emotional needs that you were not meeting are now being met by her friends, by her male friend in particular. Who can argue with that?

I don't think your wife's beliefs are at the core of your problem. What is at the core is that she has been making decisions that ignore your feelings. Her decision to stop making love to you is one of many designed to ignore your feelings and cut you out of her life. I imagine that in her three months away from you, she missed her children and perhaps the economic comforts that your home provides. It's also possible that her romantic relationship with her religious advisor didn't go as well as she had hoped. So she moved back in with you, remaining in the emotional state of withdrawal, trying to live in the same house with you without having an emotional connection with you.

If I am right about your wife's religious transformation, challenging her beliefs will prove futile. It isn't the New Age philosophy that she finds so compelling; it is the care shown by friends who meet her emotional needs that has won her over. If you are to win her back to you, you will need to learn what they do for her that she finds so irresistible. You must learn to meet her most important emotional needs; one of those seems to be her need for safe and enjoyable conversation. Ask your wife if she would be willing to read my book *Give and Take* with you. As you read the book together, she may tell you that your disrespect for her opinions (a Love Buster) drove her away from you. She may also tell you which of her emotional needs have been unmet in her relationship with you.

You won't be able to meet her needs at first, while she is in withdrawal. But you will be able to prove to her that you are a safe and pleasant person to be around by respecting her opinion. Then she will slowly come out of her defensive shell and give you opportunities to reconnect with her.

I know you have tried to be tolerant of her beliefs, but as her decisions have become increasingly hard on you, you may be showing her disrespect when you don't intend to. Be very careful that you focus attention on how her decisions affect you, rather than on the truth of the belief behind the decisions.

Remember, she is in the state of withdrawal because something you've done has convinced her that you are too dangerous to get close to. Withdrawal is a defensive strategy to guard against the Love Busters angry outbursts, disrespectful judgments, and selfish demands. Identify the Love Busters you are indulging in and protect her from them by eliminating them.

If you learn to meet your wife's emotional needs and if you overcome Love Busters, it will be much easier for her to agree to take your feelings into account whenever she makes a decision. You and your wife are probably very intelligent. If you use that intelligence for each other's welfare, your wife will become reconnected to you. You and she will be soul mates once again.

The following is D. R.'s response.

Dear Dr. Harley,

Thank you for your considerate reply to my e-mail. The language she uses is like fingernails scraping on a blackboard to me: "biospiritual energy," "detailed analysis of the chakra system," blah, blah, blah. It is a challenge for me to bite my tongue on hearing this sort of stuff and to refrain from making "disrespectful judgments."

But I agree with your assessment of the dynamics of our relationship. Beliefs are not the real issue here. I believe that trying to discuss our differences at that level only gets in the way of addressing the real cause of our turmoil—our emotional needs not being met.

What you are suggesting is a major paradigm shift for both of us, as our marriage counseling to date has been along the lines of improving communication—each of us learning the different "languages" we speak and improving our ability to argue more effectively. But this has not proven to be a productive approach in the emotionally bankrupt climate in which we are living.

I met with my wife over lunch today and we discussed taking the approach outlined in your book "Give and Take." The next step will be for us to fill out the questionnaires. I am hopeful that we are—at last—on a productive track to resolving this painful situation.

My wife's primary concern, as you might imagine, is fear of making decisions that take my feelings into account (the Policy of Joint Agreement). I will try to learn to make decisions with her feelings in mind and hope she does the same for me.

I'm certainly looking forward to the prospect of us once again becoming "soul mates"!

D. R.

Dear Dr. Harley,

My wife has moved out and filed for divorce after twenty-two years. I have read your basic concepts and I think that they would have been of great help in resolving our conflicts and restoring the love and care that we had but I think it is now too late. If only we had found you sooner!

This is a second marriage for both of us. She has two children from a previous marriage, and I have three. All of our children no longer live with us. The past four years have been particularly difficult for my wife. It all began with her mother passing away. She experienced a deep and pervasive grief over the loss of her mother and began questioning what she has done with her life. Severe migraine headaches followed and she also started menopause. To top it off, her father remarried three months after her mother's death. It was a shock to us all but it devastated my wife.

After her suffering two years with migraines, we started t'ai chi together to help her learn to relax. I dropped out after a few months due to a leg injury, but she continued on her own. From there, with the instructor's encouragement, she joined him and his nephew in attending services at the Tibetan Buddhist teaching house.

The three became inseparable, and our family-owned business suffered as my wife spent more and more time with them instead of working. Dream group/drum group, Indian temple dancing, vegetarianism, and Indian food all followed. Our close intimate relationship eroded and finally ended. The marriage counselor we saw seemed to be at a loss to know what to do.

I could see that we were growing apart, but everything I said or did was ignored. She said she was going to keep her friends, and nothing would change her mind. I started getting more upset and loud arguments ensued. She left our bedroom to move into the room across the hall. She also left our business and got a job on her own. I continued to try to talk to her but it always led to arguments. Whenever I asked if she was having an affair, it led to a fight. Then she stopped talking to me altogether, except about superficial topics.

Three months ago I shoved her onto a bed in fear and anger for her refusing to talk to me, and she moved out three days later while I was at work. I was served restraint and divorce papers, and she took half of our belongings and left the place a disaster. Tossed!

By legal agreement I can only communicate with her by e-mail or mail or if she calls me by phone. She also comes to the house to pick up things from the enclosed back porch. Last night she called me and we discussed our marriage for a while. I thought we had been soul mates and were very close, but she told me that we had never agreed on anything—I always had it my way, our family business had always been mine not hers, and that in spite of her efforts to please me, I had not met her needs. I asked her if she would be willing to see a marriage counselor with me. She responded that she "owed me at least that much" but said that legally she had to attend only once and would not commit to any more than that. She also said she did not want the restraining order to be lifted.

Since our last counseling experience ended in failure, I am looking for the right counselor for the one court-ordered session and don't know where to turn. I have almost given up hope, but is there something you could suggest for that one session?

O. S.

Dear O. S.,

From your description of the problem, the death of your wife's mother, her headaches and menopause, the remarriage of her father, and probably other crises plunged her into some serious soul searching.

Your marital problems probably all started when your wife's father remarried right after her mother's death. She may have expected him to grieve a little longer than three months, to say nothing about the possibility that he may have been in a romantic relationship with his new wife long before your mother-in-law died. Your wife may have started to think about the sacrifices her mother made for her father and how her father didn't even show her enough respect to grieve for her.

Then she took a hard look at you. She began thinking of all the work she did in your family business. Why was she sacrificing for you the same way her mother sacrificed for her father? All of her mother's loyalty and sacrifice didn't mean a thing, your wife may have thought. She decided not to waste her life the way her mother had.

Someone finally came along to whom she could talk about her feelings and he comforted her in this period of upheaval. He not only listened to her questioning but also may have given her answers that made sense to her. Your wife may have eventually fallen in love with this person. But even if she didn't have an affair, she seems to have come to the conclusion that she can't depend on you. She may believe that if she were to die, you would forget about her, just as her father forgot about her mother. She may have decided that there must be more in life than sacrifice and denial and that she must begin thinking of herself because you don't seem to be thinking of her.

She had been emotionally withdrawn from you for some time when you threw her on the bed in your effort to force her to talk to you. Your behavior confirmed her worst suspicion. You had not only failed to care for her, but you were now also a threat to her safety. You might even kill her, she thought. So she left you with divorce papers and a restraining order.

At this moment you are your wife's enemy, not her soul mate. You cannot be a part of her future because she doesn't want to turn out just like her mother. If you and she are to reconcile, you must somehow convince her that you care about her deeply and you will make every effort to help her find life safe, enjoyable, and fulfilling.

The one counseling session that she is required to attend should be used to convey to her your deepest apologies for not being there for her when she needed you the most. You should not blame her for a thing and don't expect her to respond to your apologies. Tell her that you have made many mistakes and you did not take her feelings into account when you made decisions. Ask her to give you a chance to redeem yourself by proving to her that you will put her feelings first from now on.

Read *Give and Take: The Secret to Marital Compatibility* before you get to the counseling session so that you will have insight into what it was that drove her away from you. It was probably the way you talked to her, how you tried to convince her that she was wrong, and the arguments you had with her.

Give and Take begins by laying out my basic concepts. It explains how you and she got into this mess and why your wife is responding to you the way she is. The second part of the book gets into three of the most destructive Love Busters (angry outbursts, disrespectful judgments, and selfish demands). They drove her away from you, and you need to learn how to overcome those habits. The third part of the book explains how important it is to meet emotional needs and how you can learn to identify and meet your wife's needs. I would give special attention to the chapter regarding the need for thoughtful and supportive conversation.

If you go to the counseling session with a plan for reconciliation—with a goal for making your wife's life with you safe and fulfilling—she may listen. Even if she doesn't listen at first, your appeal may sink in over time.

Of course in the end, your wife will also have to meet your emotional needs, which have gone unmet for some time. She will also have to avoid Love Busters and follow the Policy of Joint Agreement. But if you can demonstrate a willingness to form a safe and considerate partnership with her, where her feelings and future are just as important as yours, her sense of fairness will eventually prevail and you will become the soul mates that you described in your letter.

Dear Dr. Harley,

My fiancé and I are very much in love and we plan to get married around Christmas this coming year. We've been together for almost three years, and everything has worked out perfectly between us. There's just one issue about our potential marriage that I think we haven't resolved. We are of two different religious faiths. I'm a Catholic and my fiancé is a Protestant. Since we have both been very religious our entire lives, neither one of us wants to convert to the other's religion.

We've spent quite a bit of time discussing the problem and have come to some agreements. For example, we have agreed to have a wedding with both a Catholic priest and a minister present. We've even discussed attending two worship services together once we're married so we can be together and yet not abandon our own faiths. But I'm concerned that this could end up being a logistical nightmare somewhere down the line. Do you have any suggestions regarding our agreements?

The more difficult question, I think, is what to do about our children's religious development. We're both concerned that our religious differences may be confusing and contradictory to them. Plus, each religion has its own requirements (particularly mine), and some of these aren't conducive to compromise. What do you think we should do? We both love each other very much and I think we'd both be more than willing to embrace any adequate compromise.

We have an intrafaith conflict. We are both Christians but we don't agree on some of the specific details of Christianity. I'm curious to know what couples do with interfaith conflicts, where they believe in very different religions. I don't hear too much about it, which surprises me since it seems like the odds would be against one marrying someone from exactly the same faith, unless that person met the other person at a church function or something.

Thank you for helping us with this issue.

R. A.

Dear R. A.,

The reason that differences in faith can create such a problem in marriage is that faith usually affects our behavior. As you have already noticed, you and your fiancé's religious differences have not prevented you from falling in love with each other or feeling like soul mates but these differences have made it difficult for you to carry out the dictates of your respective faiths while you have been dating. For example, to satisfy the requirements of your faith and yet share your religious experiences with each other, you must both attend both Catholic and Protestant services. As you anticipate, such compromises can become "logistical nightmares" as the expression of your faith grows.

Intrafaith differences, such as between Catholics and Protestants, do not create as many marital conflicts as interfaith differences, such as between Islam and Buddhism. That's because there are fewer conflicting beliefs *within* a world religion than there are *between* world religions.

174

But sometimes the zeal with which a husband and wife believe can be more of a problem than the beliefs themselves. The stronger the religious conviction, the more troublesome the differences become. People with weak faith have little trouble respecting and accommodating their spouse's conflicting beliefs. But those with strong faith, like you, usually feel that respect and accommodation are uncaring and sinful. Your commitment to faith may make even minor intrafaith conflicts difficult to resolve.

I won't encourage you to lose your religious zeal just to accommodate each other. I am quite a religious zealot myself. But I don't want your faith to come between you and your fiancé either. There are ways to resolve your conflicts so that you can have your faith and a great relationship at the same time. That's what I will recommend to you in this letter.

I suggest a two-part plan to resolve your religious conflicts. The first part is for you to try to come to an agreement regarding your faith. Obviously, if you can reach an agreement, there will be no need to negotiate about lifestyle conflicts because you won't have any. But if your effort to come to an agreement fails, I suggest the second part of my plan, which will show you how to resolve lifestyle conflicts that your differences in faith help create.

How to Respectfully Convert Your Partner

Should you try to convert your partner to your religious beliefs? Should he try to convert you? If so, how should you go about it? It sure would make your decisions a lot simpler if you were both Catholic or both Protestant.

My Catholic grandmother married my Methodist grandfather, but neither had much religious zeal. Since their religious beliefs had little to do with their practices, they rarely created a conflict. Then one day my grandmother was converted to the Mennonite faith—those same Mennonites that believe in living a separated life, free of alcohol and tobacco, among other things. My grandfather who drank and smoked heavily was converted by my grandmother to the same Mennonite faith in one week's time. The next week he gave up smoking and drinking for life. A most miraculous transformation.

Just as my grandmother went about converting my grandfather, I recommend that you consider persuading each other to your respective religious beliefs. But the process should be safe and enjoyable and done with profound respect for each other.

Use the following steps to try to respectfully persuade each other. They may lead you to a shared religious faith.

Step 1: Clearly state your conflicting beliefs to each other. There are a myriad of details in any religious faith, so this part of the assignment may take a while. I suggest that in your effort to understand each other's convictions, you attend classes with each other that are designed to describe the faith that you have. While you study together, try to identify the beliefs you hold in common and the beliefs that conflict. You have probably already done this to some extent, since you attend each other's church services, but try to formalize your areas of religious agreement and disagreement.

This is actually a good exercise for any couple, whether or not they think they have religious differences. To know what your spouse believes and why is a critical step toward understanding your spouse.

After you have identified differences in your beliefs, describe them to each other, to check on your accuracy. Make sure you describe each other's position to each other's satisfaction so there are no misunderstandings.

Incidentally, many of your conflicts may not be rooted in beliefs but rather in habits or emotional reactions. Your beliefs may turn out to be remarkably similar, but because you've been in the habit of worshiping a certain way, you may feel some anxiety about the prospect of changing. A Catholic service may meet your emotional needs while a Protestant service does not. For your fiancé, it could be the other way around. Try to separate out religious practices that are driven by habits and emotions as opposed to those that are belief-driven. It's pointless to discuss beliefs when habits or emotions are at the root of a conflict. But whether your practices derive from beliefs or habits, respect them. Never be condescending to each other's religious practices regardless of how they're derived.

Remember, people usually don't like to be told what to do, and any effort on your part to force him to become a Catholic will backfire. For you to achieve a genuine agreement, he must know that your belief is not only in your best interest but in his best interest as well. The second step is designed to help you achieve that objective.

Step 2: Explain how your beliefs are in your fiancé's best interest. At this point respectful persuasion often disintegrates into disrespectful judgments. What would happen if you were to shout, "Can't you see how stupid you are by not participating in the sacraments? You have everything to gain and nothing to lose!" But you'd be losing love units for sure and you would be ineffective in persuading him.

Why do husbands and wives have so much trouble discussing their differences? Because the process can be so unpleasant. Rather than discovering each other's wisdom, they tend to ridicule each other. A much more enjoyable and persuasive approach would be to say, "Even though I don't agree with you, I know you have good reasons for your beliefs. But I would like to suggest some other reasons that may change your mind."

Some people have great difficulty making the above statement, because they don't believe their spouse has any good reasons for his or her beliefs. This attitude reveals an underlying disrespect. If your fiancé tries to explain the reasons for his faith, and you make them a subject of ridicule, he will eventually keep his opinions to himself.

Even after you have tried to show that your beliefs are in your fiancé's best interest, your arguments may not convince him. He may tell you that he still doesn't agree with you. But that doesn't mean you are at the end of your rope. There is one more thing you can do. You can ask him to test your belief for a brief period of time to see if he likes it. This is the third step of respectful persuasion.

Step 3: Suggest a test of your beliefs. A final argument in defense of your beliefs is, "Try it, you'll like it!"

People often make a big mistake in marital discussions when they try to force each other to make a long-term change rather than a temporary one. If your fiancé is not convinced that your beliefs are correct for him, he cannot be expected to make a commitment to your position. But his interest in your beliefs and his respect for you may encourage him to risk a test.

You could suggest to him that he participate in some of the sacraments to see how he feels about them. In advance of the test, explain

177

that habits take time to develop, so if he is comfortable with the first week's test, he may need to extend the test for about three months so that he will develop a habit of participating in one of the sacraments.

When I try to convince others to accept my faith, I encourage them to read the Book of John from the Bible and pray at least once a day. My faith assumes that God will reach out to them through that simple experience and that by meeting God personally, they will be convinced of his presence and plan for their lives. From there I encourage them to attend a church that will help them grow in the relationship they have formed with God. That simple test has helped me convert many people to my religious beliefs.

Step 4: Give your fiancé an opportunity to persuade you. Respectful persuasion is a two-way street. Your fiancé has the right to try to influence your judgment just as much as you have the right to influence his. If you want to persuade your fiancé, you must be willing to let him persuade you. After all, he could be right and you could be wrong about any issue you discuss.

Your fiancé could propose his own test to convince you that his Protestant beliefs are correct. The test that I suggested (reading the Book of John and praying for a month) is a typical test of Protestant beliefs, and he could suggest that you try that test.

Regardless of how the tests turn out, think about how much you will learn about each other and how much wisdom you will gain from each other as you follow this procedure. I firmly believe that what I am recommending to you will not only help you avoid many conflicts you could have over your different beliefs, but it will help you form an even closer relationship with each other.

Step 5: If your tests fail to persuade, drop the subject. Clearly understand the bargain: If your fiancé is not comfortable with your beliefs after the test, and you are not comfortable with your fiancé's beliefs after his test, you may each ask for yet another test. But if either of you feels that you've had enough tests, drop the subject.

At this point many couples forget the rules for respectful persuasion. The focus of attention must be on *respectful*, not *persuasion*. If your test is ineffective in persuading your fiancé, accept the fact that you've failed. You may have another opportunity someday. But at this point you should back off.

Remember, respectful persuasion does nothing that would draw love units from your fiancé's Love Bank. As soon as you do anything that your fiancé finds unpleasant, it's no longer respectful persuasion. The entire process must be pleasant and nonthreatening. If you think you must persuade your fiancé at all costs, the cost will be love units, and you will also fail to persuade. I may be able to force my wife to say she agrees with me and I may be able to force her to do what I want but I cannot force her to change her beliefs and I can't force her to love me. Only the process of respectful persuasion can achieve those objectives.

Let's assume that you are unsuccessful in persuading each other to adopt your religious beliefs. What should you do to resolve the conflicts that you described in your letter? How can you avoid the "logistical nightmare" that you anticipate? That's the second part of my plan.

How to Come to Agreements Regarding Lifestyle When You and Your Partner Maintain Differences in Religious Faith

Whether you marry someone with a conflicting religious belief, or your spouse is converted to a conflicting belief, the decisions you make must accommodate your spouse's feelings and sensitivities or your marriage will suffer.

My mother is a Democrat and my father a Republican. Their political preferences have not greatly interfered with their marriage because their opinions have not had much to do with the decisions they make. The only time their differences are noticeable is when they vote. They cancel each other out. But since their political opinions do not affect their lifestyle choices, they don't affect their marriage either.

Your religious convictions, however, have a great deal to do with the decisions you make. They have already made a difference in the way you live. For that reason, it will be difficult for you to come to an enthusiastic compromise but it can be done if you follow the steps I recommend for negotiating:

1. Set ground rules to make negotiations pleasant and safe.

2. Identify the problem from the perspectives of both you and your partner.
3. Brainstorm solutions with abandon.
4. Choose the solution that is appealing to both of you.

For more details on these steps see pages 132–33. It is the last step that will help you avoid the "logistical nightmare" that you antici-pate. Don't agree to a solution that does not work out well for both of you and under no conditions should you be disrespectful or judg-mental of your fiancé's religious convictions. Your negotiations should accept and respect your differences of opinion.

Remember, I advocate following the Policy of Joint Agreement in literally every decision you make, especially the important ones. You must put the Policy before everything, including your religious beliefs.

You are already following the Policy in the decisions you have been making, which is a credit to both of you. So far you have discussed each conflict with care and consideration for each other's feelings. That's why you are still in love with each other. As long as you con-tinue to follow the Policy under all the conditions that will change your life, your religious differences will not drive a wedge between you and you will have a life filled with love.

I am a Christian with very strong convictions but I also believe, based on the experience of the thousands of couples I've counseled, that marriage (and children) will thrive only if spouses put each other's feelings before the dictates of their religious convictions. It doesn't mean that religious convictions must be abandoned. It sim-ply means that you must live your faith in a way that accommodates the feelings of your spouse.

How to Be Honest with Your Spouse

There are two essential rules for marital negotiating and problem solving: the Policy of Joint Agreement and the Rule of Honesty. They work together to help couples accurately state the problem (honesty) and solve it with mutual consideration (enthusiastic joint agreement). So if you want to overcome conflict in your marriage, honesty is a prerequisite. The Rule of Honesty is explained on pages 27–28 and there is more information on it in appendix E.

Honesty is much more than a problem-solving rule. It also meets one of the most important emotional needs in marriage (see honesty and openness on page 268–69 in appendix A). If you want to make your spouse happy, you must be honest.

Honesty meets an important emotional need in marriage and dishonesty is one of the worst Love Busters in marriage (see dishonesty on page 290–92 in appendix C). It can ruin a relationship by destroying trust and confidence.

The letters I receive reflect the crisis that dishonesty creates in marriage. My answers are designed to help restore honesty that will resolve conflicts, meet an emotional need, and overcome a Love Buster.

Dear Dr. Harley,

Ever since day one of our relationship, I have been honest with my spouse. Recently, however, I found out that he has not been honest with me and I'm going out of my mind.

To give you a short background, when I met my husband (then boyfriend) he was dating someone we both knew. I asked him then and since whether or not they had a sexual relationship. He has always told me no, but for some reason I have always doubted the truth of his answer.

This past weekend I was cleaning out some boxes and I found a letter that told me otherwise. I read the letter out loud to him, and he finally confessed and told me the truth. I am not angry that he had a relationship with her (it's not like I did not expect him to have a "life" before me) but I can't get over the fact that he lied to me over this.

He claims that he lied to me because he was afraid of losing me at the beginning of our relationship. However, since I have asked him periodically over the years, I feel as if he should have told me a long time ago rather than my discovering the truth in this letter.

I am really bitter about this and cannot seem to get over the hurt of being lied to. I keep grilling him with questions because that lie makes me think of other things he could have lied about. He says my grilling is torturing him, but his lie feels like a stab in the back, especially because I have always been honest with him. I have risked losing him by telling him things about my past that were very painful to tell but I was honest.

How can I resolve this situation?

S. C.

Dear S. C.,

You have introduced a problem that has baffled many professional marriage counselors: lack of honesty. For years I have maintained an unpopular opinion on the subject—honesty at all costs. I have recommended to my clients that they be honest about everything, especially instances of sex with others, before or after marriage. Why? So a husband and wife can come to understand each other better and protect each other from their predispositions.

The argument made by most marriage counselors is that discussion of past sexual affairs or sexual experiences before marriage is cruel to the other spouse. I've heard it explained that the only reason one spouse would reveal his or her indiscretion to the other is to feel better, to get it off his or her chest. The caring thing to do is to lie about it, rather than cause the spouse all that pain.

I'm horrified whenever I hear such nonsense. While it's true that honesty releases a great burden of guilt, it's not true that the only reason to be honest is to gain emotional relief. Honesty is the door to understanding and it's what each of us deserves from our spouse. But I've never heard that position expressed when counselors discuss the issue. It's as if we should be honest only when no one would feel bad if confronted with truth.

So it's no wonder that your husband has kept you in the dark about his previous relationship: It's what's often suggested by counselors these days. But I, like you, feel that it is more important to know the truth than it is to avoid emotional pain. I feel that honesty is essential to the safety and success of marriage. Almost every week I am asked by husbands and wives whether they should confess to an earlier affair or, as in your husband's case, to sex before marriage.

I don't guarantee that a spouse will not be terribly upset with the truth. In fact I predict it. I don't even guarantee that the spouse will not walk out once he or she hears the truth, although no couple I've ever known divorced or even had a worse marriage after the revelation had a chance to sink in. Honesty does not take away the hurt of a harmful revelation but it does prevent another harmful act, dishonesty, from being repeated throughout marriage.

In your case, instead of your husband confessing his lie, you discovered that he'd lied. That is much harder to take than if he had just simply told you the truth at any point before you found the incriminating letter. You are not convinced that he is any more honest now than he was before you found his letter. But regardless of how it happened, you now have convincing information that he lied to you. You can now let him know that what you want in your marriage is truth at all costs.

There may be other areas where he has been dishonest with you. He should tell you about those too. You may not have been completely open with him about all of your feelings either. From now on you have an opportunity to create a relationship that places honesty above all other values, and if you do, you will have joined my wife and me and the minority of couples who place a high value on honesty.

We tend to be willing to hurt others when we think that no one will know what we are doing. I've always thought that the solution to crime and thoughtlessness itself is for all of us to sacrifice our privacy. If all our acts were videotaped for anyone to see, most crime would be a thing of the past—we would be much more thoughtful and caring.

Self-imposed honesty is the next best thing to videotape. If you know that you will reveal to your spouse whatever you do, you are far less likely to do things that are likely to hurt him. It essentially eliminates the risk of most affairs. If you go one step further and follow my Policy of Joint Agreement—*never do anything without an enthusiastic agreement between you and your spouse*—affairs are utterly impossible.

Within a few weeks you will be feeling better about this, regardless of what I say to you. But be sure that this experience is an encouragement to your husband to be honest with you in the future. Most people do the opposite. When confronted with a lie, they make their spouse pay for it. They cry; they scream; they hit; they make threats. They do all sorts of things that convince the lying spouse to cover his or her crimes more carefully in the future. Don't put him through hell because he failed to tell you the truth. That would simply encourage him to be dishonest with you next time. Instead, let him know that his honesty means a great deal to you and that you will work with him to try to achieve a more honest marriage. Use your discovery as evidence that you both need to rise to a new level of honesty.

Dear Dr. Harley,

I read your book "His Needs, Her Needs" and find your analysis of how people have affairs to be very accurate. It seemed like you were describing the affair I had several years ago. But in my case the affair is now over and I no longer have any interest in the woman. You seem to suggest that I tell my wife about it, even though it's over. I can't imagine doing such a thing to her. Since my affair is over, why torment her with unpleasant memories?

J. M.

Dear J. M.,

The fact that you were unfaithful to your wife is an extremely important thing for her to know about you. In fact your affair is one of the most memorable events of your life, however upsetting it may be to your wife were she to know about it. But it is more than an important event. It is also evidence that you can't be trusted, and your wife should know that about you. Of course, once you tell her, your wife may not trust you about anything. Then you will need to reestablish her trust in you.

Honesty is a form of protection—for others! The more people know about you, the better able they are to protect themselves from your destructive predispositions. If you want your wife protected, as you indicate in your letter, she needs to know everything about the ways that you could hurt her. If she knows about your weaknesses, you can both make adjustments that will make your failure less likely in the future. On the other hand, if she is ignorant of them, she will be left defenseless.

You may be afraid that she will leave you if she knows what you did. Are lies all that's keeping you together? If she knew you better, would she hate you and want nothing to do with you? She has the right to the truth and then she has a right to leave you, but it's very unlikely that she will. As painful as it is to find out about an affair, very few couples ever divorce because of it. In most cases, both spouses make adjustments that help avoid a repeat. But without the truth, there is little assurance that it will not happen again. Most people have affairs because of an unmet emotional need, and unless that need is now being met by your wife, you will be tempted to be unfaithful again.

When you had the affair, you knew that there was a chance that your wife would discover it and yet you went ahead anyway. In other words, you didn't care how painful it would be to your wife; all you cared about at the time was your own pleasure. The reason that the affair is over is that the woman didn't meet your needs the way you thought she would—luckily for you. But how do you or your wife know that the next woman you meet won't be better suited to you?

You and your wife need to work together to guarantee that you are both meeting each other's emotional needs and that you will never be unfaithful to her again. You may need to set rules for yourself that prevent you from developing friendships and spending time alone with women who could meet your unmet emotional needs. You need to spend most of your free time with your wife. She needs to be your best friend.

After you reveal this indiscretion to her, don't keep anything from her again. Be honest with her about everything. You'll find that honesty will not only help you create a very intimate relationship, but it will also help keep you from hurting her in the future.

Dear Dr. Harley,

I'm really hoping that you can help me. I've been married for almost two years now and as far as I can tell the whole marriage has been one lie after another.

It started with something pretty simple: My wife was a smoker when I met her, and I told her up front that I had always hated smoking and would not date a smoker. She assured me she was quitting, so we started dating. After she had convinced me she had stopped, I found out from her friends and family that she was lying and was hiding it from me. By this time we were already engaged.

She kept reassuring me that she did want to quit and would do so before our wedding. When we were married, as far as I knew, she had quit. Again her friends and family told me it was all a lie. Then I found out there were other lies: She would spend money on one thing, then lie and say it was spent on another. She would be in one place and lie and say she was somewhere else. Now she has admitted to me that since we were married, she has had more than one affair.

She explains to me that her affairs were just "one night stands" just after we had had a fight and she did it because she was lonely. She also admits that she lied about other things to prevent me from getting close to her or knowing what she was doing.

She was married before and was abused by her husband, so I believe a lot of our problems stem from defenses she's carried into our marriage. She seems really honest

186

about making things right this time, but J've heard that from her before and it just turned out to be a lie.

Everyone J talk to says she's a habitual liar and if she's cheated more than once, she'll cheat on me again, so J should divorce her. Js it possible for someone with such a history of dishonesty to change her ways? J love her and want this to work out but J'm really hurting. J feel very vulnerable right now and J don't think J could take another betrayal of any kind.

We've separated for now, with the hope that she can change, but J have been told it's wrong for me to wait for her to change and J don't know if J should subject myself to another possible harmful situation. What should J do? Jf J should stay with her, how do J make this work?

S. C.

Dear S. C.,

Apparently you are in love with your wife, so she must be doing something right. I imagine she does a good job of meeting many of your emotional needs.

There are three kinds of liars: born liars, avoid trouble liars, and protector liars. From what you've said about her, she sounds like the avoid trouble liar. These people do things that they know are unacceptable; then when confronted they lie to avoid getting into trouble. (See chapter 7 in *His Needs, Her Needs* for more information on types of liars.)

The born liar is different than the avoid trouble liar in that he or she doesn't seem to know the difference between truth and fiction and makes things up for no apparent reason or purpose. An avoid trouble liar, on the other hand, is very much aware of the truth and only lies to avoid getting into trouble.

The avoid trouble liar is used to getting his or her way. This person usually has a long history of agreeing to anything and then doing what he or she pleases. When confronted with the lie, this liar promises to never do it again—another lie, of course. This person is usually very cheerful because life is just the way he or she wants it. Avoid trouble liars think that if people would just stop telling them what to do, there would be no need for dishonesty. What they think makes them dishonest is people trying to change them. They don't think it's right, so they say whatever people want to hear just to get them off their back.

The way to help an avoid trouble liar learn to be truthful is to focus attention on honesty and to ignore everything else for a while. I encourage such liars to tell the truth in return for their spouse not telling them what to do. In other words, minimize the consequences of the acts that they are afraid will get them into trouble. Instead of trying to punish your wife for going back on her promises, I would put more emphasis on safe and pleasant negotiation, where she is free to explain what she wants to do and to give you a chance to offer alternatives that are genuinely attractive to her.

What happens now is that she feels she is *made* to agree with you. You have told her that unless she does this or that, you will leave her. Even in the beginning you explained that unless she stopped smoking, you would not even date her. She has learned to agree with anything and then do what she pleases to avoid fighting or being abandoned. But what if there were no fight? What if you didn't threaten to leave her? I recommend that you try to stop fighting with her and stop threatening to leave her. When she tells you she smokes, tell her you would appreciate it if she didn't and offer her incentives to stop. But don't use threats.

Infidelity is quite another matter, of course, but I think she has come a long way just to have told you about it. I don't think she wants to make a habit of cheating on you but she doesn't want you to threaten to kick her out either. I may sound naive on this point but I would try to create a nonthreatening environment for her first, and then see if she cheats on you.

I encourage you to read about my Policy of Joint Agreement (see pages 17–18). It would be terrific if you and your wife could follow it. But right now your wife seems to be a long way from making such a binding agreement. She is not accustomed to negotiating with commitment, but it wouldn't hurt to start trying to follow the Policy. It is far more likely that she will follow through on an agreement that she shows enthusiasm for than one that she feels forced to agree with.

There are two essential conditions that you must follow if you want her to negotiate with you honestly. Your negotiations must be safe and enjoyable. In other words, when you negotiate you should never threaten her with punishment or make the negotiations unpleasant for her. Instead, if you do not reach an agreement, you should let her do whatever she wants, without recrimination.

Try to establish a relationship with your wife where you never try to force her to do anything. Place honesty at the top of your wish list and give her freedom of choice in all other areas.

Oh yes, one more thing: Invite her to live with you again. I don't think a separation is a good idea in your case.

Dear Dr. Harley,

I've known my boyfriend for more than two years and I am deeply in love with him. We've recently looked into moving closer together, possibly moving in together and working toward a future as husband and wife. I've always trusted him and felt very loved and cherished by him, until last Sunday.

Last Sunday at about 1 A.M. we had both fallen asleep, and I was extremely tired that night. In a half-asleep daze, I heard his cell phone beep and realized my b/f was making a phone call. It was very obvious he was trying to sneak a phone call because he whispered and moved away from where I was. He did this for about twenty minutes. I casually asked him whom he was talking to, still not suspecting anything. But he lied and said he was only chatting with his brother. It got my attention because it didn't make any sense. When I confronted him, he finally admitted he was calling a girl, a pen pal, someone he's never met but has been friends with for a year. Evidently this girl had paged him earlier, and he chose the opportunity while I was asleep to return her page. He was calling another country to talk to this girl!!! He left snuggling with me to sneak off to make this call and then lied about it!

I let him know at the time that I was quite upset and hurt.

But now, one week later, I am still angry and am considering leaving him. He, on the other hand, feels I'm overreacting and have blown things out of proportion. I feel I can no longer trust him and don't know him as well as I thought. What are your views on this?

D. L.

Dear D. L.,

Honesty is something we all want from others. I'm sure your friend has reasons for his dishonesty but at the same time he wants you to be honest with him. He would have been upset if you had done the same thing to him. We all hate to be lied to. That's why I call dishonesty a Love Buster.

In your case there may be more to it than that. Honesty, for many, meets an important emotional need. In other words, what may have attracted you to this man may have been his honesty and openness. You may have fallen in love with him because you felt you knew him and because he was willing to share his deepest feelings with you. When you discovered him keeping something from you—a relationship with another woman, of all things—he was no longer meeting that need, and the man you thought you knew didn't really exist. Now you don't know whether or not you can trust him about anything.

As with all emotional needs, when the need for honesty is met, it makes a person feel very good, and when it's not met, it makes the person very unhappy. When your most important emotional needs are met, you fall in love with the person who meets them, but when they are not met, you lose that feeling of love. You may find your love for your boyfriend already slipping away now that you feel he cannot meet your need for honesty.

If your boyfriend does not have the same need for honesty, he will not understand what's wrong with you. He can understand why you were upset at first. But why continue to be upset and why would you think of ending the relationship? What he doesn't understand is that from your perspective, he is now a totally different person than he was before he lied to you. Before he lied, he met your need. Now he doesn't. If he wants your love back, he must somehow reestablish your trust in him. He must return to the days when he was meeting your need for honesty.

I suggest that you ask him to read The Five Parts to the Rule of Honesty (appendix E). Ask him if he is willing to commit to the level of honesty that is described in that rule. You and he may never have discussed honesty with each other and now you have a chance to explain your position on the subject.

I'm sure he wants to be honest with you, in principle. But the truth is he is carrying on a relationship with another woman, and perhaps with more than one. If he tells you about these relationships, you will probably express dismay and encourage him to break them off, which is something he doesn't want to do. By being dishonest, he has been able to have you and the other relationships as well.

Having a great relationship means that you adjust your behavior to suit the sensitivities of each other. And you do it with total honesty. You have probably abandoned your former lovers, in part, because it would upset your boyfriend if you hadn't. He should do the same.

My Policy of Joint Agreement is a clear-cut relationship builder. It helps create magnificent marriages where spouses are deeply in love with each other. But the Policy also invites dishonesty. People do not like to check with someone every time they turn around, even though it creates a loving marriage. People want the freedom to do what they please, without any consequences, so they may be tempted to lie while pretending to abide by the Policy. It turns out that there *are* consequences for everything we do, and a great marriage has a price. The price is limiting your behavior to habits and activities that are acceptable to both you and your spouse. To do otherwise is to invite marital disaster.

If you and your friend can agree to follow the Rule of Honesty and the Policy of Joint Agreement, taking each other into account whenever you do anything, you will be headed in a direction that leads to a great marriage.

Part 5

Living Together before Marriage

Does Living Together Prepare You for Marriage?

*M*any people who write me are unmarried and have chosen to live with their partner as a test of their compatibility. Most intend to marry eventually. But when they do marry, they almost always divorce. Because this is the likely result, I have taken a decidedly extreme position on the practice of living together before marriage: I am very much against it.

The practice is growing in popularity, partly because the media has not done a very good job of making the facts public. I'm not sure that most people realize that living together prior to marriage is one of the single best predictors of divorce. Why is this the case? Why does cohabitation (living together) ruin the chances for a happy marriage? My answers to the letters in this section make clear the reasons this has proven to be true.

Dear Dr. Harley,

I've been reading the information on your web site and just recently brought home a copy of the Emotional Needs Questionnaire to go over with my (live-in) boyfriend. We have set aside time each week to discuss one question at a time. We have just started this so we haven't gotten very far yet. We're looking at this as preventative maintenance so we do not run into problems in the future. We have been together for two years but don't feel ready to get married yet. I think these exercises may help us figure out why that is.

So far, just about everything I've seen makes a lot of sense. How do you feel about people living together before being married? Does it help couples prepare for marriage?

E. N.

Dear E. N.,

The number of unmarried couples living together has increased dramatically over the past few decades, and I expect that it will continue to increase. The rationale is simple: "By living together before marriage, we'll know how compatible we are." Presumably, if a couple can get along living in the same apartment before marriage, they will be able to get along with each other after marriage.

It's a tempting argument. After all, a date tends to be artificial. Each person is up for the occasion, and each one makes an effort to have a good time. But marriage is quite different from dating. In marriage, couples are together when they're down too. Wouldn't it make sense for a couple to live together for a while, just to see how they react to each other's down times? If they discover that they can't adjust when they live together, they don't have to go through the hassle of a divorce. Besides, isn't it easier to adjust when you don't feel trapped by marriage?

The problem with those arguments is that marriage changes everything. If couples that live together think that after marriage everything will be the same, they don't understand what marriage does to a couple, both positively and negatively.

In my experience and in reports I've read, the chances of a couple divorcing after living together are huge, much higher than for couples who have not lived together prior to marriage. If living together were a test of marital compatibility, the statistics should show opposite results—couples living together should have stronger marriages. But they don't. They have *weaker* marriages.

To understand why this is the case, I suggest that you consider why couples live together rather than marry. Ask yourself that question. Why did you choose to live with your boyfriend instead of marrying him?

The answer is that you were not yet ready to make a long-term commitment to him. First, you wanted to see if you would still love him after you cooked meals together, cleaned the apartment together, and slept together. In other words, you wanted to see what married life would be like without the commitment of marriage.

But what you don't realize is that you will never know what married life is like *unless* you're married. The commitment of marriage adds a dimension to your relationship that puts everything on its ear. Right now you are testing each other to see if you are compatible. If either of you slips up, the test is over, and you are out the door. Marriage doesn't work that way. Slip-ups don't end the marriage, they just end the love you have for each other.

What, exactly, is the commitment of marriage? It is an agreement that you will take care of each other for life, regardless of life's ups and downs. You will stick it out together through thick and thin. But the commitment of living together isn't like that at all. It is simply a month-to-month rental agreement. As long as you behave yourself and keep me happy, I'll stick around.

Habits are hard to break, and couples that live together before marriage continue the habit after marriage of following their month-to-month rental agreement. In fact they often decide to marry, not because they are willing to make a lifetime commitment to each other, but because the arrangement has worked out so well that they can't imagine breaking their lease, so to speak. They say the words of the marital agreement but they still have the terms of their rental agreement in mind.

Couples who have not lived together before marriage, on the other hand, have not lived under the terms of the month-to-month rental agreement. They begin their relationship assuming that they are in this thing for life, and all their habits usually reflect that commitment.

A newly married couple make a deliberate effort to accommodate each other, because they know their relationship will be for life. They want to *build* compatibility, not *test* it. The Policy of Joint Agreement makes all the sense in the world to a couple who are committed to living their lives together.

It's true that a couple who live together without marriage can follow the Policy of Joint Agreement from the day they move in. They can commit themselves to each other's happiness as if they were married. They can overcome Love Busters that could destroy their love for each other. But couples who live together tend not to do those things because their month-to-month rental agreement does not demand it. They lack motivation to put each other first in their lives because they are testing the relationship. They're not sure they want each other for life, and so they are usually not willing to make the all-out commitment that the Policy of Joint Agreement demands.

When a couple have lived together without the Policy of Joint Agreement, it is very difficult to apply it once they are married. What they usually do is stay the course. They figure that their month-to-month agreement has worked, so why change it.

Marriage has a very positive effect on a relationship for those who have *not* lived together, because they tend to follow the Policy of Joint Agreement without having ever heard of it. They know that they will be together for life, so they make an effort to *create* a compatible lifestyle from day one.

But marriage has a very negative effect on those who have been in the habit of following the month-to-month agreement. The commitment of marriage is seen as the "other guy's" commitment. Those who have lived together prior to marriage feel that their own behavior has passed the test, and any further accommodation should be unnecessary. Worse yet, they think they don't need to be on their best behavior because now they're married, and their spouse can't leave.

I'm not suggesting that you and your boyfriend should avoid marriage but I'm warning you that unless you break out of the habits that come from a month-to-month rental agreement, your marriage will be a disaster.

Begin by following my Policy of Joint Agreement. It's not impossible to follow when you care for each other's feelings and put them first. You will create a lifestyle that fits you both perfectly and you'll wonder why you didn't marry each other to begin with.

Living together may prove compatibility for a moment in time but it provides no evidence for your happiness together over a lifetime. The only way you can have that happiness and compatibility is if you agree to take each other's feelings into account every time you make a decision. And that's what people who marry after not having lived together are highly motivated to do.

Dear Dr. Harley,

J've often heard that living together before marriage is perilous and that statistics bear that out. My friend is planning to move in with his girlfriend. J told him what J've heard but have not actually seen the statistics. He questioned my stats. Imagine that! If it's not too much trouble, J would appreciate any hard info on these stats and their sources.

Thanks in advance.

W. K.

Dear W. K.,

One study that you may find interesting was done by Bennett, Blan, and Bloom, "Commitment and the Modern Union: Assessing the Link between Premarital Cohabitation and Subsequent Marital Stability," *American Sociological Review* 53 (1988): 127–38. The point made by the authors is that, overall, the risk of divorce after living together is 80 percent higher than the risk of divorce after not living together, which is already too high. In other words, those who lived together before marriage are almost twice as likely to divorce than those who did not live together. But they also point out that the risk of divorce is even higher if you live together fewer than three years prior to marriage. The risk of divorce decreases the longer you live together prior to marriage, until after eight years of living together, when the risk of divorce is equal to those who have not lived together.

Another interesting study was conducted by Hall and Zhao, "Cohabitation and Divorce in Canada," *Journal of Marriage and the Family* (May 1995): 421–27. They write:

> The popular belief that cohabitation is an effective strategy in a high-divorce society rests on the common-sense notion that getting to know one another before marrying should improve the quality and stability of marriage. However, in this instance, it is looking more and more as if common sense is a poor guide.

Their study showed that cohabitation itself was shown to account for a higher divorce rate, rather than factors that might have led to cohabitation, such as parental divorce, age at marriage, stepchildren, religion, and other factors. In other words, other factors being equal, you are much more likely to divorce if you live together first.

DeMaris and MacDonald, "Premarital Cohabitation and Marital Instability: A Test of the Unconventionality Hypothesis," *Journal of Marriage and the Family* (May 1993): 399–407, came to a similar conclusion. They found that the unconventionality of those who live together does not explain their subsequent struggle when married. There is something about living together first that creates marital problems later. They write:

> Despite a widespread public faith in premarital cohabitation as a testing ground for marital incompatibility, research to date indicates that cohabitors' marriages are less satisfactory and more unstable than those of noncohabitors.

Undoubtedly there are some self-selection factors that make people who live together more prone to marital problems later. But the gist of current research is that these factors are not enough to explain the astonishingly huge effect. Simply stated, if you live together before marriage, you will be fighting an uphill battle to save your marriage.

If you like to spend your evenings hidden among the periodicals of your local library, here are some other studies that show how risky it is to live together before marriage:

Balakrishnan, Rao, et al. "A Hazard Model Analysis of the Covariates of Marriage Dissolution in Canada." *Demography* 24 (1987): 395–406.

Booth and Johnson. "Premarital Cohabitation and Marital Success." *Journal of Family Issues* 9 (1988): 255–72.

Bumpass and Sweet. "National Estimates of Cohabitation." *Demography* 26 (1989): 615–25.

DeMaris and Leslie. "Cohabitation with the Future Spouse: Its Influence upon Marital Satisfaction and Communication." *Journal of Marriage and the Family* 46 (1984): 77–84.

DeMaris and Rao. "Premarital Cohabitation and Subsequent Marital Stability in the United States: A Reassessment." *Journal of Marriage and the Family* 54 (1992): 178–90.

Teachman and Polonko. "Cohabitation and Marital Stability in the United States." *Social Forces* 69 (1990): 207–20.

Teachman, Thomas, and Paasch. "Legal Status and the Stability of Coresidential Unions." *Demography* 28 (1991): 571–86.

Thompson and Colella. "Cohabitation and Marital Stability: Quality or Commitment?" *Journal of Marriage and the Family* 54 (1992): 259–67.

What Is It Like to Be Married after Living Together?

*T*here are couples who make a successful transition from living together to marriage but they are the exceptions. In most cases, marriage after cohabitation is an unexpected disaster. Since the number of couples who have chosen to live together before marriage is steadily increasing, is there anything these couples can do to avoid disaster should they decide to marry?

Dear Dr. Harley,

I was married only four months ago after having been with my husband for seven years, five of which we lived together. Since the wedding my husband has been acting completely different.

He has turned our garage into his domain, complete with carpet, couches, appliances, and everything you would need in the perfect bachelor pad. He constantly has friends over, and I am excluded. When he is not spending time in the garage, he is online or playing interactive computer games with his friends. He rarely comes to bed at the same time as me and just generally does not seem to be interested in sharing anything with me lately.

I understand that marriage is a huge change, but he never acted this way before. Why now? He is the one who really pushed getting married. I was very hesitant because of my parents' bad relationship. I even left him at one point three years ago because he was pressuring me so much. We discussed marriage at great length and both finally felt that it was the right time, so J do not understand his recent behavior.

Js this normal?

R. G.

Dear R. G.,

Your husband's transformation of the garage (and himself) is something he would not have done prior to marriage because you would have left him if he had. Before you married him, he took your feelings into account before making decisions, because he wanted you to stay with him. He put pressure on you to marry him so he could do what he pleased without fear of your leaving.

Now he thinks that you won't leave regardless of what he does, because you are married, so he does anything he wants. He's wrong, of course. If he doesn't accommodate you soon, you'll fall out of love with him and eventually leave him just as you would have done before you were married.

The solution to your problem is for both of you to take each other's feelings into account before making decisions. In other words, you should be following the Policy of Joint Agreement. Neither of you should do anything unless the other agrees to it enthusiastically! If you had both been following the Policy when you married, his "bachelor pad" would never have been created, and he would not have excluded you from his activities with friends.

If you don't follow the Policy soon, you'll become another statistic. *Give and Take* will help you learn to apply the Policy to your marriage. It will teach you how to resolve conflicts with consideration for each other's feelings. I recommend that you read it together.

Dear Dr. Harley,

My wife and J have grown apart since our marriage two years ago. Prior to marriage we lived together for two years. Six months after our marriage my wife had an affair with a coworker. She left me, claiming to want more personal freedom and to be on her own, but J eventually learned of the affair. Shortly afterward, the affair ended and she came back to me.

Then about eight months ago she had another affair with a different coworker, but this time she did not leave me. When I confronted her with it, she said it was over.

On New Year's Day we had a fight, and she decided to leave me again. She told me that she needed to be in control of her own life and her own money, and that was the only reason for her decision to leave. I decided to make the best of the situation and not fight it, keep it friendly, and work towards a resolution of our problems. Then a week later I discovered that for three weeks before she left me, she had been having an affair with the second man again.

I had not found your web site or books at that point. Now I realize I made almost all of the mistakes that you say not to when dealing with this situation. Now after visiting your site, I realize that I was not meeting her needs in many different areas, and she found someone who would.

Incidentally she had refused to seek any kind of marriage counseling until she read some of the printouts I made from your site. Now she has agreed to read your book "His Needs, Her Needs" with me.

Is there hope or am I just fooling myself? I am uncertain how to bring up the honesty issue. I gave her a copy of your Rules of Honesty in the stack of printouts and I know that she realizes this is an issue. However, she has a definite problem with honesty. She feels that honesty hurts more often than it helps and would rather mislead me and deal with the consequences later than be honest now.

What am I to do about her "friend"? I understand your approach and I think I can outlast this guy. I am deeply committed to her happiness, while his interest in her appears to be only sexual. Apparently he has not been too nice to her recently, and that will also help. But I have unbelievable hostility toward this guy and do not know what to do. I feel that I will be able to give my wife the type of relationship we had while we were dating. I love my wife

*deeply and could not imagine the rest of my life without her.
But how do J deal with this man in the meantime?*

B. K.

Dear B. K.,

You are probably turning things around in your relationship, so keep it up. Be particularly careful to avoid the Love Busters angry outbursts, disrespectful judgments, and selfish demands.

I think that reading *His Needs, Her Needs* together will help you both. Through it you will be able to discover what it is that is driving her into these other relationships. It may take you a while to develop the skill required to meet her needs, and it will also take a while for her Love Bank balance to recover, so be patient.

You are going down the same track most married couples take after having first lived together. Your wife's behavior reflects the self-centered rules you both used during your first two years together, rules that, until recently, had not changed and would have led to divorce. But you have put new rules in place, rules that will protect your wife from your selfish and destructive tendencies. Instead of making her feel trapped living with you, she will feel cared for and will find herself much more willing to care for you.

Much of her dishonesty comes from living under the old rule, Do whatever you can to make you happy and avoid anything that makes you unhappy. Her affairs reflect her self-centeredness. Her dishonesty is also due to self-centeredness—honesty usually benefits others, not ourselves. It helps others become aware of our attitudes, motives, and plans that might be harmful to them. Honesty protects others from ourselves, because it gives them warning of what we might do, or have already done, to hurt them. The more selfish we are, the more dishonest we become, because we don't want others to know we have hurt them.

Your wife has been dishonest about her affairs. If she had been honest from the beginning, she would have had a most difficult time pulling them off, because you would have tried to prevent them. That's why she lied about them. But once you both change the rules and enter into a relationship of mutual care, it will be much easier to be honest. There will be much less to cover up, since you will both be making decisions that are in your mutual interest.

How can you overcome the feelings you have toward your wife's lover? If at all possible, I recommend that your wife leave her job, and perhaps both of you should move to another city. Regular contact with a former lover is just asking for trouble. Not only will you be continually offended by any conversations your wife may have with either of her former lovers, but there is a significant chance for the relationships to rekindle even after you and she have resolved the problems that created the affairs. An affair is an addiction, and the only way to end it once and for all is to make access to it very difficult. If you move away, your attitude toward her lover and her feelings toward him will fade away.

Part 6

How to Keep Love in Your Marriage

How to Get through the First Year and Keep Love in Your Marriage

The first year of marriage can be so painful that divorce seems to be the only escape. That's why more people divorce in the first year of marriage than in any other year. But the first year can also be a couple's best year of marriage. That is also a tragedy because it means the remaining years are not as good.

In this section there are three letters from newlyweds. The first is from a man who is clearly starstruck. He represents the idealism of couples who are still on their honeymoon. Some may wish they could share his attitude, but I try to show how his idealism can undermine the strength of a lifelong marriage.

The second letter is from a man who is also starstruck, but his wife has been struck by the realities of his insensitivity. How can they turn things around quickly enough to avoid being caught in the blame-game?

The last couple has just about had it with each other. Their daughter is keeping them together, at least for a while. No idealism here. But their love for the child may force them to make their marriage sensational.

Dear Dr. Harley,

I am a newlywed—seven months—and I know God couldn't have given me a more wonderful mate for life. We are very happy, and our unconditional love is and always will be, I hope, the cord that holds us together.

We get so busy with our own schedules, though, that we don't really have time for each other. A couple of my friends have suggested that we continue to "date" each other by purposely and purposefully doing things together. Well, it's just not as easy as it sounds. It's awkward now to plan a specific time together, and yet I know that if we don't do it, we're not going to know each other anymore.

What do you suggest?

R. B.

Dear R. B.,

Your friends are right. Unless you take time to "date" after marriage, you will probably not be able to meet each other's needs that you met before your marriage. These needs probably include affection, conversation, and recreational companionship, among others. Without taking time to be with each other, you can't meet those needs. For many women, affection and conversation are preconditions for sexual fulfillment. If you spend little time talking to each other and being affectionate, I can almost guarantee you that your sexual relationship will suffer.

A date should be the time you set aside to meet each other's important emotional needs. You should be enthusiastic about what you have planned, because it should give you what you need the most. If either of you thinks it's a waste of time, it's because you are not giving each other what you should.

Before you were married, you met each other's emotional needs on dates, and what you did on dates caused you to fall in love with each other. Unless you continue to do the same thing now, you will lose the feeling of love that makes you think your love is unconditional.

Your dates don't need to be exactly the same as before marriage. In fact you may be able to meet each other's needs without actually "going out." I have found, though, that an evening at home with Joyce can easily be spent working on personal projects without spending much time with each other. For us, even though our children are married and on their own, we have to get out of the house to give each other the attention we need.

210

When you say that your schedules are too busy to get together for dates, I would interpret that to mean that you are making scheduling decisions independently of each other. After you look at your schedules, you find there is no time for dates. But if you were to put the dates in first, and then schedule everything else around them, you would solve your scheduling problem.

You or your wife may also find that the time you spend together on dates does not meet your needs the way it did before marriage. If that's the case, try doing different things until your needs are met. We all change, and what works at one time may not work at another.

Now I will tackle an issue that gets me into all kinds of trouble—unconditional love. The position I take seems almost sacrilegious, but the more I have thought about the issue, the more convinced I am that I'm right. I also believe that my position is consistent with the highest moral values.

You say in your letter that your "unconditional love is a cord that holds us together." But I believe that unconditional love usually ruins marriages instead of saving them. I explain how that can happen in *Give and Take* (chapter 12).

The gist of my argument is that unilateral love (unconditional love) lends itself to a lifestyle where one suffers for the happiness of the other. It's easy to get into the habit of living that way, and there are many well-meaning spouses who give unconditionally, only to find that their own needs are never met. They think they are the ones always giving but often their spouse thinks he or she is always giving.

It seems almost everyone thinks he or she is the Giver and hardly anyone sees the Taker in himself or herself. Most of the spouses I've counseled think they are the ones giving the most in their marriage, and that leads to deep resentment. After having given unconditionally for a while, and getting little in return, human nature seems to come up with a new idea: Why not *take* unconditionally?

So a spouse sees a counselor, who supports the idea of "taking care of myself" for a while. You know what that means? It means doing whatever makes you happy regardless of how it makes your spouse feel, a sure formula for marital disaster.

Why would any professional counselor suggest such a thing? You have to be there to understand it. Imagine you are counseling a person who is depressed to the point of suicide, and you ask what the problem is. You discover that the person's spouse is making selfish demands that are causing untold sorrow for your client. The solution is simple: "Stop doing it and start taking better care of yourself."

But what about unconditional love? Am I not supposed to do whatever I can to make my spouse happy, even if I must sacrifice? Am I not supposed to let my spouse do whatever he or she wants to do, even if it causes me pain? Many faced with their spouse's infidelity, drug addiction, gambling, or physical abuse believe in unconditional love. The counselor tries to talk them out of this belief, which is clearly destroying them.

But then the counselor goes too far. In reaction to unconditional love, the counselor suggests that the person stop being a caregiver entirely. He or she is encouraged to believe in unconditional love—for self! Those who follow that advice are headed for divorce, but in most cases, no one thinks the marriage is worth saving anyway.

There is a way to save these marriages, but it requires a new rule that is different from the two we have been discussing. First, let's review the two unhealthy rules:

1. *Unconditional love for your spouse:* Do whatever you can to make your spouse happy and avoid anything that makes your spouse unhappy (even if it makes you unhappy).
2. *Unconditional love for yourself:* Do whatever you can to make you happy and avoid anything that makes you unhappy (even if it makes your spouse unhappy).

The first rule is wrong because it does not take your own feelings into account, and the second rule is wrong because it does not take your spouse's feelings into account.

I think you can see by now where I am headed. We need a new rule that takes the feelings of both you and your spouse into account simultaneously. The rule should read: Do whatever you can to make you and your spouse happy at the same time, and avoid anything that will make either you or your spouse unhappy. This, in other words, is the Policy of Joint Agreement—*never do anything without an enthusiastic agreement between you and your spouse.*

The Policy of Joint Agreement is a healthy compromise between the two unhealthy rules because it recognizes that the feelings of both spouses are important and should be accommodated simultaneously in marriage. You can avoid running into trouble in your marriage by following the Policy now, before trouble starts to brew. I strongly recommend that you read *Give and Take* to help you make the very important decisions that will determine the success of your marriage and your compatibility as a couple.

Incidentally, the problem you are having with scheduling time together is a reflection of the fact that you do not follow the Policy of Joint Agreement. Right now your schedules are made with unconditional love as your guide. If one of you really wants to do something, the other one simply allows it to happen without any objection. As you are finding out, this way of handling your schedules leads to an insidious drift apart, and some day you will find that you are strangers. Don't let that happen. Follow the Policy of Joint Agreement now and keep following it for the rest of your married lives.

Dear Dr. Harley,

I've been married for seven and one-half months and am facing a trying time. My wife has told me that she is not happy and that the main reason is some of the "bad habits" she didn't realize I had.

It is hard for me to pinpoint any of these myself, but they are there and I accept that and am willing to try to change. Since this has started, I find myself accepting all the blame and thinking that I am the only cause for her unhappiness. There is nothing I want to do more than to reestablish her happiness and trust in me and to strengthen our marriage. I do not want to add more difficulty to this situation by placing some of the "blame" on her.

Most of the problems stem from what I have said in a normal day-to-day conversation, and she has taken them very personally. I might be insensitive, while my wife is overly sensitive. If this is the problem, do any of your methods deal with how we can reach a good balance?

I hope that you can make a recommendation so I can restore our bad relationship to what we had just a few short months ago.

K. G.

Dear K. G.,

The first year of marriage is a very good time to identify and over-come areas of incompatibility. The longer you let them grow, the more difficult they are to overcome.

If you have read The Three States of Marriage (see page 20), you will see that you are in the state of intimacy and your wife is in the state of conflict. That's why you are willing to accept all the blame for her hurt feelings, and she is blaming you. The truth is that both of you will need to make some adjustments to each other. You will need to understand what it is you do that offends her, and she may need to modify the way she reacts.

It may be helpful for your wife to discuss her sensitivities with you. Perhaps there are certain things you do or say that symbolize experiences she has had in the past that are particularly distressing to her. After you discover them, don't spend much time trying to "resolve" them. I've found that such probing won't make someone else less sensitive; it only helps you understand why that person is sensitive, so you can adjust to it.

I often begin counseling clients by telling them that if I do or say anything that offends them, let me know so that I can be more sen-sitive. You should do the same with your wife. Above all, don't be defensive by telling her you didn't mean to offend her. And don't explain how your offending opinion makes as much sense to you as her opinion. Instead, simply apologize for offending her and try to avoid it in the future.

It's likely that Love Busters are creeping into your conversation. Pay particular attention to the Love Buster disrespectful judgments. This is when you try to give your wife "constructive criticism." Mar-riage is no place to straighten someone out. Any effort you make to take charge or be a leader may be interpreted by her as disrespect. Your intentions may be pure, but if the effect is hurt feelings, stop whatever you're doing.

Give and Take: The Secret to Marital Compatibility can teach you and your wife how to take each other's feelings into account, not just in conversation, but in all the decisions you will be making in life. Ask your wife if she would be willing to read it with you, say, fifteen minutes a day. The book will not only help your wife express her frustration with you (she can highlight sentences that express her feelings particularly well), but it will also show you how to make the adjustments to accommodate her.

Dear Dr. Harley,

My husband and I have been married for less than a year and we have a two-month-old daughter. Every day we wonder if we've made a huge mistake by starting a family together so soon. I know that if it weren't for our daughter, we would have been divorced long ago, but we "try" only for her sake. I don't think that she has added any friction but she's definitely given us reason to hold on to each other. We do know that our biggest problem is communication. We have trust and honesty and there is love there but we are quickly losing hope.

My husband seems to think that divorce is the only answer if I cannot change. He doesn't think he needs to change, however. I'm willing to do whatever it takes to hold on to this marriage, and though I've tried to change my attitude toward him, I can't do it without his participation. Please give me hope. I really appreciate any response you can give me and I thank you for your time.

T. W.

Dear T. W.,

I'm sorry to hear that your new marriage is off to such a rough start. Your daughter may be the only thing keeping you together right now, but at least you haven't given up entirely. As long as you are together, you can make the adjustments to each other that will save your marriage.

While it's true that you cannot make all the changes yourself, you can learn to do your part and be an example to your husband. You should not do anything that is not in your own best interest, because that's not the example you want to give him. Instead, I recommend that you do things that are good for both of you.

Make a list of what it is he wants you to change. They will fall into two categories: things you do that bother him (Love Busters) and things he wants you to do that you are not doing to meet his emotional needs (like having sex more often).

You need to learn to stop doing anything that falls into the first category. If he objects, for example, to your going out with friends at night, leaving him with the baby so you can get a little relief, I suggest that you get your relief some other way that he would not object to. Don't allow yourself to gain at his expense, even if you cannot think of any alternatives at the time. Take a serious look at everything you do that bothers him and find another way to accomplish your objective. Whenever you do this, you will be following my Policy of Joint Agreement. When you use the Policy to make your decisions, you eliminate Love Busters from your marriage.

Your husband may be doing quite a few things that bother you, and until now, your objections may have had little effect. But if you set the example of asking him how he feels about your habits and activities, he is likely to be more considerate of your feelings when he makes his plans.

Take a different approach to the second category—things he wants you to do to meet his emotional needs. Don't do anything for him unless you enjoy doing it. If he wants more sex, explain to him what he would have to do to make it enjoyable for you. If he doesn't do it, discuss alternatives until you are both satisfied with the agreement. But until then, no sex unless you enjoy the experience too. This approach to problem solving is a good example for your husband. He should learn to meet your needs the same way. He should also be enthusiastic about whatever he does for you because if he doesn't enjoy doing it, it won't be done very often. Besides, you don't want your spouse doing things for you with resentment. This approach will help you learn to meet each other's needs in ways that build compatibility and eliminate resentment.

What if it doesn't work? What if all your efforts to change do not result in any changes in your husband? What if he becomes abusive, has affairs, spends all your money gambling? Then, I'm afraid, you will probably divorce him. But if you do what you can to avoid being the cause of his unhappiness and learn to meet as many of his needs as you can without it causing you to suffer, it's very likely that your husband will learn to do the same and will treat you with the kindness and respect that you have learned to show him.

How to Have the First Baby and Keep Love in Your Marriage

*I*t's tragic but true that the first baby often sinks a marriage. You'd think that it would be the other way around, that a baby would draw a husband and wife closer together. But there are very good reasons why children in general and babies in particular tend to make marriages worse, not better.

It has to do with problem-solving skills. Prior to the first child's arrival, a couple's ability to resolve conflicts is not really put to the test. Peace and order usually reign in marriages before children arrive. There may be conflicts but they are few and relatively easy to resolve. But after the first child, couples are faced with conflicts they've never seen before and they often do not have easy answers.

Dear Dr. Harley,

I have a three-month-old son whom I love so-o-o much that I'm having mixed feelings about going back to work full-time. I'd like to find something part-time or work at home if possible. My husband is now bearing the stress of only one income coming into the house and sometimes he drives me crazy with his constant complaining about money.

I'm getting to the point where I am starting to resent him. I want to know if this is normal when you have one working partner and the other partner is currently staying at home to take care of the baby. I lose my patience with him and I also get mad that when he comes home, he plays with the baby only a little bit and then gives him to me to hold or calm down. I've tried explaining to him that when he comes home, it feels good for someone else to take care of the baby so I can do other things, like take a shower or watch TV. I don't know if I am into a type of postpartum depression or what but I need some input on why I'm starting to resent him.

B. K.

Dear B. K.,

Since you became pregnant with your first child, your life has completely changed. Your goals have probably changed, your needs have probably changed, and your resources have undoubtedly changed. All these changes have required you and your husband to make new decisions every day. And with every decision you make, there is a risk of conflict between your interests and the interests of your husband.

Your new baby has forced you into a new lifestyle. He has been a twenty-four-hour-a-day responsibility from the moment he was born, and your life will never be the same. Your letter reflects the stress you and your husband are under trying to adjust to your new way of life.

But your letter also reflects a growing resentment. You feel abandoned by your husband now when your needs are great. Here you are, faced with one of the most demanding and stressful responsibilities of your life, and where is the man? Watching TV, no doubt. And then, to make matters worse, he is grousing about not having much money since you took a leave of absence from your job to care for your baby. Why hasn't he been more supportive of you during the first three months of your son's life? Why does he seem distant at a time that you want him to be emotionally connected to you?

The answer to those questions is found in the way you and your husband make decisions. For every problem you face, there is an array of solutions. You have solutions, and your husband has solutions. But a reasonable solution for you may not be reasonable for your husband. What may work to your advantage may work to his disadvantage, and vice versa. When that happens, you have a conflict.

218

Conflicts are very common in marriage, but much more common when the first baby arrives. That's because you become flooded with new decisions that must be made quickly, decisions you've never had to make before. It is the first real test of your problem-solving skills. From the sound of your letter, you both need to go back to school.

The success of your marriage will depend on your ability to resolve your conflicts with mutual consideration. That means whenever a decision is to be made about anything, the feelings of both you and your husband must be taken into account simultaneously.

But, sadly, that's not the way most married couples resolve their conflicts. I'll first explain what most couples do to try to resolve their conflicts and then I'll explain what couples *should* do. Finally, I will give you some advice regarding the care of your baby.

How Most Couples Resolve Conflicts

Most couples use one of three different strategies to resolve conflicts. The first and most common of the three is the *dictator* strategy. This strategy assumes that one member of the family, usually the husband, has the wisdom and compassion to make most family decisions correctly. While other members of the family can lobby to have him (or her) take their interests into account, when a decision is made, it is final.

Sometimes that strategy works. But, especially here in America, it usually doesn't work. For one thing, dictators have not been known to be all that wise or compassionate. They tend to make decisions in their own interest and at the expense of those depending on them. The same thing happens in marriage. When one spouse is given the right to make all final decisions, the other spouse usually suffers.

You may be a victim of the dictator strategy. It sounds as if your husband has decided that you are to take full responsibility for the care of the baby, especially since you are not employed. It solves the problem from his perspective but not from yours. That's the downside of the dictator strategy.

Those who have had bad experiences with a dictator often modify their approach to problem solving by creating a second strategy, the *dueling dictators* strategy. This approach raises both spouses to dictator status, and solutions to problems are decided by strength and determination. Each spouse proposes a solution to a conflict that is in his or her own best interest, and the war begins. After the dust settles, one spouse wins the decision, which means that his or her solution is put into effect. You and your husband may be moving toward this strategy at this very moment.

Unfortunately the dueling dictators strategy works well enough to be the working strategy for millions of unhappy couples. Clearly this approach makes problem solving unpleasant for all involved, but at least it ends with a solution. And it seems more fair than the dictator strategy because the pain alternates between the spouses instead of being borne by only one. With each decision one spouse wins and the other loses. Instead of one spouse being consistently victimized, both spouses have a turn at being victimized.

If you were to make the mistake of adapting the dueling dictators strategy, you would try to force your husband to care for your baby whenever you could, whether he liked it or not. You would threaten him, keep him awake at night, withhold sex, and tell his parents what a terrible father he has turned out to be. From time to time your tactics would work, and he would care for your son while you took a shower, watched TV, or went out with your friends.

The failure of the dictator strategy and the dueling dictators strategy often leads to a third approach to marital conflict resolution, the *anarchy* strategy. This strategy gives up on the idea that marital conflicts can be resolved and takes the position of "every man for himself." A husband and wife both do whatever they feel like doing. This strategy has the advantage of preventing either spouse from forcing the other to submit to his or her wishes. That's because both spouses refuse to do anything that the other wants them to do.

This strategy, of course, is only one step away from divorce, but almost everyone faced with failure to resolve conflicts tries it. An example of this strategy would be for you to drop your son off at your mother-in-law's house and tell her that it's your husband's turn to care for the child. He, in turn, would ignore his mother's telephone calls and go on with his life as if nothing had happened. In other words, this strategy doesn't resolve the conflict; it overlooks it.

There is a variation of the strategy that I call *limited anarchy*, where only one spouse completely abdicates responsibility. In this case your husband decides not to deal with the issue of child care, leaving you with the complete responsibility to raise your baby. In this scenario your husband doesn't tell you what to do; he simply ignores the problem. You, on the other hand, end up caring for the child because you have not yet abandoned your responsibility. As is the case with total anarchy, limited anarchy also leads to divorce. In fact it is the most common reason that women leave men (see appendix F).

How Couples Should Resolve Conflicts

There is another strategy. It's the *democracy* strategy. This strategy is guided by the Policy of Joint Agreement—never do anything without an enthusiastic agreement between you and your spouse. When this strategy is used to resolve a conflict, a husband and wife do not make a decision until they are both in enthusiastic agreement.

The democracy strategy is very different from the other strategies. With the dictator strategy, marital conflicts are resolved by the decisions of one spouse (usually the husband), leaving the other to suffer the consequences. In the dueling dictators strategy, conflicts are resolved by the winning spouse imposing his or her will on the losing spouse. The anarchy strategy has no winner or loser because neither spouse is willing to submit to the other's wishes, and the conflicts are never resolved. But in the democracy strategy, conflicts are not only resolved, but they are resolved with no victims. The outcome of each decision is in the best interest of *both* spouses.

Why isn't the democracy strategy used in all marriages, or even in most marriages? Self-centeredness is one answer. The most powerful person in a marriage may feel that if he or she can always prevail in a conflict, why not? That puts the dictator strategy into play. Once it's tried, the other strategies I've mentioned eventually follow.

Another reason that couples don't use the democracy strategy is that it requires more time and skill than the others. Here are the steps to successful negotiation that I recommend for successful problem solving (see pages 132–33 for more information on following these steps).

1. Set ground rules to make negotiations pleasant and safe.

2. Identify the problem from the perspectives of both you and your spouse.
3. Brainstorm solutions with abandon.
4. Choose the solution that is appealing to both of you.

These steps take effort and thought, something that the other strategies do not require. The steps will not only give you solutions to your problem, they will also draw you much closer to each other emotionally.

How to Resolve Your Conflict over Care for Your Baby

You love your new son and love caring for him. So much so that you want a job that keeps you at home so that you can provide the quality of care you feel he needs. But you also want your husband to share in your joy, and in the responsibility for his care. You are feeling abandoned by your husband, because, when you need a break from the care of your son, he refuses to help.

I made the mistake of making my wife, Joyce, feel abandoned when we had our first baby, Jennifer. I was a full-time graduate student and had a full-time job to support our new family. I reasoned that with all that work, Joyce, who quit her job to be a full-time mom, should take full responsibility for our daughter until I finished graduate school. It seemed reasonable to me at the time, but Joyce still remembers how I didn't help her care for our baby.

It was the first time our problem-solving skills were really put to the test, and I found myself dropping into the dictator strategy of conflict resolution. I told Joyce the way it was going to be, and she accepted it, with resentment. If I had it to do over again, she and I would have thought it through until we arrived at a mutually agreeable solution. After considering the alternatives, Joyce may have enthusiastically agreed to take full responsibility for the baby until I finished graduate school. If we had come to a mutual agreement first, there would not have been resentment later.

But she may have explained to me that my active role in caring for our new baby was more important to her than my job or my schooling. If that were the case, I would have needed to rethink my priorities and reorganize my schedule to accommodate caring for our new baby. Perhaps I would need to slow down the pace of my education or work a little less. I had incorrectly assumed that my schedule was something I was doing for both of us. I was wrong. I certainly wasn't doing it for Joyce if my schedule had crowded out fulfillment of her emotional needs.

Your husband's helping to care for your baby is one of your emotional needs. You've never had it before because this is your first baby. But you've now discovered that you need your husband to join you in taking full responsibility for the care of your son. When he does that, he deposits love units into his account in your Love Bank and when he doesn't, your frustration withdraws love units. He doesn't realize it but every time he refuses to watch your baby so that you can take a shower or watch TV, you lose a little love for your husband.

I squandered some of the love Joyce had for me when I didn't help her with our first baby. If she had explained it to me in those terms, I'm sure that I would have adjusted my schedule to accommodate her. But I didn't think it mattered that much. I thought she would adjust to it. I was wrong, because you can't adjust to an unmet emotional need.

I suggest that you explain to your husband (1) that you *need* his active involvement in the care of your new baby and (2) what he should do to meet that need. All of his arguments about working to support you and being tired when he comes home don't negate the fact that he is not meeting your emotional needs right now. If he expects you to continue to be in love with him, he must learn to meet this very powerful, but new, emotional need.

Then I would try to help him meet your need by explaining that you don't want him to suffer when he helps you with the baby. You want him to enjoy meeting your need. So, by discussing a variety of alternatives with him, you can create ways that he can enthusiastically join you in the care of your son. That will require you to implement the democracy strategy to help you resolve this conflict. When you use that strategy, your husband can learn to meet your emotional need with enthusiasm. That's the way he wants you to meet his needs too.

My book *Give and Take* will guide you in the implementation of the democracy strategy. I suggest that you and your husband read the book together and follow my advice. If you do, you will not only be able to overcome your resentment, but your baby will grow up with parents who are in love with each other.

How to Divide Domestic Responsibilities and Keep Love in Your Marriage

*M*ost of the letters I receive reflect marital disaster. Complaints of infidelity are common. But there are more mundane issues that, if ignored, can lead to marital disaster. One of these issues is the division of domestic responsibilities. I introduce this issue with two short letters, one from a wife and the other from a husband.

Dear Dr. Harley,

My husband thinks because he cooked dinner last month that he should be excused from all other responsibilities. (I can't even get him to take out the trash without a fight!) All I want is a little help. I have tried asking him sweetly, but he still calls me a nag. I am at the end of my rope! What do you suggest I do?

T. G.

Dear Dr. Harley,

We have been married for six years and have two children. During the first year of marriage, my wife and I both worked, but when our children arrived, my wife stayed at home to care for them. Now she has gone back to work, and we spend much of our time together fighting over who's going to take care of our children, cook the meals, wash and iron the clothes, clean the house, etc. At this rate our marriage will not survive spring cleaning. Can you help us?

D. K.

224

Dear T. G. and D. K.,

With the proliferation of so many dual-career marriages, the division of domestic responsibilities has become a major source of marital conflict. Changes in our cultural values have contributed greatly to the problem, because there is more agreement that both a husband and wife should share the domestic responsibilities, particularly child care. But change in behavior has not kept pace with the change in values.

Traditionally wives have assumed most household and child care responsibilities, while husbands have taken the responsibility of providing income for the family. When couples could afford it, housekeepers and nannies were employed to relieve the wife's burden.

But today, at least in America, there are fewer live-in housekeepers and nannies, and women are much more committed to working outside the home. So there is a gap to fill and husbands are the most obvious source of help. While men are changing the diapers, wielding the mop, and tending the stove more often than ever before, it still isn't enough. In dual-career marriages, men on average do only half as much child care and housework as their working wives.

As most women have figured out by now, men are not very motivated to do child care and housekeeping. T. G., you indicate in your letter that your husband thinks *any* effort on his part to help you with household responsibilities represents a monumental sacrifice and contribution to your happiness. From your perspective, he is simply doing a small part of his fair share of the work.

In your letter, D. K., you and your wife each have a totally different perspective on who should do what and you find yourselves fighting about it. You are apparently demanding that she do most of the work, and she is demanding that you do it. Neither of you feels it is your responsibility.

Domestic responsibilities are a time bomb in many marriages. Marriage usually begins with a willingness of both spouses to share domestic responsibilities. Newlyweds commonly wash dishes together, make the bed together, and divide many household tasks. The groom welcomes the help he gets from his wife because, prior to marriage, he'd been doing it all alone as a bachelor. At this point in marriage, neither of them regard domestic responsibilities as an important marital issue. But the time bomb is ticking.

When does it explode? It's when the children arrive! Children create huge needs, both a greater need for income and greater domestic responsibilities. The previous division of labor becomes obsolete. Both spouses must take on new responsibilities. Which ones should they take? In most modern marriages, both spouses opt for income, leaving the domestic responsibilities to whoever will volunteer. It's a recipe for disaster, at least for most working women, because they end up doing most of the housework and child care, resenting their husband's lack of support.

If household responsibilities are given to whoever is in the mood to do them, nothing much will be done. If one spouse demands help from the other, that will also have an unsatisfactory outcome. But if assignment of these tasks can be mutually agreed on by willing spouses who accept responsibility, everything will run smoothly.

I would like to propose to you a solution based on the Policy of Joint Agreement. As it does with all marital conflicts, the Policy will not only resolve your conflict over domestic responsibility, but it will help you increase your love for each other.

This solution will require you to do something you may rarely do: Get organized. It means you must think through your problem carefully and systematically. You will need to write down your objectives and create solutions that take each other's feelings into account. While you may find all of this awkward and terribly "not you," there is no other way. Besides, when you're done, you may find it to be more comfortable than you anticipated.

Step 1: Identify your household responsibilities. First, make a list of all of your household responsibilities, including child care. The list should (1) name each responsibility; (2) briefly describe what must be done and when to accomplish it; (3) name the spouse who wants it accomplished; and (4) indicate how important it is to that spouse (use a scale from 1–5, with 1 least important and 5 most important).

Both spouses should work on this list, and it will take several days to cover the bases. You will add items each day as you find yourself accomplishing various tasks or wanting them accomplished.

Each time a task is added to the list and the work described, the spouse wanting it done must be named. Of course many of the tasks will be mutually desired, such as diapering the baby. In that case the names of both spouses should accompany the item with the importance rating of each one. You will probably find that many tasks will be the concern of only one spouse.

Here are some examples of items on the list:

Washing the breakfast dishes: Every morning clearing off the breakfast table and washing, drying, and putting away all the breakfast dishes and utensils. Becky (4); John (2)

Feeding the cat: At 8:00 A.M. and 5:00 P.M. put cat food and water in the cat's dishes. John (5)

When you have finished your list, both of you should be satisfied that it includes all of the housekeeping and child care responsibilities that you share. You may have as many as one hundred items listed. Just this part of the exercise alone will help you understand what you're up against with regard to the work that you feel must be done.

Step 2: Assume responsibility for items that you would enjoy doing or prefer doing yourself. Make a second copy of your final list, so that both you and your spouse can have a copy. Then, independently of each other, put your own name in front of each item that you would like to do yourself. These are tasks that you would enjoy doing, don't mind doing, or want to do yourself so they can be done a certain way.

When you compare your two lists, if both you and your spouse have named the same items, you can either take turns doing them, or arbitrarily divide them between you. But you must approve each other's selections before they become that person's responsibility. If one of you does not feel that the other will perform the task well enough, you can give each other a trial period to demonstrate competence. Once you have taken responsibility for an item, your spouse should be able to hold you accountable for doing it according to his or her expectations.

Begin two new lists of household responsibilities, one representing the husband's responsibilities, and the other, the wife's. Items from the original list that have been selected by a spouse and mutually agreed to as a responsibility should be written on these new lists and taken off the original list.

Now you have three lists: the husband's list of responsibilities, the wife's list of responsibilities, and the list of household responsibilities that are not yet assigned.

Step 3: Assign the remaining responsibilities to the one wanting each done the most. Assuming that all tasks you would not mind doing have been assigned, you are left with those that would be unpleasant for either of you to perform. These are items that neither of you want to do but at least one of you thinks should be done.

These unpleasant responsibilities should be assigned to the person who wants them done. If both of you want something done, the one giving it the highest value should take responsibility for doing it. If you think that this is unfair, consider for a moment why you want the other person to do these tasks for you. Even though *you* are the one who wants them done, you want the other person to relieve you of the discomfort you suffer when you do them. In other words, you want to gain at your spouse's expense.

You may argue that what you want is really not for you but for the children. In that argument you imply that your spouse is so uncaring and insensitive that he or she doesn't even know, or doesn't care, what's best for the children. If that's your argument, you are making a disrespectful judgment. You are assuming that your view of the situation is superior to that of your spouse. Disrespectful judgment is a Love Buster. Whenever you try to impose your way of thinking on your spouse, you will withdraw love units and you won't win the argument; that's for sure.

If you then insist that your spouse care for the children's needs the way you perceive them, you are making a selfish demand. You are not only trying to impose your perspective on your spouse, but you are also trying to force your spouse to do something that he or she will find unpleasant. A selfish demand is another Love Buster that will withdraw love units every time.

After seeing my solution to the domestic responsibility problem, you may not be entirely happy with my approach. You probably feel that something's missing. Well, there is something missing, but it can only be added when you reach this stage in your effort to divide household responsibilities fairly.

Step 4: Learn to enthusiastically help each other with your household responsibilities. Up to this point the assignment of household responsibilities is fair. You are dividing responsibilities according to willingness and according to who benefits most from their accomplishment. But marriage takes you one step further. In marriage you do things for each other because you care about each other's feelings. You may not be willing to take responsibility for a certain task because, quite frankly, you don't think it needs to be done. But if your spouse thinks it needs to be done, you will sometimes help him or her with it because you care for your spouse.

Let's suppose that you have been assigned cooking dinner because you want dinner more than your spouse wants it. You hate cooking dinner but you want it done so you have to do it. Then one day your spouse comes into the kitchen and tells you to take a day off. Your spouse will cook for you today. Do you know what happens? Love units are deposited in your Love Bank big time!

Does your spouse's offer mean that your spouse is now in charge of dinner? Not at all. It simply means that he or she is willing to help alleviate your burden once in a while. But if your spouse loved you enough, wouldn't he or she want to relieve you of your burden every day and take charge of dinner? Wouldn't your spouse want to spare you the pain of it all? Well, it might be tempting for your spouse to do just that. But then it would withdraw love units from his or her Love Bank and could cause your spouse to lose love for you.

The one wanting something done the most will lose the fewest love units doing it. After all, he or she is doing it *for self.* It's much more painful to do something unpleasant for someone else.

There are many ways to get things done, and you may not have considered the best possibilities. You and your spouse should discuss how the burdensome responsibilities can be accomplished in ways that are not so burdensome. Maybe one of you would not mind doing one part of dinner preparation, and the other would not mind doing another part. Or maybe you would agree that going out to dinner is the ultimate solution to the problem.

The items left on your list of responsibilities that are unpleasant to perform should be regularly discussed. Brainstorm all kinds of alternatives that might get the job done without either of you suffering.

There are certain household tasks that are so unpleasant for both spouses that hiring someone to do them is a reasonable alternative, especially when both spouses work full-time. Hiring a housekeeper to do only the most unpleasant cleaning chores once a week is money well spent. The same thing may be true of maintaining the yard. Having someone mow and trim the lawn can turn a burdensome Saturday into an opportunity to enjoy the day with the family.

On a related subject, be sure that you do not assign your children tasks that both you and your spouse find too unpleasant to do. It doesn't build character to give your kids jobs that you hate to do; it builds resentment. If you want your children to help around the house, have them choose tasks from your list of household responsibilities that they would enjoy doing. Make lists for them, as well as for you and your spouse. There will be plenty to keep them busy.

To summarize my solution to the division of household responsibilities, the Policy of Joint Agreement should be your guide. Assume household responsibilities that you can do enthusiastically. And then, when you help each other with the unpleasant tasks that are left, help only if you can do it enthusiastically.

By following the Policy, you may decide to change your attitude about some of the responsibilities on your list. When you know that the only way to do something is to do it yourself, you may decide that it doesn't need to be done after all. In fact you may find that what kept you convinced of its importance was the notion that your spouse was supposed to do it.

The Policy guarantees your mutual care, especially when you feel like being uncaring. It prevents you from gaining at your spouse's expense and trying to force your spouse into an unpleasant way of life with you. It points you in a direction that will give you both happiness, fulfillment, and, best of all, the feeling of love for each other.

I received quite a few e-mail letters from unhappy readers of my answer to the questions concerning domestic responsibility. This issue is a common problem in marriage—how to decide who does what with regard to housework and child care. The solution should not only resolve the conflict but also make the couple more compatible and build their love for each other.

My answer to the first letter is a defense of the solution I offered earlier. In my answer to the second letter I explain why this problem can be so upsetting when it is not resolved and why it is so important to negotiate a solution.

Dear Dr. Harley,

I think you are just plain off on this one. My husband would eat cereal every night for dinner, let the litter box go indefinitely, and go to the store for paper plates before emptying the dishwasher—if left to his own devices. And because these chores don't matter to him, and he doesn't like doing them, I'm supposed to put them on my list by default? Not only that, I'm supposed to be enthusiastic too?

I was really hoping for some help. I'm already living with letting him do what he feels like when he feels like it, and I assure you, it's not working. Any other suggestions?

R. W.

Dear R. W.,

Why don't you try my solution for a few weeks? You might like it! While you don't think it will work, what you've been doing hasn't been working either. I think the results will surprise you.

Let me clarify a few points for you. It is at step 3 that you choked on my recommendation. I suggested that the unpleasant responsibilities should be assigned to the person who wants them done the most. It's a reasonable solution, since to do otherwise would force responsibility on the one who doesn't care about them.

By the way, I did not mean to imply that you were supposed to be enthusiastic about taking responsibility for tasks that only you wanted accomplished. I simply feel that if you don't take responsibility for them yourself, the only one left would be your husband, who doesn't have any interest in them. And, as you've noticed, the only way you can get him to do them for you is to make demands on him.

Demands, as I have explained, always withdraw love units and never solve a problem. So until you have a better way of getting these things done, like hiring someone to do them, I suggested that you take these unwanted tasks yourself.

Bear with me as I explain why I recommend this solution. Consider for a moment *why* you want the other person to do these unpleasant tasks for you. Even though *you* are the one who wants them done, you want your spouse to relieve you of the pain you suffer when you do them. In other words, you want to enjoy the benefit of having them done but you are not willing to suffer for them yourself. You would rather see your spouse suffer. You want to gain the benefits of having these unpleasant tasks accomplished at your husband's expense.

You may argue that these tasks are not really what you *want* done, but rather, what *should* be done because they benefit your children, or for some other reason. But when you use that argument, you imply that your spouse is such a slob, and so out of touch, that he doesn't even know or care what's right or what's best for the children.

While that may be precisely the way you feel, it's what I call a disrespectful judgment. You are assuming that your view of the situation is superior to that of your spouse. You are trying to straighten him out. Disrespectful judgments are Love Busters because they always make your spouse feel bad when you use them. Whenever you try to impose your way of thinking on your spouse, you will withdraw love units and you won't win the argument. My solution to your problem does not cause a fight; it causes love. Let me reword step 4.

Revised Step 4: Negotiate an agreement to help each other with your household and child care responsibilities. Step 3 leaves you both with a list of household and child care responsibilities. Some of them you don't mind doing, and others are unpleasant for you. But the unpleasant responsibilities are assigned to the one who wants them done the most.

If we were to leave it at that, I believe it would be a fair division of labor. But we can go one step further, and that step will improve your compatibility and increase your love for each other.

There are many items on your list that your husband would help you accomplish, if you presented your requests in the right way. I'm sure you have tried demands with him, and you already know they don't work very well. You also may have tried to nicely ask him to help and you've probably found that it doesn't work either. That's because asking nicely can actually be a demand in disguise, unless you are willing to accept no for an answer.

You must learn how to negotiate with your husband. There are many ways to get things done, and you may not have considered ways that take your husband's feelings into account. You and your spouse should discuss with each other how these burdensome responsibilities can be accomplished in ways that are not so burdensome. If you discuss them with him, he may be willing to help you do a part, or maybe all of one, if he can do it in a way that won't bother him.

To successfully negotiate with your husband, review the basic steps to successful negotiation found on pages 132–33.

Remember, every time you try to force your husband to do something unpleasant, you are chipping away at his love for you. Not only is it a thoughtless way to accomplish your objectives, but it also won't get the job done. Sooner or later he will figure out a way of escaping you and your demands. A far better way to accomplish the same objectives is to find a way that takes his feelings into account. When you do this, you will build your love for each other. To do otherwise destroys your love.

The method I am suggesting will stand up to the test of time. It will make neither of you a slave or a master. And you won't feel alone or abandoned in your effort to achieve your important objectives. Your husband will become a willing helper who loves and cares for you.

Dear Dr. Harley,

In reading this week's Q&As at your web site, I have come away very frustrated. Tell me, why is it so common for the male head of the house to be totally disinterested in doing what is commonly referred to as routine maintenance of his own house?

I am not speaking of domestic chores—I think those are my responsibility. My husband and I agreed that I would stay home and raise our daughter. I "retired" from a career in electronics when she was born. I am speaking of things such as repairing woodwork in our house, helping hang wallpaper in our bathroom that has been prepped for four years, painting, mowing, keeping up the vehicles, changing a light bulb, helping me file his paperwork, repairing the washer or getting someone else to, helping clean the garage or the three vehicles we have, and helping me carry in the groceries (he has helped with that about four times in our eighteen years of marriage).

My husband seems to have no interest in helping me even when he can see I am struggling. I have done almost everything around the house, inside and out, all these years and now I'm just tired. I'm tired and frustrated and hurt that he seems so oblivious to my need for his involvement as a partner in these chores. He works hard to support me financially but when he's home, he has plenty of time to help me keep our home looking nice.

We live in a middle-class neighborhood where the houses and yards are well maintained. Ninety-nine percent of the time, I am the only female in the neighborhood doing the outside chores. I get embarrassed and hurt by that because sometimes he is in the living room watching TV while I am mowing or doing some other chore. Our daughter and I were on the roof in December hanging Christmas lights, and he got in his truck and went to his mother's.

He goes to his mom's on Saturday and Sunday and stays all day and most of the night instead of staying home and working with me to keep our home nice. At his mom's, he fishes, watches TV, or catnaps. I know you have said that the home usually means more to the woman than to the man, but isn't this ridiculous?

I am not a nagging wife. We have always been good recreational partners; we have wonderful sex (even though I am losing my desire because of my frustration with his lack of help); and I have done all the work around the house in the past because I did not "work" away from the home.

But I am frustrated! I'm sure this all sounds selfish but I am just tired of not having a helpmate. I have prayed hard; I have asked God to change my attitude and I know I must be willing but I have been increasingly frustrated for the past five years and I need help trying to understand what's wrong with me.

Can you help me?

S. N.

Dear S. N.,

You are probably doing an outstanding job meeting your husband's most important emotional needs, and he probably loves you very much. But he doesn't seem to be doing a good job meeting your emotional needs. One of your most important emotional needs may be domestic support, because your husband's help would deposit so many love units if he ever got around to it. Have you ever discussed your emotional needs with your husband? Have you ever told your husband that what would make you love him the most would be his putting up Christmas lights or mowing the lawn or hanging wallpaper? This would give your husband a whole new perspective on the importance to you of these tasks.

Domestic support can be the same as any other emotional need. If it's not met, the marriage can be at risk. If your husband does not meet your need for domestic support, you may lose the feeling of love you once had for him. The losses of love units over the past five years have already taken their toll on your sexual response to him, and if it continues, you may find yourself without any sexual interest at all.

It is crucial for your husband to meet your need for domestic support, but he must do it in a way that he finds enjoyable, or it won't work. When you are trying to meet the emotional needs of your spouse, your goal must be to make your spouse happy in a way that makes you happy as well. Sacrifice is shortsighted. You can do it once in a while, but your motivation will not endure. If you want help around the house from your husband, you want him to do it cheerfully, because that's the only way you will get consistent help from him.

That brings us to the Policy of Joint Agreement—*never do anything without an enthusiastic agreement between you and your spouse.* Your husband can learn to meet your need for domestic support if you follow the Policy.

It is evident that you have not been following this policy because he does things, such as go to his mother's, with which you do not enthusiastically agree.

You made a deal with your husband years ago that if he supported you financially, you would support him domestically. You now know that deal does not work for you. It is no longer a deal that you enthusiastically agree to, so it should be revised using the Policy of Joint Agreement.

There's nothing wrong with you, I can assure you of that. Your frustration comes not only from having to do difficult and unpleasant work, but from the feeling that you have been abandoned by your husband, because he is not meeting one of your important emotional needs. What you want is the feeling that you and he are partners in this business called life. You consider it very important for him to help you with household responsibilities, so I would negotiate with him to get the help you need.

Use the steps for negotiation (see page 132) and you may find that he will cheerfully take on some of the responsibilities. Negotiate with him to help you with some of those that are left, and I think you will find him to be far more helpful than you imagined.

You may not have confronted the issue before because you have an underlying feeling of guilt for wanting him to do things that you feel are your responsibility. Forget all of that and focus on what he could do for you that would make you the happiest. Then bargain in his best interest to get it done. You will both have a happier and more compatible marriage as a result of your effort.

How to Raise Children
and Keep Love in Your Marriage

These letters regard the problem of raising children. But instead of dealing with how to get kids to turn out okay, I will focus my attention on how parents can raise children while still loving each other. The first letter is written by a young mother who feels abandoned by her husband. The second is written by a man whose stepson has ADHD (attention deficit/hyperactive disorder). In both cases the parents want their children to flourish. In the end children tend to turn out okay only if their parents love each other.

Continuing on the theme of raising children, the third letter regards blended families and the unique problems they create in marriage. Again I focus my attention on the care parents show each other, especially when they are tempted to give their children from a previous marriage a higher priority than they give their spouse.

Trying to blend families is one of the greatest causes of divorce. Very few of these marriages survive five years. However, I have witnessed many couples who have learned to beat the odds and create a wonderful, love-filled marriage. The secret is in following the Policy of Joint Agreement.

Dear Dr. Harley,

I gave birth to a beautiful and healthy baby girl last month. We already have a three-year-old son. My husband has never been the world's best father with our first child but he was very excited while I was pregnant and

237

pitched in every once in a while when John was an infant. Now that our son is three, my husband usually spends a few hours on Sundays with him. However, he has been extremely uninterested in our new daughter. He never could get excited during the pregnancy and barely has any time for her now that she's with us. He didn't even want to be in the delivery room. He was there for our son.

This is causing a lot of stress in our relationship. I can't deal with the fact that he has such little interest in his new child. This lack of interest has also been transferred to me. My priorities right now are my children, especially my daughter who needs ALL of me, but my husband's lack of support is driving me crazy. It's gotten so bad that I'm considering moving in with my parents for a while. At least they'll be willing to help out. I've tried talking to him about it, but as far as he's concerned, raising children is a woman's job. I'm at a loss. HELP!

B. K.

Dear B. K.,

The feeling of love is essential for a happy marriage but it is very fragile. Most couples lose it within a few years of marriage, especially after children arrive. Love is created before marriage when a man and woman are successful in meeting each other's most important emotional needs. But after marriage those needs often go unmet and when they do, couples fall out of love with each other.

Sometimes after marriage, spouses are simply lazy about the way they try to meet each other's needs. But more often it's not laziness that gets them in trouble—it's ignorance. After children arrive, new emotional needs are created that come very unexpectedly. And most spouses are not only ignorant of their importance but also unprepared to meet them.

If our needs were the same after children as they were before, the problem would be easy to fix—go back to what you were doing before the children arrived. But emotional needs change dramatically when we become parents.

One of the emotional needs that develops with parenthood is often a big surprise to couples, particularly men. It is what I have called the need for family commitment. I have defined this need as a craving to have your spouse put time and energy into the care and development of your children. Using my theoretical terminology, every time your husband takes time to be with your children and contribute to their care, he deposits love units into his account in your Love Bank, because he is meeting one of your most important emotional needs. Since you feel so good whenever it's met, he deposits carloads full of love units.

Conversely, when he does not meet that need and your craving goes unfulfilled, he inadvertently withdraws love units from his account—carloads of them. The frustration and anger you are experiencing reflect your unfulfilled emotional need and the resulting loss of love units from your Love Bank. You probably don't like him as much as you used to. Before long, your love for him may be gone entirely. And this is all over one issue: his failure to meet your emotional need for family commitment.

Since he is not meeting your emotional need for family commitment, you are not very encouraged to meet his emotional needs either. So you are probably not meeting them, or at least not very often. He may be confused as to what it was he did to deserve your cold shoulder. Where is the woman that couldn't get enough of him just a few years ago? As soon as she became a mother, her interest seemed to be so focused on her children that he was completely ignored. Now he's simply around for money and chores around the house. Not exactly what he had in mind when he married you.

He may really believe that raising children is "a woman's job" and he is doing his part by earning a living to support the family. He may think that what you are asking of him goes beyond the call of duty, something he never bargained for. He is not only ignorant of your emotional need for family commitment, but he also does not know how to meet it (you mentioned that he wasn't the world's best father when you had your first child).

Ironically it is your emotional need for his support in raising your children that may cause your loss of love for him and, ultimately, your divorce. The very thing that will secure the most happiness for your children, parents in love with each other, is being threatened by your need for them to be happy.

There is a very good solution to your problem, however, and if you and your husband will implement it soon, your marriage, and the happiness of your children, will be secure.

Most spouses start their marriages wanting to meet each other's most important emotional needs. But the needs often change, and spouses no longer know what the needs are. Each spouse ends up meeting needs that he or she thinks are important. For example, your husband probably feels he is doing a good job caring for you by earning a living or by being affectionate.

But if he is to hit the mark right in the center, he must ask you what he can do that would make you the happiest now. What is your most important emotional need? You would tell him that, at this moment, it would be his commitment to care for your children.

Then he tells you what his most important emotional need is—what would make him the happiest. For most men it's sexual fulfillment, but he will have to let you know what his most important need is. I'm sure that with all of the added responsibilities of motherhood, your ability and willingness to meet his needs have suffered. It may be much more difficult to meet needs that, prior to the arrival of your children, were a snap. And yet if your marriage is to survive, you need to meet his needs as much as he needs to meet yours.

After each of you have identified your most important emotional need, you make a swap. You'll meet his most important emotional need if he meets yours. If both of you do it, you will be depositing the most love units for the least amount of effort, because you will be hitting each other's target at dead center. Both of you will feel much better about the way your marriage is turning out. And the better you feel, the easier it is to meet each other's needs. Not only will you be happy, but your children will be the ultimate benefactors of your renewed relationship.

There is one hurdle you will need to overcome before any of this will work. You must learn to meet each other's needs in a way that follows my Policy of Joint Agreement—*never do anything without an enthusiastic agreement between you and your spouse.*

That means that whatever your husband does for your children must be done with his enthusiastic agreement. And whatever you do for him must be with your enthusiastic agreement. To be honest, that is the only way that you and he will ever get into the habit

240

of meeting each other's needs—to do it in ways that you both find enjoyable.

So you can't ask each other to sacrifice as you're learning to meet these needs. Instead, you must discover a way of meeting each other's needs that not only does the job but also fits your predispositions. This may take both of you a while to figure out, but in the end, you'll have a formula that may last for life.

What could your husband do for your children that would mean the most to you, that would make you the happiest? Describe it as clearly as you can so that he understands what you need. Make a list of the ways he could care for your children that would mean a lot to you. You may even give each item a number from 1 to 10 indicating how important it is to you. Then your husband could divide the items into three groups: (1) things he would have no trouble doing; (2) things that may take a little effort to learn to enjoy; and (3) things that he thinks would be unpleasant no matter how long he worked at them.

He could tackle the easy items first, proving to you and himself that they are already enjoyable for him and he has no problem doing them to meet your need. Then he might take three from the second group, items that will take some thought to discover ways to enjoy. He could start with those three with your highest rating, so that his effort brings you the greatest satisfaction. After he learns to enjoy doing the first three items, he can then continue until all of them are learned. By then, you may find that those in the third group, those he cannot imagine ever being pleasant, are not that important to you, as long as he is doing all the rest.

I'm sure that your husband loves your children just as you do and wants to play an active role in their development. Once he has learned to meet your need for family commitment, he will find that his new skills are fulfilling for him too. You'll actually be doing him a favor by encouraging him to become a good father, even though at this time he doesn't think it's that important.

You probably feel the same way about having sex with him. I'm sure you don't want to be celibate the rest of your life and you would like to have a fulfilling sexual relationship with him. But you may also feel that with the pressures of children, sex isn't that important. And yet if sexual fulfillment is your husband's most important emotional need, it's as important to him as his help raising your children is important to you.

So he should explain to you how you can meet his need for sex, or whatever his need happens to be, without either of you sacrificing to do it. You had your baby just one month ago, so you will need to take your physical condition into account. Remember, don't ever try to meet his need for sex in a way that is at all uncomfortable for you. That would violate the Policy of Joint Agreement.

Right now he probably feels that whatever it is you want from him is more than he can give. And you may feel that his emotional needs will have to wait a while. Neither of those ideas is true. He can meet your need for family commitment in a way that fits his emotional predispositions, and you can meet his needs in a way that fits yours. The sooner you get started, the sooner you will be depositing love units again.

Dear Dr. Harley,

I need some help with my marriage. I have read your books: "Love Busters;" "His Needs, Her Needs," and "5 Steps to Romantic Love." These books were great and have been a big help to my wife and me.

However there is a Love Buster that I don't quite know how to deal with. That Love Buster is my stepson. He suffers from attention deficit/hyperactive disorder (ADHD) and it is really draining on my marriage. I am not really sure what category of Love Buster this would fall into, but it is a big Love Buster in my house. The heart of the problem is that my wife feels that I don't treat our son fairly or show him enough love, and I of course think the opposite.

Dr. Harley, our son is a terror on two feet. He is only ten and he really wants to please us, but because of his handicap he does poorly in school, the dog does not get along with him, he is always breaking my wife's and my own personal belongings, and he steals from us. When I come home from work, I never know what to expect. There is always bad news regarding something he did. Since the bad news hurts me so much, I feel myself emotionally withdrawn from my son, and because I am withdrawn, my wife tells me that this is a Love Buster for her, and then she starts to withdraw from me. It's a vicious cycle.

We have tried support groups for ADHD and sought other counseling too, but so far it has not worked. I would greatly appreciate any advice that you can give me.

R. D.

Dear R. D.,

Reading between the lines, I assume that your wife wants you to react to your stepson's inconsiderate behavior with patience and love. I'm sure that she does not always react that way herself, but whenever she sees you upset with him, she feels as if you are upset with her. So she withdraws from you to escape the pain.

One approach to your problems is to count the years before he is out of the house. If your marriage can survive until he is old enough to leave, you can pick up the pieces and try to rebuild what your "Love Buster" almost destroyed.

But I have a more proactive approach to your problem that may not only prevent the loss of love units but also guide your stepson into a successful life.

My approach to child rearing is found in both *Love Busters* (chapter 10, Resolving Conflicts over Children) and *His Needs, Her Needs* (chapter 11, Family Commitment).

I make two recommendations. The first is all decisions made regarding children must follow the Policy of Joint Agreement. The second is that each week parents set aside what I call "quality family time," when the family is together. This time is always especially planned to be enjoyable and educational with an emphasis on taking other people's feelings into account. In other words, the primary purpose of quality family time is to teach children the values of behaving in a way that is cooperative and thoughtful.

I don't believe that you and your wife are following the Policy of Joint Agreement when it comes to raising your son and you are certainly not spending much time in quality family time. You have probably had conflicts about discipline. You have had your way one time, and your wife has had her way the next. Your stepson is probably getting mixed signals. And your wife's reaction about your fairness and love may reflect the fact that you don't spend much quality time with him.

I've never been convinced that the factors leading to the diagnosis of ADHD are inherited. There are so many similarities in the conditions under which ADHD kids are raised that I believe environment plays the crucial role. My entire family is full of high-energy people. I could hardly sit still in school and even today find lectures intolerable. But I was trained to be considerate of others. My father would not allow me to behave in any other way.

My personal opinion is that ADHD kids are not simply high-energy children. They are *inconsiderate* high-energy children. What makes your son a Love Buster is not his high energy or his failure in school or his short attention span. It's his stealing, lying, disrespect, temper tantrums, abuse, and many other traits characteristic of those who have never been taught to be considerate. Thoughtfulness isn't an instinct. It is learned and most often taught by parents.

What will solve your marital problems and your stepson's social problems is for you and your wife to make a commitment to train your child consistently and with an emphasis on cooperation and thoughtfulness.

Start by agreeing that from now on you and your wife will never discipline your son unless you both enthusiastically agree. No more mixed signals. He will be getting all of his reprimands from both of you or he won't get any at all. That means that you and your wife will spend many hours discussing how to handle this "terror on two feet," but you'll do it together.

You should also set aside time together (you, your son, and your wife) each week for quality family time. The time should be spent in an enjoyable activity and the time should be devoted to teaching your son to be cooperative and thoughtful. Once you have set aside time for your family, you'll find that the Policy of Joint Agreement will be much easier to implement. Your wife will be thrilled that you are taking leadership in your son's development and will want it to work for him. What had been a Love Buster will turn into a love builder. Your effort will not only deposit love units in your wife's Love Bank, but you will see your son's selfish pattern of behavior begin to change as he shows signs of thoughtfulness.

The Policy of Joint Agreement will not only help you and your wife overcome conflicts over discipline but will also set an example for your son. It is a rule that insures thoughtfulness because it forces you to take each other's feelings into account. During your quality family time the Policy can apply to your son too. Ask him to help plan each outing so that all three of you will have a good time. In the process of coming to an agreement, he will have to consider your feelings just as much as you will have to consider his. You don't go anywhere or do anything until you have an enthusiastic agreement from all three of you.

Plan ahead for your son's misbehavior so that it does not ruin your experience together, or alienate you from your wife. Have contingency plans if he does not cooperate with you. Since this is an educational experience, expect your son to make mistakes. But you and your wife will also see his growth. The longer you have this time together as a family, the more enjoyable it will be for all of you, because your son will learn to be more thoughtful.

Dear Dr. Harley,

This is the second marriage for each of us. We each have two children, all of whom are older teens except one. We seem to constantly disagree on simple child rearing issues (i.e., cleaning the room, household chores, curfew, etc.). My largest complaint is that since we have blended our families, it seems my children have had to make the most adjustments while my husband's children just seem to run wild when they are here (they live with their mother most of the time). My husband is always very critical of my children and their "conformance" to house rules, yet his children seem to make their own rules. While I have tried to stress that no two children can be reared the same, he continues to punish my children for seemingly minor infractions. This is causing a great deal of distrust among all of us. Is there anything we can do to rebuild trust between us? I am beginning to question my faithfulness to someone so unwilling to compromise.

D. K.

Dear D. K.,

Marriages with blended families tend to be very unsuccessful, one of the best predictors of divorce. And you have firsthand experience to see why this is the case. It is common for each spouse to put his or her own children's interests first. It is often in an effort to compensate for the trauma children experience when there is a divorce. But when the children's interests are put first, the interests of the other spouse and the other spouse's children are pushed somewhere down the list, and that's a formula for marital disaster.

However, in cases that I have witnessed, these marriages can be saved if both spouses are willing to follow my Policy of Joint Agreement. In effect, whenever you follow the Policy, you put your spouse's interests first, where they should be.

Following the Policy means that neither you nor your husband act to reprimand or discipline any child until the two of you have reached an enthusiastic agreement. At first, you may not agree about much of anything, in which case you are not to discipline the children (they may do whatever they please). But as you practice applying the Policy, you and your husband will begin to establish guidelines in child rearing issues, and agreements will start to form. Eventually you will agree on how to discipline your children in ways that take each other's feelings into account, and your marriage will be saved.

Child rearing is a huge problem in blended families, but it's not the only issue in your marriage, I'm sure. Regardless of your conflicts, however, you'll find that you can resolve them all when you have learned to negotiate with the Policy of Joint Agreement. Incidentally, the guidelines that will help you negotiate an enthusiastic agreement can be found on pages 132–33.

The reason you argue is that you are incompatible—you have not learned how to act in the interest of both of you at the same time. But if you follow the Policy of Joint Agreement and use the guidelines for negotiation, you will find yourselves in greater and greater agreement. Eventually your marriage will turn out better than you could have ever hoped.

If you don't follow the Policy, however, you will eventually make each other so miserable that you will lose your love for each other and divorce, like most couples with blended families. This process has already begun. Stop it before it goes any further.

Dear Dr. Harley,

My wife and I were married in December of 1995 after a very short three-month dating relationship. This is a second marriage for both. I had been divorced for two years, she for four. I have two children (a girl seven, a boy eleven), and she has one (a girl six). We have all the normal challenges I have read about with second-marriage blended families, which I think we are handling fairly well. However, we are really struggling with the issue of what I will call "conflicting independence." We both lived on our own and were independent and caring for our children alone.

Now we are really struggling with how to merge our lives and define our roles in our new family. In my time alone, I had to do the man, woman, daddy, and mommy chores. My wife had the same role. We learned to do it all. I find myself on a regular basis trying to decide who should be doing what, and it is causing real problems when either we both want to do it, or neither wants to do it. What would your approach be to even begin a discussion on this issue?

Your assistance would be appreciated!

D. R.

Dear D. R.,

What a great term: "conflicting independence." That pretty much sums up what I've always called marital incompatibility.

Having counseled for more than thirty years now, I am convinced that marital compatibility is a problem of gigantic proportions in most marriages. Couples are usually most compatible the day of their wedding, and things go downhill from there. Why? Because prior to marriage the couple make a great effort to become compatible. They try to understand each other's likes and dislikes and then try to accommodate those feelings. Then they are usually willing to change their behavior to become more compatible. And it works so well that they decide to be together for life.

247

Trouble is most couples stop trying to be compatible as soon as they're married. Mission accomplished! We're married, so now I can set my sights on other objectives in life. My career, my children, my health, my . . .

At first, one spouse is particularly hurt by the other's neglect. The hurt spouse feels that he or she is not the highest priority as before. After having time to let it sink in, the hurt spouse figures that the honeymoon is over and the most mature thing to do is to become resigned to the obvious: Love just doesn't last.

So instead of doing something to improve compatibility, he or she makes the spouse less important, just as the hurt spouse felt less important. You can see what happens: a negative feedback loop. The more neglected you feel, the more neglectful you become. Eventually you can't remember what you saw in each other. A sad story indeed!

There is one and only one solution, as far as I'm concerned. It's my Policy of Joint Agreement. With this one rule, you and your spouse put each other first in your life, whether you feel like it or not. It's where you should have been all along. This rule more than any other creates compatibility. It eliminates everything that is good for one of you and bad for the other. In its place, you create situations that are good for both of you, and they become your standard operating procedures.

Whatever you cannot agree on defines an area of incompatibility. It needs to be replaced with a compatible alternative. And you'll find that each resolution solves a repeating problem. Your conflicts are not usually isolated. They revolve around an issue that comes up again and again. Once you find the answer, you sweep many future arguments out the door.

The only way you will be able to merge your lives is to follow the Policy of Joint Agreement. Everything you do should be predicated with the question, "How would you feel if I . . . ?" If the answer is not an enthusiastic, "I'd feel fine," you don't do it. Pure and simple. Granted, you won't be independent anymore; you will be interdependent. There is simply no way you can merge your independent lifestyles. You must bite the bullet and recreate a lifestyle that takes the feelings of both of you into account simultaneously.

At first, it may be very difficult to follow the Policy because you are in the habit of doing so many incompatible things. But if you follow it at all costs for a few weeks, you will find it easier and easier. You will also come to grips with the temptation of trying to gain at each other's expense. When one of you feels that it's okay to go ahead with plans even if the other person objects, you are simply saying, "I don't really care how you feel; I'm going to do it anyway because I'm willing to gain at your expense."

As you wrestle with the issues of a blended family, give the Policy of Joint Agreement a shot. Personally, I think it's your only hope for a happy marriage.

How to Develop Your Career
and Keep Love in Your Marriage

I strongly encourage both husbands and wives to develop challenging careers for themselves, but the Policy of Joint Agreement should be their guide. Spouses should remember that throughout marriage no career objective is so important that to achieve it you can't meet each other's most important emotional needs.

Dear Dr. Harley,

I hope you can help me. This morning my husband told me he doesn't love me anymore. I love him very much and want to do what I can to save our marriage.

I have just earned a doctorate degree in chemistry. While I was in school, my husband supported me and was willing to move so that I could get the education I needed. But he has recently found a job he really enjoys and has talent for. My training is very specialized and there are very few jobs available in my area of expertise. I have been offered a job I would love to have, but my husband doesn't want to leave the area we're in because he loves his job so much.

I am hurt that after my being in college so very long and training so hard, he is not absolutely supportive of my career. Now the hard part is over and it is time for us to reap the financial rewards of years of diligence. Can you offer assistance? I would be so grateful.

E. H.

250

Dear E. H.,

I think if you and your husband were to have a heart-to-heart talk, he might tell you that he does not feel that your educational efforts were in his best interest. He might tell you that they were in your best interest. Your achievements were not for you as a couple; they were for you as an individual. He may not even feel he had a choice in the matter. Or he may have supported your educational objectives because he loved you, not because he felt there was something in it for him too.

Romantic love affects our state of mind. When your husband loved you, he was in the state of marriage I call intimacy and he was willing to make sacrifices to make you happy. (See the section on the Three States of Marriage, beginning on page 20.) But because his emotional needs have not been met, his love for you has faded and he is either in the state of conflict or withdrawal, probably withdrawal. In either of these states of mind, he will be more concerned about his own interests and will tend to ignore yours. That's why he wants to pursue his own vocational goals independently of yours.

He lost his love for you because while you were pursuing your education, his most important emotional needs were not being met. I've been to graduate school too and I know that it takes long hours of study to be successful, hours away from your spouse. One day, perhaps years ago, he woke up and realized he didn't love you anymore. He may have admitted it only now because you were expecting him to move to another city.

In the state of conflict, he may have thought to himself, *She cares more about her career than she does about me. If she cared about me, she would have been more concerned about me and my career development and would have at least considered staying here.* The evidence at hand would have supported his argument.

We marry to be with someone who cares more about us than anything or anyone else. Both men and women feel that way. If your career interests are more important than your husband's needs, he will eventually conclude that he is missing what he needs most in marriage, someone who puts him first.

Incidentally, that applies not just to career interests but to any interests. If children are considered most important, they will come between spouses. The same is true for friends, in-laws, money, or what you do on weekends. Anything will ruin your marriage if it is considered more important than your spouse's feelings. Your most important consideration in life should be the interests of your spouse, or your marriage will suffer.

If your career really is your first priority, your marriage does not have much of a chance. I don't think it's possible to love anyone for any length of time whose career is his or her highest priority. But if you put your husband's interests first, your marriage will flourish and you'll find your career flourishing as well. That's because if you're happily married, your zest for life will have a positive impact on your career.

Refocus your efforts in life to prove to your husband that you care more about him than you do about your education or your career. That's what my Policy of Joint Agreement is all about. It helps spouses put each other's interests before all other considerations, even when they don't feel like it or don't have the sense to.

Your husband may not be in the mood to follow the Policy himself at this time, but that doesn't mean that you can't take the initiative and follow it unilaterally. Tell him that from now on you will not try to make him do anything unless he is enthusiastic about it—unless he sees it is in his best interest too. And that includes moving to take a job that will advance your career objectives.

Your husband's telling you that he doesn't love you may be a very timely warning of disaster on the horizon. Refocus your efforts so that your educational pursuits don't end up costing you your marriage.

Dear Dr. Harley,

I am a twenty-nine-year-old woman who has been married for six years and I really love my husband. I am a medical student, and he works to support my education. I appreciate what he is doing to help me financially but I am not getting enough emotional support from him.

I really feel overworked and I am frustrated that my husband is not more supportive. When we decided that I would go to medical school, I thought that he was making a commitment to help me get through. Instead, I feel that he has abandoned me.

The cleaning and grocery shopping fall primarily to me because I have trouble keeping my thoughts organized when the house is a mess and when meals are not planned. When I repeatedly ask him for more help, he says he will but he either does nothing or does a crappy job. School has been tough and I feel that my husband does not understand my increased need for his support during this difficult period. I have repeatedly expressed my frustration, but it seems as though he takes my need for partnership as a demand and as an expression of his failure.

My husband also refuses to tell me what he wants or how he feels about practically anything. I have tried to make him feel less threatened and more willing to explore his own emotions but to no avail. I know that my frustrations are not his responsibility. But he just waits for me to get over whatever's bothering me instead of trying to fix the problem.

He spends hours solving problems at work, trying everything he can think of. But if our marriage has a problem, he's satisfied to say "I don't know." After every fight, he comes to me and apologizes in tears. I feel really desperate. What do you suggest?

G. R.

Dear G. R.,

If I were to talk to your husband about your marriage, he would probably tell me that he has done all he can do to make you happy but he has been a total failure. All his efforts are getting him nowhere. Each conversation he has with you leaves him feeling increasingly inadequate.

You say in your letter that your frustrations are not his responsibility and yet what you say in the rest of the letter suggests that you think they are his responsibility. Which is it? I'm sure he feels that your unhappiness is something he should fix, but I doubt that helping to clean the house and doing grocery shopping would help. Besides, it's something he probably never liked doing, even when you were very happy with him. We go to our spouse for help when we are unhappy. That's normal. But what could he do to make you happy?

When you ask him what he wants or how he feels, he probably wants to share his frustration with you. He may want to say, "What do you think I'm getting out of all of this? You never seem to be too concerned about how much stress I'm under. All you ever think about is yourself. Do you think I'm satisfied with the lack of attention I get from you?" But if he were to say that, it would make you even more upset. He wants you to be happy and feels terrible that you are not but he doesn't want to make you even more unhappy by loading you down with his own frustration.

He thought that his financial support would make you happy. He's making a big sacrifice putting you through medical school, and you're making a big sacrifice by going. You are probably both over-worked and living on a tight budget. Furthermore, you have years of education ahead of you that will require even greater sacrifices. The very thought of it probably puts knots in both of your stomachs.

You complain to him about the fact that he is not helping you with housework and grocery shopping. But he doesn't understand that what is most upsetting is that you have emotional needs that he is not meeting. And you are probably not meeting his needs either because of your busy schedule. Put simply, your lifestyle is preventing both of you from meeting each other's emotional needs. He is probably as upset about it as you are but he is trying to tough it out by keeping his nose to the grindstone and ignoring your problems because he feels that while you are in medical school, there's nothing either of you can do about them. When you do have time to talk to each other, all you ever talk about are problems, so he doesn't say anything. You don't use the opportunities you have to support and encourage each other.

I'd like you to reflect on the time when you and he did meet each other's needs. You probably spent much more time with each other in meaningful conversation because you simply had more time with each other. Now you try to sneak it in between all of your responsibilities and it doesn't work.

Here's the solution to your problem: Spend fifteen hours a week with each other engaged in affection, sex, conversation, and recreational companionship (not all at the same time!). In other words, take fifteen hours a week out of your busy schedules to have fun with each other. Take a vacation from your problems. Don't bring up unpleasant topics for a while. Instead, enjoy your time together.

If you can't find the time to be together just to talk, be affectionate, share recreational activities, and find sexual fulfillment, you've discovered why your marriage will ultimately fail—your career development prevents you from meeting each other's emotional needs. It's just that simple. Whenever your education, children, career, finances, or anything else prevents you from meeting each other's needs, your marriage does not have much of a chance of survival. If you can't meet each other's needs and go to medical school too, you should abandon medical school, not your marriage.

If you decide to spend those fifteen hours a week together, but just don't enjoy each other's company as much as you used to, your problem is creeping incompatibility. Over the past few years you have been growing apart. The solution is to keep spending fifteen hours a week together, but learn to grow together by following the Policy of Joint Agreement. You have been trying to force your husband into a lifestyle that is increasingly unpleasant for him (and you too). The Policy will prevent you from doing that. Within a month you will find your time together much more enjoyable. But most important you will be meeting each other's most important emotional needs. If you follow my advice, by the time you finish medical school, you will both be as much in love as you've ever been, and there will be no complaining about emotional abandonment.

Throughout your life, you and your husband will have important objectives that will tempt you to abandon each other's emotional needs. Never yield to those temptations. No objective is important enough to risk the love you have for each other.

The following letter is from a woman whose husband is trying to complete his education. The husband has made his education his highest priority, higher than the interests of his wife.

The preceding letters also focus attention on how education and career decisions can ruin a marriage when the interests of a spouse are not taken into account but they were from the perspective of wives who were putting their careers before their spouse's interests. To some extent, the following letter is more of the same.

In my answer I put more emphasis on neglect as the primary reason that the marriage is being destroyed. It gives me an opportunity to point to a crucial reason why women are leaving men. The letters I receive dramatically illustrate the frustration of women throughout America who find themselves married to men who have misplaced priorities. How can these women reach their husbands with their desperate cry for help before they decide that their love is misplaced?

I hear from men almost every day whose wives have just left them because the wives were neglected. The husbands are beside themselves with grief. They will do anything to encourage their wives to return to them. Why can't men see what is happening before wives leave, often never to return?

In an effort to reach these men before it was too late, I wrote "Why Women Leave Men," which appeared in the July-August 1996 issue of *New Man*. There is an edited version of that article in appendix F to encourage you to avoid the tragic results of neglect.

Dear Dr. Harley,

My husband works full-time while he is getting his master's degree. He is always stressed and busy. I am proud of his endurance and hard work and I try very hard to keep any extra stress away from him. I handle all the housework, bills, and yard work. I also work full-time and am trying to work on my novel (which is my career goal).

When my husband does take time off to do something fun, he usually spends the time with his friends. I tried going out with his friends just to be able to spend some time with him, but he said maybe two words to me and most of the time I spent talking to his friends. This did not do anything for me. I was wasting writing time.

Every once in a while he will take time out to do something with me; however, the whole time he is in a serious mood. He says he is thinking about work and school and that he cannot help it. He isn't this way when he is with his friends. He has fun and laughs with his friends, so I think that it is me. When we go out together I can tell that to him it is just another chore he has to get in before the day is over, like walking the dog before bedtime. Sometimes he is too tired to go out with his friends and he stays home and sleeps. This, he claims, is spending time with me.

So I feel more like a maid and prostitute than a wife. I got up the courage and told him how I felt the other night, and he got angry. He said that it is just the time he is going through right now. He said that he loves me more than anything and that I am his best friend. He went out with his friends anyway, saying he was already in trouble with me, so it didn't matter. I am at a loss. I am afraid that if we keep going this way, we will no longer know each other. But I am also afraid that if I push the issue, he will just leave or get more mad and really won't want to spend time with me. I love him with my whole self and I will do anything for him.

Please, I am open to any suggestions.

J. N.

Dear J. N.,

Marriages are very fragile when one or both spouses are finishing their education because the couple are tempted to spend very little time together. They often make work and studying their highest priorities and often feel that they cannot afford to take time to be together. Three hours together on Saturday afternoon translates to thirty dollars lost income.

You and your husband need to spend time with each other to meet each other's emotional needs. If you don't, you will lose your love for each other and risk divorce.

You introduce a problem that goes beyond just not having enough time to be together. Your husband does have some free time, but it is spent away from you, with his friends. When he could be with you, meeting your emotional needs, he chooses, instead, to have his needs met by others.

Actually this problem is more common than most people think. Those who burn the candle at both ends very often neglect their spouse and children, even when they have time for them. It's probably a form of escape from all their responsibility. Your husband's friends expect nothing of him and so they are the only ones with whom he feels he can be totally relaxed.

You and your husband have grown apart and you are no longer each other's best friend. You have become incompatible, as is evident in what happens when you go out alone together. But you can steer your marriage back on the right track if you both decide to create a new lifestyle that both of you can enjoy together.

The Policy of Joint Agreement helps create that lifestyle. It makes both of you each other's highest priority because you cannot do anything unless you both agree enthusiastically. It will bring you and your husband back into a relationship where you become each other's best friend.

You will either grow apart or grow together. If you make decisions that do not take each other's feelings into account, you will grow apart. If, on the other hand, you consult with each other about all of your lifestyle decisions and take each other's feelings into account, you will grow together.

Right now you still love him and you want to avoid divorce, but given time, your feelings will evaporate and even if you remain married after his master's degree, you may harbor deep resentment about the way he treated you.

I hear from men almost daily who have treated their wife the way you have been treated. After their wife has suffered enough neglect, she leaves, sometimes with another man. These husbands are devastated. They've lost the most precious part of their life, but their wife surely never felt very precious. While these marriages can be saved, it's a long and hard struggle back. How much easier it would have been if they had responded to their wife's cry for help when she still felt the way you do!

How can you reach your husband before you end up leaving him? You already see the need to be together more often, but he doesn't. When you try to talk to him about the problem, he responds with anger.

I hope he reads this letter or talks to someone who can intervene on your behalf. In many cases, that's all it takes. He thinks he's doing the right thing but he needs to be shown what disaster lies ahead.

I suggest that you read *Give and Take*. It explains how a couple can learn to grow together instead of growing apart and it tackles the most important issues, including how to become each other's best friend.

Your problem is real and if you don't do something about it, things will get worse. Women are usually the first to identify a marital problem, and sometimes it's hard to convince men that it's their problem too. They're easily convinced once their wife leaves them, but by then, in many cases, it's too late.

How to Resolve Financial Conflicts and Keep Love in Your Marriage

*O*ne great test of your ability to keep love in your marriage is to try to make financial decisions together. If you make them easily with mutual consideration, chances are your love for each other is in good shape. If, on the other hand, you can't seem to agree on how to spend your money, or worse yet you put your individual incomes into separate accounts so you don't have to agree, your love for each other has probably taken a beating.

The following letters are from people who are struggling with financial conflicts. But their conflicts are not just about money. They are about what is important in marriage—consideration of each other's feelings. For these couples, money has taken priority. If they don't change their priorities soon, they may lose their love for each other in an effort to control the purse strings.

Dear Dr. Harley,

My husband and I have been married almost seven years and we have two beautiful daughters. Throughout our marriage we have had separate bank accounts and credit card accounts. We both work full-time and both share in the responsibilities for our children and household. We rent a house since we are unable to buy one at this time due to our separate debts and the high cost of rent and day care. It seems we can never get ahead.

260

J have suggested we get help from a financial planner, but he refuses. He is always depressed about money but he won't do anything about it. We are both at fault because we spend more than we can afford. We mainly fight about money and it's been getting more frequent.

My husband has a second job and now he is always angry that he has to work so hard. He says he loves me but he feels J am not pulling my weight as far as finances are concerned. J make approximately sixteen thousand dollars less a year than he does but J help pay rent, some day care, and the groceries. He wants me to do all the housework, but after a day at work J'd rather spend the time with my kids and save the cleaning for the weekend.

Where do J go from here?

B. W.

Dear B. W.,

From your description, you and your husband have been growing increasingly incompatible over the few years you've been married, and your approach to financial planning is probably the rule for all areas of your marriage. Instead of learning how to accommodate each other with joint financial accounts, you separate them so that you do not have to take each other's feelings into account when you spend money. You probably do the same with other decisions you make, such as what you do after work, how you discipline your children, when you see relatives, and so forth.

You're not building a relationship; you're preparing for the day when you will go your separate ways. Your husband's reaction to your income (that you do not earn enough) reflects his emotional distance. If you are still in love with each other, it won't be for long. You will soon be just putting up with each other for the sake of your children.

Imagine how difficult it would be for you to follow my Policy of Joint Agreement at this point in your marriage. The more incompatible a couple is, the more difficult it is for them to follow the Policy, and you're at the point where it would be almost impossible. But if you and your husband would agree to follow the Policy for just one week, you would begin to see the light at the end of the tunnel. Within a year, by following the Policy, you would be more compatible than you have ever been at any point in your marriage, and your financial problems would be solved.

The Policy of Joint Agreement is simply your willingness to take his feelings into account before you do something and his willingness to do the same for you. You ask how he feels about whatever you do, and if he doesn't like it, you don't do it. Then you discuss what else you could do that would be more to his liking and you settle on something that you both like. Marriage cannot survive without thoughtfulness, and the Policy of Joint Agreement forces you to be thoughtful, even when you don't feel like it.

When you say that you fight about money and you have separate checking and credit card accounts, you are telling me that you are not bargaining for each other's happiness. You are bargaining for your own happiness at each other's expense, otherwise there would be no fighting. But if you had been following the Policy of Joint Agreement from the beginning of your marriage, there would have been no need for separate accounts. Regardless of who earned the money, the decision to spend it would have been made jointly.

One of the best ways to get your finances under control is to make joint decisions about how your money is to be spent. First, get rid of your individual checking and credit card accounts and get joint accounts. All the money either of you earns should go into your joint checking account—every penny! Then, whenever you buy something, check with each other to be sure you both agree. I usually recommend a weekly allowance that is taken out of the checking account so that each spouse has money to spend as he or she chooses. The allowance should not exceed fifty dollars a week and it should be equal for both spouses.

When you pay your bills, you should do it together. Every check you write should be written with each other's approval—which bills to pay first, how much to pay on a credit card account, and so forth.

At this point in your marriage, my advice will be difficult to implement. You are already living separate lives and are learning to treasure your independence. Why would either of you want to give up the freedom you have writing checks out of your own checking accounts and using your own credit cards at will? To get each other's

permission to spend money will, at first, seem childish and humil-
iating. Furthermore, you may find yourselves refusing permission
on almost everything, because so much of what you have been buy-
ing has been thoughtless. For a while you may be discouraged
because it's so hard to agree on much of anything! That's because in
the past you have not needed to negotiate with each other. You've
gone ahead and done what you pleased. Your fights are a reflection
of your poor negotiating skills.

But if you stick to the Policy of Joint Agreement, little by little,
agreements begin to form. There are areas right now on which you
can agree, and as you negotiate, keeping each other's feelings in
mind, all the areas of incompatibility will eventually be replaced
with compatible decisions. Your finances will probably be in great
shape in no time because together you are wiser than either of you
is separately. But what's more important, your marriage will also be
in great shape.

Start today using the Policy of Joint Agreement to make your financial decisions and all your decisions.

Appendix A

The Most Important Emotional Needs

Before you complete the Emotional Needs Questionnaire in appendix B, review the following ten most important emotional needs.

Affection

Quite simply, affection is the expression of love. It symbolizes security, protection, comfort, and approval—vitally important ingredients in any relationship. When one spouse is affectionate to the other, the following messages are sent:

1. You are important to me, and I will care for you and protect you.
2. I'm concerned about the problems you face and will be there for you when you need me.

A hug can say those things. When we hug our friends and relatives, we are demonstrating our care for them. And there are other ways to show our affection—a greeting card, an "I love you" note, a bouquet of flowers, holding hands, walks after dinner, back rubs, phone calls, and conversations with thoughtful and loving expressions can all communicate affection.

Affection is, for many, the essential cement of a relationship. Without it many people feel totally alienated. With it they become emotionally bonded. If you feel terrific when your spouse is affectionate and you feel terrible when there is not enough of it, you have the emotional need for affection.

Sexual Fulfillment

We often confuse sex and affection. Affection is an act of love that is nonsexual and can be received from friends, relatives, children, and even pets. However, acts that can show affection, such as hugging and kissing, that are done with a sexual motive are actually sex, not affection.

Most people know whether or not they have a need for sex, but in case there is any uncertainty, I will point out some of the most obvious symptoms.

A sexual need usually predates your current relationship and is somewhat independent of your relationship. While you may have discovered a deep desire to make love to your spouse since you've been in love, it isn't quite the same thing as a sexual need. Wanting to make love when you are in love is sometimes merely a reflection of wanting to be emotionally and physically close.

Sexual fantasies are usually a dead giveaway for a sexual need. Fantasies in general are good indicators of emotional needs—your most common fantasies usually reflecting your most important needs. If you have imagined what it would be like having your sexual need met in the most fulfilling ways, you probably have a sexual need. The more the fantasy is employed, the greater your need. And the way your sexual need is met in your fantasy is usually a good indicator of your sexual predispositions and orientation.

When you married, you and your spouse both promised to be faithful to each other for life. This means that you agreed to be each other's only sexual partner "until death do us part." You made this commitment because you trusted each other to meet your sexual needs, to be sexually available and responsive. The need for sex, then, is a very exclusive need, and if you have it, you will be very dependent on your spouse to meet it for you. You have no other ethical choice.

Conversation

Unlike sex, conversation is not a need that can be met exclusively in marriage. Our need for conversation can be ethically met by almost anyone. But if it is one of your most important emotional needs, whoever meets it best will deposit so many love units, you may fall in love with that person. So if it's your need, be sure that your spouse is the one who meets it the best and most often.

Men and women don't have too much difficulty talking to each other during courtship. That's a time of information gathering for both partners. Both are highly motivated to discover each other's likes and dislikes, personal background, current interests, and plans for the future.

But after marriage many women find that the man who would spend hours talking to her on the telephone, now seems to have lost all interest in talking to her and spends his spare time watching television or reading. If your need for conversation was fulfilled during courtship, you expect it to be met after marriage.

If you see conversation as a practical necessity, primarily as a means to an end, you probably don't have much of a need for it. But if you have a craving just to talk to someone, if you pick up the telephone just because you feel like talking, if you enjoy conversation in its own right, consider conversation to be one of your most important emotional needs.

Recreational Companionship

A need for recreational companionship combines two needs into one: the need to engage in recreational activities and the need to have a companion.

During your courtship, you and your spouse were probably each other's favorite recreational companions. It's not uncommon for women to join men in hunting, fishing, watching football, or other activities they would never choose on their own. They simply want to spend as much time as possible with the men they like and that means going where they go.

The same is true of men. Shopping centers are no strangers to men in love. They will also take their dates out to dinner, watch romantic movies, and attend concerts and plays. They take every opportunity to be with someone they like and try to enjoy the activity to guarantee more dates in the future.

I won't deny that marriage changes a relationship considerably. But does it have to end the activities that helped make the relationship so compatible? Can't a husband's favorite recreational companion be his wife and vice versa?

If recreational activities are important to you and you like to have someone join you for them to be fulfilling, include recreational companionship on your list of needs. Think about it for a moment in terms of the Love Bank. How much do you enjoy these activities and how many love units would your spouse be depositing whenever you enjoyed them together? What a waste it would be if someone else got credit for all those love units! And if it is someone of the opposite sex, it would be downright dangerous.

Who should get credit for all those love units? The one you should love the most, your spouse. That's precisely why I encourage couples to be each other's favorite recreational companions. It's one of the simplest ways to deposit love units.

Honesty and Openness

Most of us want an honest relationship with our spouse. But some of us have a need for such a relationship because honesty and openness give us a sense of security.

To feel secure, we want accurate information about our spouse's thoughts, feelings, habits, likes, dislikes, personal history, daily activities, and plans for the future. If a spouse does not provide honest and open communication, trust can be undermined and the feelings of security can eventually be destroyed. We can't trust the signals that are being sent and we have no foundation on which to build a solid relationship. Instead of adjusting to each other, we feel off balance; instead of growing together, we grow apart.

268

Aside from the practical considerations of honesty and openness, there are some of us who feel happy and fulfilled when our spouse reveals his or her most private thoughts to us. And we feel very frustrated when they are hidden. That reaction is evidence of an emotional need, one that can and should be met in marriage.

An Attractive Spouse

For many people, physical appearance can become one of the greatest sources of love units. If you have this need, an attractive person will not only get your attention but may distract you from whatever you're doing. In fact that's what may have first drawn you to your spouse—his or her physical appearance.

There are some who consider this need to be temporary and important only in the beginning of a relationship. After a couple get to know each other better, some feel that physical attractiveness should take a backseat to deeper and more intimate needs.

But that's not been my experience, nor has it been the experience of many people whom I've counseled, particularly men. For many, the need for an attractive spouse continues on throughout marriage, and just seeing the spouse looking attractive deposits love units.

Among the various aspects of physical attractiveness, weight generally gets the most attention. However, choice of clothing, hairstyle, makeup, and personal hygiene also come together to make a person attractive. It can be very subjective, and you are the judge of what is attractive to you.

If the attractiveness of your spouse makes you feel great, and loss of that attractiveness would make you feel very frustrated, you should probably include this category on your list of important emotional needs.

Financial Support

People often marry for the financial security that their spouse provides them. In other words, part of the reason they marry is for money. Is financial support one of your important emotional needs?

It may be difficult for you to know how much you need financial support, especially if your spouse has always been gainfully employed. But what if, before marriage, your spouse had told you not to expect any income from him or her? Would it have affected your decision to marry? Or what if your spouse could not find work, and you had to financially support him or her throughout life? Would that withdraw love units?

You may have a need for financial support if you expect your spouse to earn a living. But you definitely have that need if you do not expect to be earning a living yourself, at least during part of your marriage.

What constitutes financial support? Earning enough to buy everything you could possibly desire or earning just enough to get by? Different couples would answer this differently, and the same couples might answer differently in different stages of life. But, like many of these emotional needs, financial support is sometimes hard to talk about. As a result, many couples have hidden expectations, assumptions, and resentments. Try to understand what you expect from your spouse financially to feel fulfilled. And what would it take for you to feel frustrated? Your analysis will help you determine if you have a need for financial support.

Domestic Support

The need for domestic support is a time bomb. At first it seems irrelevant, a throwback to more primitive times. But for many couples, the need explodes after a few years of marriage, surprising both husband and wife.

Domestic support involves the creation of a peaceful and well-managed home environment. It includes cooking meals, washing dishes, washing and ironing clothes, cleaning house, and child care. If you feel very fulfilled when your spouse does these things and very annoyed when they are not done, you have the need for domestic support.

In earlier generations, it was assumed that all husbands had this need and all wives would naturally meet it. Times have changed, and needs have changed along with them. Now many of the men I counsel would rather have their wives meet their needs for affection or conversation, needs that have traditionally been more characteristic of women. And many women, especially career women, gain a great deal of pleasure having their husbands create a peaceful and well-managed home environment.

Marriage usually begins with a willingness of both spouses to share domestic responsibilities. Newlyweds commonly wash dishes together, make the bed together, and divide many household tasks. The groom welcomes his wife's help in doing what he had to do by himself as a bachelor. At this point in marriage, neither of them would identify domestic support as an important emotional need. But the time bomb is ticking.

When does the need for domestic support explode? When the children arrive! Children create huge needs—both a greater need for income and greater domestic responsibilities. The previous division of labor becomes obsolete. Both spouses must take on new responsibilities—and which ones will they take?

At this point in your marriage, you may find no need for domestic support at all. But that may change later when you have children. In fact as soon as you are expecting your first child, you will find yourselves dramatically changing your priorities.

Family Commitment

In addition to a greater need for income and domestic responsibilities, the arrival of children create in many people the need for family commitment. Again, if you don't have children yet, you may not sense this need, but when the first child arrives, a change may take place that you didn't anticipate.

Family commitment is not just child care—feeding, clothing, or watching over children to keep them safe. Child care falls under the category of domestic support. Family commitment, on the other hand, is a responsibility for the development of the children, teaching them the values of cooperation and care for each other.

271

It is spending quality time with your children to help them develop into successful adults.

Evidence of this need is a craving for your spouse's involvement in the educational and moral development of your children. When he or she is helping care for them, you feel very fulfilled, and when he or she neglects their development, you feel very frustrated.

We all want our children to be successful, but if you have the need for family commitment, your spouse's participation in family activities will deposit carloads of love units. And your spouse's neglect of your children will noticeably withdraw them.

Admiration

If you have the need for admiration, you may have fallen in love with your spouse partly because of his or her compliments to you. Some people just love to be told that they are appreciated. Your spouse may also have been careful not to criticize you. If you have a need for admiration, criticism may hurt you deeply.

Many of us have a deep desire to be respected, valued, and appreciated by our spouse. We need to be affirmed clearly and often. There's nothing wrong with feeling that way. Even God wants us to appreciate him!

Appreciation is one of the easiest needs to meet. Just a compliment, and presto, you've made your spouse's day. On the other hand, it's also easy to be critical. A trivial word of rebuke can be very upsetting to some people, ruining their day and withdrawing love units at an alarming rate.

Your spouse may have the power to build up or deplete his or her account in your Love Bank with just a few words. If you can be affected that easily, be sure to add admiration to your list of important emotional needs.

Appendix B

Emotional Needs Questionnaire

© 1986 by Willard F. Harley, Jr.

Name _____ Date _____

This questionnaire is designed to help you determine your most important emotional needs and evaluate your spouse's effectiveness in meeting those needs. Make two enlarged copies of the questionnaire, one for you and one for your spouse. Before you complete this questionnaire, review the ten most important emotional needs described in appendix A. Answer all the questions as candidly as possible. Do not try to minimize any needs that you feel have been unmet. If your answers require more space, use and attach a separate sheet of paper. Your spouse should complete an Emotional Needs Questionnaire so that you can discover his or her needs and evaluate your effectiveness in meeting those needs.

When you have completed this questionnaire, go through it a second time to be certain your answers accurately reflect your feelings. Do not erase your original answers, but cross them out lightly so that your spouse can see the corrections and discuss them with you.

The final page of this questionnaire asks you to identify and rank five of the ten needs in order of their importance to you. The most important emotional needs are those that give you the most pleasure when met and frustrate you the most when unmet. Resist the temptation to identify as most important only those needs that your spouse is *not* presently meeting. Include *all* your emotional needs in your consideration of those that are most important.

273

1. **Affection.** Expressing love through words, cards, gifts, hugs, kisses, and courtesies; creating an environment that clearly and repeatedly expresses love.

   A. **Need for affection:** Indicate how much you need affection by circling the appropriate number.

   | 0 | 1 | 2 | 3 | 4 | 5 | 6 |

   I have no need   I have a moderate   I have a great need
   for affection   need for affection   for affection

   If or when your spouse is *not* affectionate with you, how do you feel? (Circle the appropriate letter.)
   a. Very unhappy   c. Neither happy nor unhappy
   b. Somewhat unhappy   d. Happy not to be shown affection

   If or when your spouse is affectionate to you, how do you feel? (Circle the appropriate letter.)
   a. Very happy   c. Neither happy nor unhappy
   b. Somewhat happy   d. Unhappy to be shown affection

   B. **Evaluation of spouse's affection:** Indicate your satisfaction with your spouse's affection toward you by circling the appropriate number.

   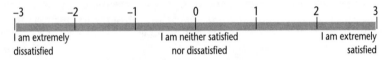

   | -3 | -2 | -1 | 0 | 1 | 2 | 3 |

   I am extremely   I am neither satisfied   I am extremely
   dissatisfied   nor dissatisfied   satisfied

   My spouse gives me all the affection I need. Yes No

   If your answer is no, how often would you like your spouse to be affectionate with you?
   _____(write number) times each day/week/month (circle one)

   I like the way my spouse gives me affection.   Yes   No

   If your answer is no, explain how your need for affection could be better satisfied in your marriage. _____
   _____
   _____
   _____
   _____

2. **Sexual Fulfillment.** A sexual relationship that brings out a predictably enjoyable sexual response in both of you that is frequent enough for both of you.

A. **Need for sexual fulfillment:** Indicate how much you need sexual fulfillment by circling the appropriate number.

0	1	2	3	4	5	6

I have no need for sexual fulfillment　　I have a moderate need for sexual fulfillment　　I have a great need for sexual fulfillment

If or when your spouse is *not* willing to engage in sexual relations with you, how do you feel? (Circle the appropriate letter.)
a. Very unhappy　　　　　c. Neither happy nor unhappy
b. Somewhat unhappy　　　d. Happy not to engage in sexual relations

If or when your spouse engages in sexual relations with you, how do you feel? (Circle the appropriate letter.)
a. Very happy　　　　　　c. Neither happy nor unhappy
b. Somewhat happy　　　　d. Unhappy to engage in sexual relations

B. **Evaluation of sexual relations with your spouse:** Indicate your satisfaction with your spouse's sexual relations with you by circling the appropriate number.

–3	–2	–1	0	1	2	3

I am extremely dissatisfied　　　I am neither satisfied nor dissatisfied　　　I am extremely satisfied

My spouse has sexual relations with me as often as I need. Yes　No

If your answer is no, how often would you like your spouse to have sex with you?
_____(write number) times each day/week/month (circle one)

I like the way my spouse has sexual relations with me.　Yes　　No

If your answer is no, explain how your need for sexual fulfillment could be better satisfied in your marriage. _____
_____
_____
_____
_____

3. **Conversation.** Talking about events of the day, feelings, and plans; avoiding angry or judgmental statements or dwelling on past mistakes; showing interest in your favorite topics of conversation; balancing conversation; using it to inform, investigate, and understand you; and giving you undivided attention.

A. **Need for conversation:** Indicate how much you need conversation by circling the appropriate number.

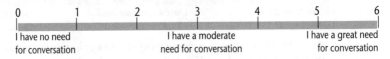

| 0 | 1 | 2 | 3 | 4 | 5 | 6 |

I have no need
for conversation

I have a moderate
need for conversation

I have a great need
for conversation

If or when your spouse is *not* willing to talk with you, how do you feel? (Circle the appropriate letter.)
a. Very unhappy   c. Neither happy nor unhappy
b. Somewhat unhappy   d. Happy not to talk

If or when your spouse talks to you, how do you feel? (Circle the appropriate letter.)
a. Very happy   c. Neither happy nor unhappy
b. Somewhat happy   d. Unhappy to talk

B. **Evaluation of conversation with your spouse:** Indicate your satisfaction with your spouse's conversation with you by circling the appropriate number.

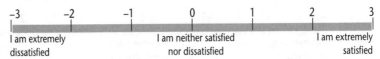

| -3 | -2 | -1 | 0 | 1 | 2 | 3 |

I am extremely
dissatisfied

I am neither satisfied
nor dissatisfied

I am extremely
satisfied

My spouse talks to me as often as I need.   Yes   No

If your answer is no, how often would you like your spouse to talk to you?
_____(write number) times each day/week/month (circle one)
_____(write number) hours each day/week/month (circle one)

I like the way my spouse talks to me.   Yes   No

If your answer is no, explain how your need for conversation could be better satisfied in your marriage. _____

_____

_____

_____

4. **Recreational Companionship.** Developing interest in your favorite recreational activities, learning to be proficient in them, and joining you in those activities. If any prove to be unpleasant to your spouse after an effort has been made, negotiating new recreational activities that are mutually enjoyable.

A. **Need for recreational companionship:** Indicate how much you need recreational companionship by circling the appropriate number.

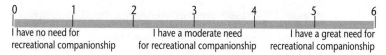

| 0 | 1 | 2 | 3 | 4 | 5 | 6 |

I have no need for
recreational companionship

I have a moderate need
for recreational companionship

I have a great need for
recreational companionship

If or when your spouse is *not* willing to join you in recreational activities, how do you feel? (Circle the appropriate letter.)
a. Very unhappy   c. Neither happy nor unhappy
b. Somewhat unhappy   d. Happy not to include my spouse

If or when your spouse joins you in recreational activities, how do you feel? (Circle the appropriate letter.)
a. Very happy   c. Neither happy nor unhappy
b. Somewhat happy   d. Unhappy to have my spouse join me in
                          recreational activities

B. **Evaluation of recreational companionship with your spouse:** Indicate your satisfaction with your spouse's recreational companionship by circling the appropriate number.

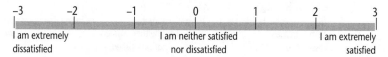

| -3 | -2 | -1 | 0 | 1 | 2 | 3 |

I am extremely
dissatisfied

I am neither satisfied
nor dissatisfied

I am extremely
satisfied

My spouse joins me in recreational activities as often as I need. Yes No

If your answer is no, how often would you like your spouse to join you in recreational activities?
_____(write number) times each day/week/month (circle one)
_____(write number) hours each day/week/month (circle one)

I like the way my spouse joins me in recreational activities.   Yes   No

If your answer is no, explain how your need for recreational companionship could be better satisfied in your marriage. _____
_____
_____
_____

5. **Honesty and Openness.** Revealing positive and negative feelings, events of the past, daily events and schedule, plans for the future; not leaving you with a false impression; answering your questions truthfully.

A. **Need for honesty and openness:** Indicate how much you need honesty and openness by circling the appropriate number.

0	1	2	3	4	5	6

I have no need for honesty and openness   I have a moderate need for honesty and openness   I have a great need for honesty and openness

If or when your spouse is *not* open and honest with you, how do you feel? (Circle the appropriate letter.)
a. Very unhappy
b. Somewhat unhappy
c. Neither happy nor unhappy
d. Happy for spouse not to be honest and open

If or when your spouse is open and honest with you, how do you feel? (Circle the appropriate letter.)
a. Very happy
b. Somewhat happy
c. Neither happy nor unhappy
d. Unhappy for spouse to be honest and open

B. **Evaluation of spouse's honesty and openness:** Indicate your satisfaction with your spouse's honesty and openness by circling the appropriate number.

−3	−2	−1	0	1	2	3

I am extremely dissatisfied   I am neither satisfied nor dissatisfied   I am extremely satisfied

In which of the following areas of honesty and openness would you like to see improvement from your spouse? (Circle the letters that apply to you.)
a. Sharing positive and negative emotional reactions to significant aspects of life
b. Sharing information regarding his/her personal history
c. Sharing information about his/her daily activities
d. Sharing information about his/her future schedule and plans

If you circled any of the above, explain how your need for honesty and openness could be better satisfied in your marriage. _____

_____

_____

_____

6. **Attractiveness of Spouse.** Keeping physically fit with diet and exercise; wearing hair, clothing, and (if female) makeup in a way that you find attractive and tasteful.

A. **Need for an attractive spouse:** Indicate how much you need an attractive spouse by circling the appropriate number.

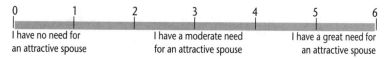

| 0 | 1 | 2 | 3 | 4 | 5 | 6 |

I have no need for an attractive spouse   I have a moderate need for an attractive spouse   I have a great need for an attractive spouse

If or when your spouse is *not* willing to make the most of his or her physical attractiveness, how do you feel? (Circle the appropriate letter.)
a. Very unhappy
b. Somewhat unhappy
c. Neither happy nor unhappy
d. Happy he or she does not make an effort

When your spouse makes the most of his or her physical attractiveness, how do you feel? (Circle the appropriate letter.)
a. Very happy
b. Somewhat happy
c. Neither happy nor unhappy
d. Unhappy to see that he or she makes an effort

B. **Evaluation of spouse's attractiveness:** Indicate your satisfaction with your spouse's attractiveness by circling the appropriate number.

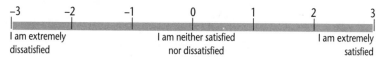

| -3 | -2 | -1 | 0 | 1 | 2 | 3 |

I am extremely dissatisfied   I am neither satisfied nor dissatisfied   I am extremely satisfied

In which of the following characteristics of attractiveness would you like to see improvement from your spouse? (Circle the letters that apply to you.)
a. Physical fitness and normal weight
b. Attractive choice of clothes
c. Attractive hairstyle
d. Good physical hygiene
e. Attractive facial makeup
f. Other _____

If you circled any of the above, explain how your need for an attractive spouse could be better satisfied in your marriage. _____
_____
_____
_____

7. **Financial Support.** Provision of the financial resources to house, feed, and clothe your family at a standard of living acceptable to you, but avoiding travel and working hours that are unacceptable to you.

A. **Need for financial support:** Indicate how much you need financial support by circling the appropriate number.

0	1	2	3	4	5	6
I have no need for financial support			I have a moderate need for financial support			I have a great need for financial support

If or when your spouse is *not* willing to support you financially, how do you feel? (Circle the appropriate letter.)
a. Very unhappy   c. Neither happy nor unhappy
b. Somewhat unhappy   d. Happy not to be financially supported

If or when your spouse supports you financially, how do you feel? (Circle the appropriate letter.)
a. Very happy   c. Neither happy nor unhappy
b. Somewhat happy   d. Unhappy to be financially supported

B. **Evaluation of spouse's financial support:** Indicate your satisfaction with your spouse's financial support by circling the appropriate number.

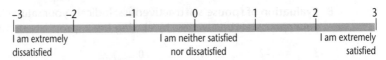

−3	−2	−1	0	1	2	3
I am extremely dissatisfied			I am neither satisfied nor dissatisfied			I am extremely satisfied

How much money would you like your spouse to earn to support you?

_____

How many hours each week would you like your spouse to work?

_____

If your spouse is not earning as much as you would like, is not working the hours you would like, does not budget the way you would like, or does not earn an income the way you would like, explain how your need for financial support could be better satisfied in your marriage.

_____
_____
_____
_____
_____

8. **Domestic Support.** Creation of a home environment for you that offers a refuge from the stresses of life; managing the home and care of the children—if any are at home—including but not limited to cooking meals, washing dishes, washing and ironing clothes, and housecleaning.

A. **Need for domestic support:** Indicate how much you need domestic support by circling the appropriate number.

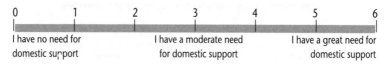

| 0 | 1 | 2 | 3 | 4 | 5 | 6 |

I have no need for domestic support

I have a moderate need for domestic support

I have a great need for domestic support

If your spouse is *not* willing to provide you with domestic support, how do you feel? (Circle the appropriate letter.)
a. Very unhappy
b. Somewhat unhappy
c. Neither happy nor unhappy
d. Happy not to have domestic support

If or when your spouse provides you with domestic support, how do you feel? (Circle the appropriate letter.)
a. Very happy
b. Somewhat happy
c. Neither happy nor unhappy
d. Unhappy to be domestically supported

B. **Evaluation of spouse's domestic support:** Indicate your satisfaction with your spouse's domestic support by circling the appropriate number.

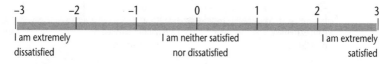

| −3 | −2 | −1 | 0 | 1 | 2 | 3 |

I am extremely dissatisfied

I am neither satisfied nor dissatisfied

I am extremely satisfied

My spouse provides me with all the domestic support I need. Yes No

I like the way my spouse provides domestic support.   Yes   No

If your answer is no to either of the above questions, explain how your need for domestic support could be better satisfied in your marriage.

_____

_____

_____

_____

_____

9. **Family Commitment.** Scheduling sufficient time and energy for the moral and educational development of your children; reading to them, taking them on frequent outings, educating himself or herself in appropriate child-training methods and discussing those methods with you; avoiding any child-training method or disciplinary action that does not have your enthusiastic support.

A. **Need for family commitment:** Indicate how much you need family commitment by circling the appropriate number.

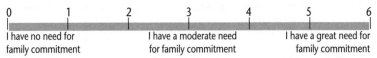

0	1	2	3	4	5	6
I have no need for family commitment			I have a moderate need for family commitment			I have a great need for family commitment

If or when your spouse is *not* willing to provide family commitment, how do you feel? (Circle the appropriate letter.)
a. Very unhappy   c. Neither happy nor unhappy
b. Somewhat unhappy   d. Happy he or she is not involved

If or when your spouse provides family commitment, how do you feel? (Circle the appropriate letter.)
a. Very happy   c. Neither happy nor unhappy
b. Somewhat happy   d. Unhappy he or she's involved in the family

B. **Evaluation of spouse's family commitment:** Indicate your satisfaction with your spouse's family commitment by circling the appropriate number.

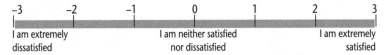

-3	-2	-1	0	1	2	3
I am extremely dissatisfied			I am neither satisfied nor dissatisfied			I am extremely satisfied

My spouse commits enough time to the family.   Yes   No

If your answer is no, how often would you like your spouse to join in family activities?
_____(write number) times each day/week/month (circle one)
_____(write number) hours each day/week/month (circle one)

I like the way my spouse spends time with the family.   Yes   No

If your answer is no, explain how your need for family commitment could be better satisfied in your marriage.

_____

_____

_____

10. **Admiration.** Respecting, valuing, and appreciating you; rarely critical and expressing admiration to you clearly and often.

   A. **Need for admiration:** Indicate how much you need admiration by circling the appropriate number.

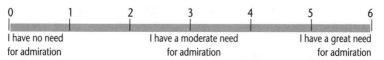

| 0 | 1 | 2 | 3 | 4 | 5 | 6 |

I have no need   I have a moderate need   I have a great need
for admiration   for admiration   for admiration

   If or when your spouse *does not* admire you, how do you feel? (Circle the appropriate letter.)
   a. Very unhappy   c. Neither happy nor unhappy
   b. Somewhat unhappy   d. Happy not to be admired

   If or when your spouse *does* admire you, how do you feel? (Circle the appropriate letter.)
   a. Very happy   c. Neither happy nor unhappy
   b. Somewhat happy   d. Unhappy to be admired

   B. **Evaluation of spouse's admiration:** Indicate your satisfaction with your spouse's admiration of you by circling the appropriate number.

| −3 | −2 | −1 | 0 | 1 | 2 | 3 |

I am extremely   I am neither satisfied   I am extremely
dissatisfied   nor dissatisfied   satisfied

   My spouse gives me all the admiration I need. Yes No

   If your answer is no, how often would you like your spouse to admire you? _____(write number) times each day/week/month (circle one)

   I like the way my spouse admires me.   Yes   No

If your answer is no, explain how your need for admiration could be better satisfied in your marriage.

_____
_____
_____
_____
_____

Ranking of Your Emotional Needs

The ten basic emotional needs are listed below. There is also space for you to add other emotional needs that you feel are essential to your marital happiness.

In the space provided before each need, write a number from 1 to 5 that ranks the need's importance to your happiness. Write a 1 before the most important need, a 2 before the next important, and so on until you have ranked your five most important needs.

To help you rank these needs, imagine that you will have only one need met in your marriage. Which would make you the happiest, knowing that all the others would go unmet? That need should be 1. If only two needs will be met, what would your second selection be? Which five needs, when met, would make you the happiest?

_____ Affection

_____ Sexual Fulfillment

_____ Conversation

_____ Recreational Companionship

_____ Honesty and Openness

_____ Attractiveness of Spouse

_____ Financial Support

_____ Domestic Support

_____ Family Commitment

_____ Admiration

_____ _____

_____ _____

_____ _____

_____ _____

Appendix C

The Five Love Busters

Before you complete the Love Busters Questionnaire in appendix D, review the following Love Busters.

Angry Outbursts

Anger usually occurs when you feel that someone is making you unhappy and that what he or she is doing just isn't fair. In your angry state, you're convinced that reasoning won't work, and the offender will keep upsetting you until he or she is taught a lesson. The only thing such people understand is punishment, you assume. Then they'll think twice about making you unhappy again!

You use anger to protect yourself and it offers a simple solution to your problem—destroy the troublemaker. If your spouse turns out to be the troublemaker, you'll find yourself hurting the one you've promised to cherish and protect. When you're angry, you don't care about your spouse's feelings and you are willing to scorch the culprit if it prevents you from being hurt again.

In the end you have nothing to gain from anger. Punishment does not solve marital problems; it only makes your punished spouse want to inflict punishment on you, or if that doesn't work, leave you. When you become angry with your spouse, you

285

threaten your spouse's safety and security; you fail to provide protection. Your spouse rises to the challenge and tries to destroy you in retaliation. When anger wins, love loses.

Each of us has an arsenal of weapons we use when we're angry. If we think someone deserves to be punished, we unlock the gate and select an appropriate weapon. Sometimes the weapon is verbal (ridicule and sarcasm), sometimes it's devious plots to cause suffering, and sometimes it's physical. But all the weapons have one thing in common: the ability to hurt people. Since our spouse is at such close range, our weapons can hurt him or her the most.

Some of the husbands and wives I've counseled have fairly harmless arsenals, maybe just a few awkward efforts at ridicule. Others are armed to nuclear proportions; their spouse's life is in danger. The more dangerous your weapons are, the more important it is to control your temper.

Remember, in marriage you can be your spouse's greatest source of pleasure but you can also be your spouse's greatest source of pain. If you've ever lost your temper in a way that has caused your spouse great pain and suffering, you know you cannot afford to lose your temper again. You must go to extreme lengths to protect your spouse from yourself.

Disrespectful Judgments

Have you ever tried to "straighten out" your spouse? We're all occasionally tempted to do that sort of thing. At the time we think we're doing our spouse a big favor, to lift him or her from the darkness of confusion into the light of our "superior perspective." If our spouse would only follow our advice, we assume, he or she could avoid many of life's pitfalls.

Yet, if we're not careful, our effort to keep our spouse from making mistakes can lead to a much bigger mistake, one that withdraws love units and destroys romantic love. The mistake is called disrespectful judgments.

A disrespectful judgment occurs whenever someone tries to force someone else to adopt a system of values and beliefs. When a husband tries to force his point of view on his wife, he's just asking for trouble. When a wife assumes that her own views are right and her husband is woefully misguided—and tells him so—she enters a minefield.

This is a way of interacting that's very easy to slip into—and hard to escape. We usually believe our opinions are correct and any opposing opinions are incorrect. When we believe strongly in our own opinions, we may want to correct the person who doesn't agree with us. We may honestly believe that the "incorrect" opinion will get him or her into trouble someday. We're just trying to help. If it's our spouse who needs to be corrected, we're motivated by our love. So why is it such a problem?

The trouble starts in marriage when we think we have the right—even the responsibility—to impose our view on our spouse. Almost invariably, our spouse will regard such imposition as personally threatening, arrogant, rude, and incredibly disrespectful. That's when we lose units in our Love Bank accounts.

When we impose our opinions on our spouse, we imply that he or she has poor judgment. That's disrespectful. We may not say this in so many words, but it's the clear message we convey. If we valued our spouse's judgment more, we might question our own opinions. What if our spouse is right, and we're wrong? That seldom occurs to us, because we trust our own judgment more than we trust our spouse's judgment.

I'm not saying that you can't disagree with your spouse. But disagree respectfully. Try to understand your spouse's reasoning. Present the information that brought you to your opinion and listen to the information that influenced your spouse. Entertain the possibility that you might change your own mind, instead of just pointing out how wrong your spouse is.

You see, each of us brings two things into a marriage—wisdom and foolishness. A marriage thrives when a husband and wife can blend their value systems, with each one's wisdom overriding the other's foolishness. That's how respectful persuasion works. By sharing ideas and sorting through the pros and cons, a couple can create a belief system superior to what either partner had alone. Unless they approach the task with mutual respect, the process won't work and they'll destroy their love for each other in the process.

Annoying Behavior

When was the last time your spouse did something that annoyed you? Last week? Yesterday? An hour ago? Maybe your mate is humming that irritating tune this very minute!

One of the most annoying things about annoying behavior is that it doesn't seem all that important—but it still drives you bananas! It's not abuse or abandonment, just annoyance. You should be able to shrug it off, but you can't. It's like the steady drip-drip of water torture. Annoying behavior will nickel and dime your Love Bank into bankruptcy.

When we're annoyed, we usually consider others inconsiderate, particularly after we've explained that their behavior bothers us and they continue to do it. It's not just the behavior itself, but the thought behind it—the idea that they just don't care.

But when our behavior annoys others, we try to minimize the whole problem. It's just a little thing. Why make a federal case out of it? Why can't other people adjust?

As a counselor, I try to help couples become more empathetic, to see through each other's eyes. Of course, no one can fully imagine what someone else feels, and that's a great part of the problem. I often wish I could switch a couple's minds: Joe becomes Jane for a day and Jane becomes Joe. If they could only know what it feels like to experience their own insensitive behavior, they would change their ways in a hurry.

I've found it helpful to divide annoying behavior into two categories. If behavior is repeated without much thought, I call it an annoying habit. If it's usually scheduled and requires thought to complete, I call it an annoying activity. Annoying habits include personal mannerisms such as the way you eat, the way you clean up after yourself (or don't!), and the way you talk. Annoying activities, on the other hand, may include sporting events you attend, your choice of church, or your personal exercise program.

Every annoying habit or activity drives a wedge between you and your spouse, creating and sustaining incompatibility. If you want compatibility in your marriage, you must get rid of your annoying behavior.

288

Selfish Demands

Our parents made demands on us when we were children; teachers made demands in school; and employers make demands at work. Most of us didn't like them as children and we still don't.

Demands carry a threat of punishment. If you refuse me, you'll regret it. In other words, you may dislike doing what I want, but if you don't do it, I'll see to it that you suffer even greater pain. In the words of the Godfather, a demand is "an offer you can't refuse."

People who make demands don't seem to care how others feel. They think only of their own needs. If you find it unpleasant to do what I want, tough! And if you refuse, I'll make it even tougher.

Demands depend on power. They don't work unless the demanding one has the power to make good on his threats. The Godfather had the power to make those "unrefusable" offers. A four-year-old who demands a new toy does not have power— unless you count the ability to embarrass you by screaming unrelentingly in the middle of a crowded store.

But who has power in marriage? Ideally there is shared power, the husband and wife working together to accomplish mutual objectives. But when one spouse starts making demands—along with threats that are at least implied—it's a power play. The threatened spouse often strikes back, fighting fire with fire, power with power. Suddenly the marriage is a tug-of-war instead of a bicycle built for two. It's a test of power. Who will win?

If the demanding partner doesn't have enough power to follow through with the threat, he or she often receives punishment, at least in the form of ridicule. But if power is fairly equal between a husband and wife, a battle rages until one or the other surrenders. In the end, the one meeting the demand feels deep resentment and is less likely to meet the need in the future. When the demand is not met, both spouses feel resentment.

Does this mean that you should never ask your spouse for a favor? Isn't it good to communicate your needs? Yes, communicate but don't demand. You may make requests but not threats. When I ask my wife, Joyce, to do something for me, she may cheerfully agree to it or she may express her reluctance. This reluctance may be due to any number of things—her own needs, her comfort level, her sense of what's wise or fair.

If I push my request, making it a demand, what am I doing? I'm overriding her reluctance. I am declaring that my wishes are more important than her feelings and I'm threatening to cause her some distress if she doesn't do what I want.

She now must choose the lesser of two evils—my "punishment" on the one hand or whatever made her reluctant on the other. She may ultimately agree to my demand but she won't be happy about it. I may get my way but I gain at her expense, and she will feel used.

"But you don't know my husband!" some wife may say. "He lies around the house all night and I can't get him to do a thing. The only time he lifts a finger is to press the remote control. If I don't demand that he get up and help me, nothing would get done."

"You can't be talking about my wife," a husband might say. "She only thinks about herself! She spends her whole life shopping and going out with her girlfriends. If I didn't demand that she stay at home once in a while, I'd never see her."

There are some major conflicts in these brief examples, but I still maintain that demands hurt more than they help. If you force your spouse to meet your needs, it becomes a temporary solution at best, and resentment is sure to rear its ugly head. Threats, lectures, and other forms of manipulation do not build compatibility. They build resentment.

Dishonesty

If your spouse had an affair ten years ago that was a brief indiscretion, would you want to know about it? If you had an affair ten years ago that you ended because you knew it was wrong, should you tell your spouse about it? These are tough questions that go to the heart of our fifth Love Buster—dishonesty.

Dishonesty is the strangest of the five Love Busters. Obviously, no one likes dishonesty, but sometimes honesty seems more damaging. What if the truth is more painful than a lie?

When a wife first learns that her husband has been unfaithful, the pain is often so great that she wishes she had been left in ignorance. When a husband discovers his wife's affair, it's like a knife in his heart. He thinks it would be better not knowing. In fact many marriage counselors advise clients to avoid telling spouses about past infidelity, because it's too painful for people to handle. Besides, if it's over and done with, why dredge up the sewage of the past?

It's this sort of confusion that leads some of the most well-intentioned husbands and wives to lie to each other, or at least give each other false impressions. They feel that dishonesty will help them protect each other's feelings. But what kind of a relationship is that? The lie is a wall that comes between the two partners, something hidden, a secret that cannot be mentioned, yet is right under the surface of every conversation.

Dishonesty can be as addictive as a drug. One secret leads to another. If you start using dishonesty to protect each other's feelings, where will it end? That's why dishonesty is a strange Love Buster. Lies clearly hurt a relationship over the long term, but truth can also hurt, especially in the short term. That's why many couples continue in dishonesty. One spouse believes he or she must protect the other from the shock of the truth. As a result ignorance leads the marriage to a slow death.

Honesty can be like a flu shot. You may experience a short, sharp pain, but it keeps you healthier over the following months.

In the case of infidelity, the fact of your affair is an important piece of information about you. How could you ever expect to have an intimate relationship with someone to whom you cannot reveal something so important about yourself? This is an extreme example. There are many other issues in marriage that are less serious, but I use this extreme case to underscore the curious nature of this Love Buster. Dishonesty may protect you and your spouse from pain for the moment, but eventually your marriage will suffer more from the dishonesty than it would have from the truth.

Honesty sometimes creates some pain, the pain of knowing. But it is really the thoughtless act (about which a spouse is tempted to be dishonest) that causes the pain. Dishonesty may defer some of that pain, but often it compounds the pain. The truth often comes out eventually, and the months or years of hiding it makes everything worse.

Dishonesty strangles compatibility. To create and sustain compatibility in marriage, both husband and wife must be honest about thoughts, feelings, habits, likes, dislikes, personal history, daily activities, and plans for the future. When misinformation is part of the mix, a couple have little hope of making successful adjustments to each other. Dishonesty not only makes solutions hard to find, but it often leaves couples ignorant of the problems that need to be solved.

There's another very important reason to be honest. Honesty makes our behavior more thoughtful. If we knew that everything we do and say would be televised and reviewed by all our friends, we would be far less likely to engage in thoughtless acts. Criminals would not steal and commit violent acts if they knew they would be caught each time they did. Honesty is the television camera in our lives. If we are honest about what we do, we tend not to engage in thoughtless acts because others will know about them. We won't cover them up.

In an honest relationship, thoughtless acts are revealed, forgiven, and corrected. In this way bad habits are nipped in the bud, and as incompatible attitudes and behaviors are revealed, they become targets for elimination. If these attitudes and behaviors remain hidden, they are left to grow out of control and to destroy the marriage. Honesty keeps a couple from drifting into incompatibility.

Spouses are often confused as to how honest they should be. To end the confusion, I have written the Rule of Honesty for a successful marriage. This can be found in appendix E.

Appendix D

Love Busters Questionnaire

© 1992 by Willard F. Harley, Jr.

Name _____ Date _____

This questionnaire is designed to help identify your spouse's Love Busters. Your spouse engages in a Love Buster whenever one of his or her habits causes you to be unhappy. By causing your unhappiness, he or she withdraws love units from his or her account in your Love Bank, and that, in turn, threatens your romantic love.

There are five categories of Love Busters (see appendix C for a complete description). Each category has its own set of questions in this questionnaire. Make two enlarged copies of the questionnaire, one for you and one for your spouse. Answer all the questions as candidly as possible. Do not try to minimize your unhappiness with your spouse's behavior. If your answers require more space, use and attach a separate sheet of paper. Your spouse should also complete a Love Busters Questionnaire so that you can discover your own Love Busters.

When you have completed this questionnaire, go through it a second time to be certain your answers accurately reflect your feelings. Do not erase your original answers, but cross them out lightly so that your spouse can see the corrections and discuss them with you.

The final page of this questionnaire asks you to rank the five Love Busters in order of their importance to you. When you complete the ranking of the Love Busters, you may find that your answers to the questions regarding each Love Buster are inconsistent with your final ranking. This inconsistency is common. It often reflects a less than perfect understanding of your feelings. If you notice inconsistencies, discuss them with your spouse to help clarify your feelings.

1. **Angry Outbursts.** Deliberate attempts by your spouse to hurt you because of anger toward you. They are usually in the form of verbal or physical attacks.

   A. **Angry outbursts as a cause of unhappiness:** Indicate how much unhappiness you tend to experience when your spouse attacks you with an angry outburst.

| 0 | 1 | 2 | 3 | 4 | 5 | 6 |

I experience no unhappiness   I experience moderate unhappiness   I experience extreme unhappiness

   B. **Frequency of spouse's angry outbursts:** Indicate how often your spouse tends to engage in angry outbursts toward you. ____(write number) angry outbursts each day/week/month/year (circle one)

   C. **Form(s) angry outbursts take:** When your spouse engages in angry outbursts toward you, what does he/she typically do? _____
   _____
   _____

   D. **Form(s) of angry outbursts that causes the greatest unhappiness:** Which of the above forms of angry outbursts cause you the greatest unhappiness? _____
   _____
   _____

   E. **Onset of angry outbursts:** When did your spouse first engage in angry outbursts toward you?_____
   _____
   _____

   F. **Development of angry outbursts:** Have your spouse's angry outbursts increased or decreased in intensity and/or frequency since they first began? How do recent angry outbursts compare with those of the past? _____
   _____
   _____
   _____
   _____
   _____
   _____
   _____

2. **Disrespectful Judgments.** Attempts by your spouse to change your attitudes, beliefs, and behavior by trying to force you into his/her way of thinking. If (1) he/she lectures you instead of respectfully discussing issues, (2) feels that his/her opinion is superior to yours, (3) talks over you or prevents you from having a chance to explain your position, or (4) ridicules your point of view, he/she is engaging in disrespectful judgments.

A. **Disrespectful judgments as a cause of unhappiness:** Indicate how much unhappiness you tend to experience when your spouse engages in disrespectful judgments toward you.

| 0 | 1 | 2 | 3 | 4 | 5 | 6 |

I experience
no unhappiness

I experience
moderate unhappiness

I experience
extreme unhappiness

B. **Frequency of spouse's disrespectful judgments:** Indicate how often your spouse tends to engage in disrespectful judgments toward you. _____(write number) disrespectful judgments each day/week/month/ year (circle one)

C. **Form(s) disrespectful judgments take:** When your spouse engages in disrespectful judgments toward you, what does he/she typically do?

_____
_____
_____

D. **Form(s) of disrespectful judgments that causes the greatest unhappiness:** Which of the above forms of disrespectful judgments cause you the greatest unhappiness? _____

_____
_____
_____

E. **Onset of disrespectful judgments:** When did your spouse first engage in disrespectful judgments toward you? _____

_____
_____
_____

F. **Development of disrespectful judgments:** Have your spouse's disrespectful judgments increased or decreased in intensity and/or frequency since they first began? How do recent disrespectful judgments compare with those of the past? _____

_____
_____

3. **Annoying Behavior.** The two basic types of annoying behavior are habits and activities. Habits are repeated without much thought, such as the way your spouse eats or sits in a chair. Activities are usually scheduled and require thought to complete, such as attending sporting events or a personal exercise program. Your spouse's habits and activities are "annoying behavior" if they cause you to feel unhappy. They can be as innocent as snoring or as destructive as infidelity or alcohol addiction.

A. **Annoying behavior as a cause of unhappiness:** Indicate how much unhappiness you tend to experience when your spouse engages in annoying behavior.

B. **Frequency of spouse's annoying behavior:** Indicate how often your spouse tends to engage in annoying behavior. _____(write number) annoying behaviors each day/week/month/year (circle one)

C. **Form(s) annoying behavior takes:** When your spouse engages in annoying behavior, what does he/she typically do? _____
_____
_____
_____

D. **Form(s) of annoying behavior that causes the greatest unhappiness:** Which of the above forms of annoying behavior cause you the greatest unhappiness?_____
_____
_____
_____

E. **Onset of annoying behavior:** When did your spouse first engage in annoying behavior? _____
_____
_____
_____

F. **Development of annoying behavior:** Has your spouse's annoying behavior increased or decreased in intensity and/or frequency since it first began? How does recent annoying behavior compare with that of the past? _____
_____
_____
_____

4. **Selfish Demands.** Attempts by your spouse to force you to do something for him/her, usually with implied threat of punishment if you refuse.

A. **Selfish demands as a cause of unhappiness:** Indicate how much unhappiness you tend to experience when your spouse makes selfish demands of you.

| 0 | 1 | 2 | 3 | 4 | 5 | 6 |

I experience
no unhappiness

I experience
moderate unhappiness

I experience
extreme unhappiness

B. **Frequency of spouse's selfish demands:** Indicate how often your spouse tends to make selfish demands of you. _____(write number) selfish demands each day/week/month/year (circle one)

C. **Form(s) selfish demands take:** When your spouse makes selfish demands of you, what does he/she typically do? _____
_____
_____
_____
_____

D. **Form(s) of selfish demands that causes the greatest unhappiness:** Which of the above forms of selfish demands cause you the greatest unhappiness? _____
_____
_____
_____
_____

E. **Onset of selfish demands:** When did your spouse first make selfish demands of you? _____
_____
_____
_____
_____

F. **Development of selfish demands:** Have your spouse's selfish demands increased or decreased in intensity and/or frequency since they first began? How do recent selfish demands compare to those of the past?
_____
_____
_____
_____

5. **Dishonesty.** Failure of your spouse to reveal his/her thoughts, feelings, habits, likes, dislikes, personal history, daily activities, and plans for the future. Dishonesty is not only providing false information about any of the above topics, but it is also leaving you with what he/she knows is a false impression.

A. **Dishonesty as a cause of unhappiness:** Indicate how much unhappiness you tend to experience when your spouse is dishonest with you.

| 0 | 1 | 2 | 3 | 4 | 5 | 6 |

I experience   I experience   I experience
no unhappiness   moderate unhappiness   extreme unhappiness

B. **Frequency of spouse's dishonesty:** Indicate how often your spouse tends to be dishonest with you. _____(write number) instances of dishonesty each day/week/month/year (circle one)

C. **Form(s) dishonesty takes:** When your spouse is dishonest with you, what does he/she typically do? _____

_____

_____

_____

_____

D. **Form(s) of dishonesty that causes the greatest unhappiness:** Which of the above forms of dishonesty cause you the greatest unhappiness?

_____

_____

_____

_____

E. **Onset of dishonesty:** When was your spouse first dishonest with you?

_____

_____

_____

_____

F. **Development of dishonesty:** Has your spouse's dishonesty increased or decreased in intensity and/or frequency since it first began? How do recent instances of dishonesty compare with those of the past?

_____

_____

_____

_____

Ranking Your Spouse's Love Busters

The five basic categories of Love Busters are listed below. There is also space for you to add other categories of Love Busters not included in the list that you feel contribute to your marital unhappiness. In the space provided before each Love Buster, write a number from 1 to 5 that ranks its relative contribution to your unhappiness. Write a 1 before the Love Buster that causes you the greatest unhappiness, a 2 before the one causing the next greatest unhappiness, and so on until you have ranked all five.

_____ Angry Outbursts

_____ Disrespectful Judgments

_____ Annoying Behavior

_____ Selfish Demands

_____ Dishonesty

____ _____

____ _____

Appendix E

The Five Parts to the Rule of Honesty

The Rule of Honesty

Reveal to your spouse as much information about yourself as you know: your thoughts, feelings, habits, likes, dislikes, personal history, daily activities, and plans for the future.

---

1. Emotional Honesty. Reveal your emotional reactions—both positive and negative—to the events of your life, particularly to your spouse's behavior.

One of the most important reasons honesty is a basic requirement for a successful marriage is that *it enables a couple to learn to make appropriate adjustments to each other.* The circumstances that led a couple into a happy marriage are going to change over the years. A long-term happy marriage requires that both a husband and a wife make a considerable number of adjustments. But those adjustments will not be made unless both parties honestly and accurately explain their feelings to each other. While some couples may fail to make a successful adjustment after feelings are honestly explained, failure is *guaranteed* when the need for adjustment is *never* communicated.

The commitment to honesty means feelings are openly expressed, whether the problem is resolved or even seems resolvable. Honesty must continue through the process of seeking a resolution.

Your emotional reactions are a gauge of whether you are making a good adjustment to each other. If you feel good, you need no adjustment. If you feel bad, a change is indicated.

Some people find it difficult to openly express negative reactions. They may fear that their response will be interpreted as criticism. Or they may feel ashamed of their own reactions, telling themselves they should not feel the way they do. They may want unconditional acceptance from their spouse and consider that their negative reactions prove their own inability to be unconditionally accepting. Whatever the reasons, many couples try to avoid expressing negative emotions.

While positive reactions are easier to communicate, many couples have not learned to express these feelings either. This failure misses an important opportunity to *deposit* love units. Whenever your spouse has made you feel good, if you express those feelings clearly and enthusiastically, you'll make your spouse feel good.

Expressing a feeling differs from expressing an opinion. Feelings are emotional reactions to life, while opinions are attitudes or beliefs. If your spouse does something that bothers you, the correct way to express your feeling is to simply say that it bothers you. If you say your spouse made a mistake, you have made a disrespectful judgment. If you say your spouse should not do it again, you're making a selfish demand. The expression of feeling should not carry judgmental or demanding baggage with it. Negative feelings are not disrespectful judgments and they're not selfish demands. They simply provide evidence that a couple has not yet achieved a successful marital adjustment. More work is needed.

Failure to express negative feelings is a Love Buster because it perpetuates the withdrawal of love units. It prevents a resolution to a marital conflict because the conflict is not expressed.

The first part of the Rule of Honesty—emotional honesty—helps us express our emotional reactions and understand the emotional reactions of our spouse. As we become aware of each other's reactions, we make adjustments to meet each other's needs and build a strong marriage.

2. Historical Honesty. Reveal information about your personal history, particularly events that demonstrate personal weakness or failure.

Many people feel that embarrassing experiences or serious mistakes of the past should be forgotten, but most psychologists recognize that past mistakes can be indicators of present weakness. For example, if someone has ever had an affair, he may be vulnerable to another one. If someone has ever been chemically dependent, he is vulnerable to drugs or alcohol abuse in the future. When you openly admit to past mistakes, your spouse can understand your weaknesses, and together you can avoid situations that may create problems for you.

No area of your life should be kept secret. All questions asked by your spouse should be answered fully and completely. Periods of poor adjustment in your past should be given special attention. Those previous conditions should be carefully understood, since problems of the past are commonly problems of the future.

Not only should *you* explain your past to your spouse, but you should encourage your spouse to gather information from *those who knew you* before you met your spouse. I have encouraged couples who are considering marriage to meet with several significant people from each other's past. It's often a real eye-opener!

I carry this Rule of Honesty about your past all the way to the disclosure of all premarital and extramarital sexual relations. My position is that a husband and a wife *must* confide in each other, regardless of the consequences.

I've had clients argue that if they tell their spouse about mistakes made decades earlier, their spouse will be crushed and never trust them again. Why not just leave that little demon alone?

My answer is that it's not a little demon. It's an extremely important part of their personal history, and it says something about their character.

But what if you haven't strayed since it happened? What if you've seen a pastor regularly to hold you accountable? Why put your spouse through the agony of a revelation that could ruin your relationship forever?

I'd say you don't give your spouse much credit! Honesty does not drive a spouse away—*dishonesty* does. People in general, and women in particular, want to know exactly what their spouse is thinking and feeling. When you hold something back, your spouse tries to guess what it is. If he or she is right, then you must continually lie to cover your tracks. If he or she is wrong, an incorrect understanding of you and your predispositions develops.

Maybe you don't really want to be known for who you are. That's the saddest position of all to be in. You'd rather keep your secret than experience one of life's greatest joys—to be loved and accepted in spite of known weaknesses.

Some counselors have argued that the only reason people reveal past infidelity is because of anger. They are deliberately trying to hurt their spouse with the revelation. Or they may be doing it to relieve their own guilt at the expense of their spouse's feelings.

While it's true that the spouse usually feels hurt, and vengeance or feelings of guilt motivate some people's honesty, whenever correct information is revealed, an opportunity for understanding and change is presented. That opportunity is more important than unhealthy motivations or momentary unhappiness.

These revelations may need to be made in the presence of a professional counselor to help control the emotional damage. Some spouses have difficulty adjusting to revelations that have been kept secret for years. In many cases, they're reacting to the fact that they'd been lied to all that time.

Some spouses with emotional weaknesses may need personal counseling to help them adjust to the reality of their spouse's past. The saint they thought they married turns out to be not so saintly. But the most negative reactions to truth that I've witnessed have never destroyed a marriage. It's dishonesty that destroys intimacy, romantic love, and marriages.

3. Current Honesty. Reveal information about the events of your day. Provide your spouse with a calendar of your activities, with special emphasis on those that may affect your spouse.

After six years of marriage, Ed discovered that it was easier to have a sexual relationship with a woman at the office than with his wife, Jennifer. He found Peggy a welcome solution to his sexual frustration. He spent time alone with her several times a week, and their sexual relationship was as fulfilling as he could have ever imagined.

Ed justified this infidelity by assuming he was doing Jennifer a favor by not imposing his sexual requirements on her. Whenever Jennifer wanted to make love to him, he happily accommodated her, but she didn't feel a sexual need more than two or three times a month.

Ed didn't *want* to share information about his daily activities with Jennifer, since honesty would have ruined any hope of continuing this very satisfying solution. Moreover, the announcement of this relationship would have upset his wife. He still loved her very much and would not have wanted to put her through the grief of such a disclosure. So to preserve a temporary solution to his problem and to keep Jennifer from experiencing intense emotional pain, he felt that dishonesty was justified.

In good marriages, couples become so interdependent that sharing a daily schedule is essential to their coordination of activities. But in weak marriages, couples are reluctant to provide their schedules, because they are often engaged in an assortment of Love Busters. They may know that their spouse would object to their activities, so they tell themselves it's better not to be honest.

Even when activities are innocent, it's extremely important for your spouse to understand what you do with your time. You should be easy to find in an emergency. Give each other your daily schedules so you can communicate about how you spend your time. Almost everything you do will affect your spouse, so it is important to explain what you do each day.

If Jennifer and Ed had established a habit of exchanging daily information early in their marriage, his affair would have been almost impossible to arrange. In fact if they had practiced the Rule of Honesty, his problem would probably not even have existed.

Honesty is a terrific way to protect your spouse from potentially damaging activities. When you know that you'll be telling your spouse what you've been up to, you're far less likely to get either of you into trouble.

4. Future Honesty. Reveal your thoughts and plans regarding future activities and objectives.

After I've made such a big issue of revealing past indiscretions, you can imagine how I feel about revealing future plans. They're *much* easier to discuss with your spouse, yet many couples make plans independently of each other.

Some couples don't explain their plans because they don't want to change them, even if their spouse expresses a negative reaction. Some don't explain their future plans because they don't think their spouse would be interested.

Even if your plans are innocent, when you fail to tell your spouse about them, you're engaging in a Love Buster. It's destructive because you don't really know what your spouse's reaction will be and by failing to give advance notice, you may create a problem for the future.

You may feel your plans are best for both you and your spouse. Once your spouse sees the plan succeed, he or she will be grateful that you went ahead with it. Or you may feel that if you wait for your spouse's approval, you'll never accomplish anything. Perhaps your wife is so conservative that if you wait for her approval, you think you'll miss every opportunity that comes your way.

Regardless of how you feel about revealing your plans, failure to do so is a Love Buster because you deliberately leave your spouse in the dark. While no love units are withdrawn at the time you're deceitful, they're almost sure to be withdrawn when your spouse realizes you've held back information and failed to take his or her feelings into account.

The Policy of Joint Agreement is certainly relevant in discussions of your future plans. It just makes sense to follow the Policy when you make your plans if you want to deposit love units and avoid withdrawing them.

5. Complete Honesty. Do not leave your spouse with a false impression about your thoughts, feelings, habits, likes, dislikes, personal history, daily activities, or plans for the future. Do not deliberately keep personal information from your spouse.

False impressions are just as deceitful as outright lies! The purpose of honesty is having the facts in front of you. Without them, you'll fail to solve the simplest marital problems. Why should it make a difference how you fail to reveal the facts to each other, whether by lies or by giving false impressions? Either one will leave your spouse ignorant.

I need to ask probing questions during premarital counseling. I know the categories where people tend to leave false impressions and I search in each of these areas for truth. Since most marital problems originate with serious misconceptions, I do what I can to dig out these little weeds that eventually choke the plant.

In most marriages, the biggest false impression is that your spouse is doing a good job meeting your needs. The truth is that in some areas you may be very dissatisfied. No one ever wants to be told they're failing at something, so your expression of dissatisfaction carries the risk of withdrawing love units. But if it's expressed in a nonthreatening, nonjudgmental way, you minimize the risk.

The alternative to expressing dissatisfaction is to leave your spouse with a false impression. But the truth is a map to a solution. Deception will lead only to continuing misery. You cripple your spouse when you fail to reveal the truth because he or she is forced to act on the basis of false assumptions. Do you want your spouse to have a map that leads to solutions or a map that leads nowhere?

Appendix F

Why Women Leave Men

"I hurt all the time because I feel alone and abandoned."

"My husband is no longer my friend."

"The only time he pays attention to me is when he wants sex."

"He is never there for me when I need him the most."

"When he hurts my feelings he doesn't apologize."

"He lives his life as if we weren't married; he rarely considers me."

"We're like ships passing in the night, he goes his way and I go mine."

"My husband has become a stranger to me. I don't even know who he is anymore."

"He doesn't show any interest in me or in what I do."

Women tend to be more concerned about their marriage than are men. They buy most of the books on improving their marriage and initiate most marriage counseling. They often complain about their marriage to their closest friends or to anyone who will listen. And they file for divorce twice as often as men.

Why are women so dissatisfied with marriage? What do they want from their husband? What bothers them so much about marriage that many are willing to risk the future of their family to escape it? Why do women leave men?

Each day I am confronted by women who are extremely frustrated with their marriage. They usually express no hope that their husband will ever understand what it is that frustrates them, let alone change enough to solve the problem. From their perspective, marital problems are created by husbands who do little or nothing to solve them. Wives tend to see themselves as the ones who push for resolving conflicts, and when they give up their effort, the marriage is usually over.

When I talk to their husbands, they usually have a very different explanation as to why the wives feel the way they do. They often feel that the expectations of women in general, and their wife in particular, have grown completely out of reach. These men, who feel that they've made a gigantic effort to be caring and sensitive to their wife, get no credit whatsoever for their sizable contribution to the family. They feel under enormous pressure to improve their financial support, improve the way they raise their children, and improve the way they treat their wives. Many men I see are emotionally exhausted and feel that for all their effort, they get nothing but criticism.

The role of husbands today is much more complex and confusing than it was a few decades ago, especially in their relationship to their wives. Some men conclude that women are born to complain, and men must ignore it to survive. Others feel that women have come to expect so much of men that they are impossible to please, so there's no point in even trying. Very few men feel that they have learned to become the husband that their wife wants.

Grounds for Divorce

When a woman is unhappy with her marriage, she will tend to file for divorce. In other words, she doesn't live with her unhappiness in marriage. She gets out of it.

The most common reason women give for leaving their husband is "mental cruelty." When legal grounds for divorce are stated, about half report they have been emotionally abused. This mental cruelty is rarely their husband's efforts to drive them crazy. It is usually husbands being indifferent, failing to communicate, and demonstrating other forms of neglect.

Another reason often given by women who are seeking divorce is neglect. Women feel neglected by their husband. This includes emotional abandonment and physical abandonment. (Husbands who work away from the home, sometimes leaving their wife alone for weeks at a time, fall into this category.)

Surprisingly few women divorce because of physical abuse, infidelity, alcoholism, criminal behavior, fraud, or other serious moral or ethical defects. The most common reason is some form of neglect. In fact I'm often bewildered by women who are in serious physical danger but who refuse to leave the men who threaten their safety. But women who feel neglected leave.

It is difficult for a man to understand that his neglect of his wife is a reason for her to leave. Most men have little trouble understanding that verbal and physical abuse are legitimate reasons for a wife to leave. Lately the increasing social pressure on men to avoid hurting their wives physically and verbally has increased their awareness of the problem.

Neglect is a much tougher sell, however, and it is also much more difficult to overcome than abuse. While it is the most important reason women leave men, it is hard to convince men that it is a legitimate reason, something they should avoid at all costs.

Some of the common complaints I hear from women are, "He ignores me except when he wants sex; he sits and watches television when he could be talking to me; he rarely calls me to see how I'm doing; he hurts my feelings and then never apologizes; instead, he tells me I'm too sensitive."

Most husbands are mystified by these complaints. They feel that their wives demand too much and that most other women would be ecstatic if married to them. Their wives have become spoiled, take their efforts for granted, and have unrealistic expectations.

Do women expect too much of husbands, or are men doing less for wives than they should? I've proven to husbands over and over again that their wives usually do not expect too much of them, and when they understand and respond to their wives' frustration, the complaining ends and a terrific marriage begins.

What's more, their wife is not expecting *more* effort from them. Instead, she's looking for effort in a different direction. It isn't more difficult to please women these days; it simply requires a change in the priority of effort.

What are women looking for in a man? They want a soul mate, someone they trust who is there for them when they have a problem and who takes their feelings into account when decisions are being made, someone to whom they feel emotionally connected.

A Man's House

I use a house as an illustration to help husbands understand how their wife feels. Each room in the house represents one of the husband's roles in life. There is a room for his job, another for golf, another for his new sports car, one for his garden, one for his children, one for church, and, yes, one for his wife.

As he makes his way through an average day, he visits various rooms where he is faced with the role the room defines. When he's in a certain room, the others are blocked out of his mind so that he can focus his undivided attention on the role he plays in that room. He does his best when not distracted and prefers to deal with each problem with all his energy and creativity so that he successfully fulfills each role he plays.

The husband role usually takes up only one of many rooms in this imaginary house. When a man is in that room, he usually tries to give his wife undivided attention and makes a special effort to meet her needs. He also goes to that room to have his own needs met, particularly the need for sex.

What frustrates many wives is that they are relegated to only one room in their husband's imaginary house. They want to be in every room. In other words, they want to be integrated into their husband's entire life, not restricted to one corner. Without such integration, there can be no emotional bonding, no uniting of the spirit, no feeling of intimacy and, in many cases, no sex.

To help husbands learn to avoid this unpleasant outcome, I have tried to show them how to become and stay emotionally connected to their wife by inviting her into each room of their house. The wife then joins her husband in the other roles he fulfills. She rides in his sports car, plants the garden with him, and understands the challenges and frustrations of his job. She becomes integrated into every aspect of his life.

When I counsel a husband, I explain that he is to invite his wife into each room of his house. Regardless of his role or responsibility, his wife should be considered in and aware of each decision he makes. Once he invites his wife to join him in each room, the results are startling! She helps change his priorities. She reminds him that her feelings are very different from his. As a result, he begins to live his life in a way that is compatible to her needs and values.

He learns how to avoid habits that cause his wife to be unhappy and he learns how to meet her most important emotional needs. He also learns how to give his undivided attention to her and schedule time to be alone with her.

The Policy of Joint Agreement

To help men integrate their wives into each room, I have encouraged husbands to follow the Policy of Joint Agreement.

The Policy helps men take their wife's feelings into account whenever they make a decision. They avoid thoughtless habits, learn to meet emotional needs with mutual enjoyment, and resolve conflicts. All of this creates marital compatibility and emotional bonding.

The Policy states, Never do anything without an enthusiastic agreement between you and your spouse. The word *anything* in the Policy applies to all the activities of a husband that go on in each of his rooms. So whenever he follows the Policy, he learns to think about his wife's reaction to everything he does, not just what goes on in the husband room.

Some argue that just an agreement would be a big help, why insist on an *enthusiastic* agreement? It's because I want couples to avoid agreements that are coerced or self-sacrificing. I want couples to learn how to come to agreements that take the interests of both of them into account at once. I have encouraged couples to continue to negotiate until they arrive at an enthusiastic agreement because that's the kind of agreement that stands up to the test of time.

Most men complain that if they invite their wife into every room of their imaginary house, their wife will take over completely and they will lose all their peace and freedom. They imagine their identities shriveling away and finding themselves a shadow of their former self.

But the Policy of Joint Agreement prevents that unfortunate outcome. Joint agreement means that both husband and wife must be enthusiastic together. No one risks losing his or her identity or being subjected to servanthood when there must be an enthusiastic agreement of both spouses about each decision. The goal is to become united in purpose and spirit, not to overpower or control each other.

How Easy Is It?

Couples that are already emotionally bonded have little or no trouble following the Policy because they have already learned how to behave in sensitive and caring ways in each of their life's roles. But emotionally distant couples have great difficulty with the Policy at first. They are accustomed to doing what they please regardless of its effect on each other, especially when they play certain roles. If they follow the Policy for even one day, however, they begin to see how their thoughtlessness has created emotional distance. As couples apply the Policy to each of their daily plans and activities, they begin to feel cared for by each other and are encouraged by each other's thoughtfulness. Over time their emotional bonding becomes more and more firm, and the Policy becomes easier and easier to follow as they become soul mates.

Men who follow the Policy of Joint Agreement think about their wife throughout the day, because as they make decisions they ask themselves how their wife would feel. Phone calls are made whenever there is any doubt. As time passes, these men become increasingly sensitive to their wife's feelings.

If men consider their wife's feelings in each decision they make, asking her when there is any uncertainty, they create a compatible lifestyle. The Policy of Joint Agreement helps create understanding, emotional bonding, intimacy, and romantic love in marriage. Men who learn to take their wife's feelings into account meet their wife's most important emotional needs. They also learn to overcome the selfish habits that make their wife so unhappy. If a couple is following the policy, selfish habits do not meet the standard of mutual agreement. Over time they experience what every couple hopes to create in marriage: a loving and compatible relationship.

A woman doesn't have to leave the man who has invited her into every room of his house. That's because she doesn't stand outside the rooms of his house feeling like a stranger. She is welcomed into his entire home as his cherished life partner.

His Needs, Her Needs: Building an Affair-proof Marriage

MORE THAN 500,000 COPIES IN PRINT!

H·I·S NEEDS H·E·R NEEDS

Building An Affair-proof Marriage

Willard F. Harley, Jr.

In a successful marriage, a husband and wife meet each other's emotional needs. But when these needs are not met in marriage, a husband and wife are tempted to go outside the marriage to satisfy them.

Ignorance of what these emotional needs are often contributes to a couple's failure to meet them. Men try to meet needs that they value, and women do the same. The needs of men and women, however, are often very different, and husbands and wives end up trying to meet the wrong needs.

In *His Needs, Her Needs* Dr. Harley describes ten important emotional needs for men and women. He helps you identify which are the most important to you and your spouse, explains how to communicate your needs to each other, and guides you in learning how to meet each other's needs.

A successful marriage requires skill in caring for the one you promised to cherish throughout life. *His Needs, Her Needs* will teach you how to care for your spouse, eliminating the major cause of infidelity. Once you have learned the lessons in *His Needs, Her Needs*, your spouse will find you irresistible.

(Hardcover—216 pages)
0-8007-1478-4 Retail $16.99

His Needs, Her Needs is available in condensed form on two 90-minute audiotapes.

0-8007-4400-4 Retail $14.99

Love Busters: Overcoming Habits That Destroy Romantic Love

Love Busters are habits that destroy romantic love. They usually develop soon after marriage and, before long, destroy intimacy, safety, trust . . . and romantic love.

In *Love Busters* Dr. Harley shows couples how to avoid losing romantic love by recognizing and overcoming five common but dangerous Love Busters: angry outbursts, disrespectful judgments, annoying behavior, selfish demands, and dishonesty. When these are unchecked, consideration and thoughtfulness turn into self-centeredness and thoughtlessness. Romantic love is the victim and with it goes all hope for a fulfilling marriage.

Romantic love is not the only victim, however. Dr. Harley also demonstrates how Love Busters prevent couples from resolving common marital conflicts involving friends and relatives, career choices, financial planning, children, and sex. When Love Busters are overcome, these conflicts are easily resolved.

(Hardcover—192 pages)
0-8007-1739-2 Retail $16.99

Five Steps to Romantic Love: A Workbook for Readers of Love Busters *and* His Needs, Her Needs

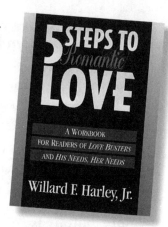

Marriage can last a lifetime if couples apply two rules to their relationships: (1) Meet each other's most important emotional needs, and (2) avoid hurting each other. Dr. Harley wrote the international best-seller, *His Needs, Her Needs,* to help couples learn to identify and meet each other's most important emotional needs. Then, he wrote *Love Busters* to help couples learn to avoid being the cause of each other's unhappiness.

Now he has written *Five Steps to Romantic Love* to help couples apply the principles found in his first two books. The contracts, questionnaires, inventories, and worksheets that Dr. Harley has used in his counseling practice are arranged in a logical sequence to help couples follow five steps:

1. Make a commitment to overcome marital conflicts.
2. Identify habits that cause unhappiness.
3. Learn to overcome those habits.
4. Identify the most important emotional needs.
5. Learn to meet those needs.

Follow these *Five Steps to Romantic Love* and you'll be on the road to having a marriage that is passionate and free of conflict. It's well worth the effort.

(Paperback—192 pages)
0-8007-5623-1 Retail $12.99

Give and Take: The Secret to Marital Compatibility

Most couples begin marriage blissfully compatible and deeply in love. But they usually don't stay that way. Why?

In *Give & Take* you will find out why you and your spouse may have lost the compatibility you had when you married. Then you will learn how to restore it, making you as much in love with each other as you ever were.

You will learn about your Giver and Taker (and about your spouse's Giver and Taker). They certainly can wreak havoc on your marriage, but you can educate these characters and turn them into heroes.

You will become acquainted with the Three States of Marriage and realize how tough it is to negotiate in any of them. Although they can prevent you from getting what you need, their destructive influence can be overcome, and you'll learn how to do it.

By learning how to give and take fairly and effectively, you can give your spouse what he or she needs the most and in return take what you need the most. The lessons of *Give and Take* will make your marriage what it was meant to be—a safe and caring relationship that brings out the best in both of you.

(Hardcover—304 pages)
0-8007-1726-0 Retail $16.99

Give and Take is also available in condensed form on two 90-minute audiotapes. Questionnaires are not included, but all of the essential concepts in their original form are preserved.

0-8007-4405-5 Retail $14.99

Visit Dr. Harley's web site

http://marriagebuilders.com

In this Marriage Builders site you will be introduced to some of the best ways to overcome marital conflict and some of the quickest ways to restore love. And it's *free!*

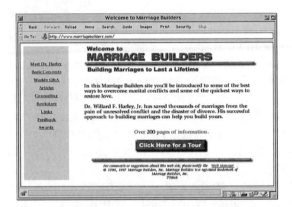

Dr. Harley has helped thousands of couples with his revolutionary concepts. These are all clearly explained in the "Basic Concepts" section of the site. Then in his weekly Q&A columns, he explains how these concepts can be used to solve just about every marital problem. And if that's not enough—if you have a problem that is not addressed in his Q&A columns or are uncertain how to proceed—you can e-mail your questions to him.

Marriage Builders also provides a telephone counseling service at a reasonable fee for those who feel they need personal encouragement to improve their marriage. The toll-free number is 888-639-1639.

Let Marriage Builders help you build your marriage to last a lifetime!

About the Author

Willard F. Harley, Jr., Ph.D., is a clinical psychologist and marriage counselor. Over the past twenty-five years he has helped thousands of couples overcome marital conflict and restore their love for each other. His innovative counseling methods are described in the books and articles he writes. One of his books, *His Needs, Her Needs,* has been a best-seller since it was published in 1986 and has been translated into German, French, Dutch, and Chinese. Dr. Harley also leads training workshops for couples and marriage counselors and has appeared on hundreds of radio and television programs.

Willard Harley and Joyce, his wife of more than thirty years, live in White Bear Lake, Minnesota. They are parents of two married children who also are marriage counselors.